APPLYING
MICROECONOMIC
PRINCIPLES

APPLYING MICROECONOMIC PRINCIPLES

A Student Guide to Analyzing Economic News

Richard J. Kieffer

Lee C. Spector

State University College at Buffalo

Harper & Row, Publishers

New York Hagerstown Philadelphia San Francisco London

Editor: George Provol

Special Projects Editor: Susan Schader

Project Editor: Carol Pritchard-Martinez

Designer: Donna Davis

Artist: Tim Keenan

Cover Artist: Dare Porter

Production Coordinator: Laura Argento

Compositors: Nora Helfgott and Typeset Services

Applying Microeconomic Principles: A Student Guide to

Analyzing Economic News

Library of Congress Cataloging in Publication Data

Kieffer, Richard J   1932-
    Applying microeconomic principles.

    1. Microeconomics--Addresses, essays, lectures.
2. Economic history--1945-   Addresses, essays,
lectures. I. Spector, Lee C., 1947-   joint author.
II. Title.
HB171.5.K475   338.5   78-27709
ISBN 0-06-388577-8

To Ann, Dan, and Doug Kieffer

and

To Kristine Spector

Contents

Preface

Many students are attracted to principles of economics courses
believing that the material learned can be used in making analyses of current economic events. In order to do this, however,
students need to learn how to apply economic theory to both magazine and newspaper articles. Unfortunately, neither textbooks
nor books of readings have accomplished this task. Textbooks
generally present the necessary theory but rarely show students
how to use it. Most supplementary readers also have limitations:
First, they almost never help students analyze the articles they
contain; and second, readers infrequently contain the kinds of
articles likely to be read by the average person. Consequently,
upon finishing their principles of economics courses, students
are generally unable to put the economics they have learned to
practical use.

This book meets these needs not only by presenting articles
from current, typical, and interesting periodicals and
newspapers, but also by teaching students how to analyze them.
For more practical and efficient use in the classroom, the

chapters of this book are organized to correspond to those of most principles texts. Each chapter contains:

* An <u>Introduction</u> showing how the material presented in the chapter relates to real-world problems and situations.

* A <u>Checklist</u> containing:

  * <u>Definitions of New Terms</u> which must be understood in order to analyze most articles.

  * <u>Concepts</u>, a step-by-step discussion of both the important concepts contained in the articles and of those needed for making the analyses.

  * <u>A Guide to Analyzing Articles</u>, showing how the concepts should be logically applied in analyzing the particular kinds of articles found in that chapter.

  * <u>Three current articles</u>, each drawing upon the topics and concepts of the chapter. The articles are always presented in the following order:

    1) <u>An Analyzed Article</u>. Preceded by an introductory overview, this article is analyzed for students using the steps from the chapter's Guide to Analyzing Articles. The sample analysis reinforces the Guide steps and further instructs students in the art of applying theory to real events.

    2) <u>An Article with Questions</u>. This article is followed by a series of questions designed to direct students to the important issues and concepts in the article and provides a foundation for their own analysis of it.

Answers to the questions are found at the end of the book.

3) <u>An Article for Student Analysis</u>. The third article
is provided for the student's own analysis. A brief
overview preceding the article elicits students'
interest in the pertinent issues.

In writing a book such as this one there are, of course, many
people to thank. These include William Ganley who was a large
help in the initial stages of this project; our colleagues at
the State University College at Buffalo, Gary Garofalo, George
Blackford, and Alex Ratkowski, who helped us in our quest to
find articles and to analyze them as succinctly as possible;
and the gang at Harper & Row, past and present, including Jerry
Papke, and George Provol, Susan Schader, and Carol
Pritchard-Martinez.

Finally, we'd like to point out that there are an enormous
number of articles that could be used in a book such as this
one. If you have articles which you find both informative and
challenging, please send them to us at the State University
College at Buffalo for possible inclusion in the next edition.
Such help can only make this volume more useful and your
contribution will gratefully be acknowledged.

Introduction: The Purpose and Use of This Book

It seemed that whenever Nancy and Chuck Rankin read their local
newspaper, they would find some mention of an economic problem.
Headlines warned that the dollar was declining, the national debt
was rising, domestic prices were increasing, and the ranks of the
unemployed were growing. Since Nancy and Chuck were soon going to
be working full time and eventually wanted to raise a family, they
thought it might be helpful for them to learn what these economic
problems mean and how they would be affected by them. Luckily,
they both had some room in their schedules and were able to sign
up for a Principles of Economics course in their senior year. In
doing so, they hoped they would be able to learn enough about
economics to understand the articles they were reading in the
newspaper.

Once in the course, however, they found, much to their
consternation, that what they were learning in class did not seem
to help them understand what they read in the paper. Sure, they
recognized some of the terms and they found they could follow some
of the discussion, but they were not satisfied with their ability
to fully comprehend the articles they read. The experience left
them feeling frustrated.

One of the major reasons for their frustration is that news
articles are rarely organized as clearly as the discussions of
economic problems found in textbooks and lectures. Nor are
articles limited to the terms and concepts discussed in the course.

The purpose of this volume is to remedy this situation and
bridge the gap between economic theory and newspaper and magazine
articles by teaching students how to apply economic theory to
their daily reading. To do this, each chapter is organized around
a series of articles which require a common method of analysis.
That is, after the presentation of some key terms and concepts,
you will be provided with a list of application steps which will
show you how to analyze the articles. Moreover, to make sure you
understand how to use these steps, you will be provided with a

sample analysis of one of these articles in each chapter.

Each chapter contains several sections which are designed to help you with the transition from theory to application. The purpose of each section is described below.

INTRODUCTION

To help you start thinking about applying economic theory, each chapter begins with a hypothetical situation in which individuals are confronted with a problem or are involved in some activity that relates to the type of economic theory contained in that chapter. When you read each story, ask yourself if you can answer the questions which are raised, and, if you are able to, point out how economic theory could be used to explain what is happening.

CHECKLIST

Definitions of New Terms

Although most of the terms provided in the checklist of key terms may be familiar, you should review the definitions provided in this section because these definitions will be used in the application material.

Concepts

It is assumed you know most of the concepts that relate to each chapter of this book. However, some concepts are more important in application situations than others. We have selected these key concepts and provided an application-oriented explanation of each. In some chapters we may also present some additional concepts with which you may not be familiar, but which are especially useful for analyzing the included articles.

GUIDE FOR ANALYZING ARTICLES

One of the major problems that people confront when attempting to apply economic theory to real-world situations is the discrepancy between the organization of theory in traditional textbooks and the description of economic events in news items. People simply do not know how to apply the theory. To remedy this problem, this section provides you with specific steps that will guide you over the gap between theory and application. These steps should be followed closely when analyzing an article: they will help you organize the material and assist you in relating economic concepts to specific economic problems.

THE ARTICLES

Each chapter has three articles which relate to the theory found

in that particular chapter. The first article is followed by a
sample analysis; the second is followed by questions and answers;
and the third is for your analysis.

An Analyzed Article

The sample analysis that follows the first article enables you to
see how to use the application steps. Perhaps the best way to use
this sample analysis is review the application steps immediately
after reading the article and then formulate your own analysis.
Then read the sample analysis and compare it with your analysis.
You may have done some things somewhat differently in arriving at
a comparable explanation--that's fine. Or you may have found some
additional things to explain--that's great. Whatever the result,
the experience of seeing the steps actually applied to an article
should help you learn how to apply the steps to other articles.

An Article with Questions

Now that you have seen a sample analysis, you should be about
ready to do one by yourself. Read the second article, review the
steps, and begin applying the steps to the article. If you wonder
whether you are proceeding in the right direction, you can check
your work with the questions provided. When you finish your work,
you can check your results with the answers to the questions,
which are supplied chapter-by-chapter at the end of the book. But
remember, neither the questions nor the answers are intended to be
as complete or as exhaustive as possible.

An Article for Student Analysis

The third article is all yours. The only help you are given is an
overview which states the purpose of the article and warns of any
unusual situations. However, if you follow the steps closely, you
should not have any serious difficulty in analyzing the article.
Also, it may help to go back and read the sample analysis; although
this will not provide you with specific answers to the questions
you have, it may give you some ideas.

Logical Thinking and Economic Analysis

Gary Simpson was raised by fairly conservative parents and generally agreed with them on most important issues--that is, until he went to college. At college most of Gary's friends were quite liberal and before long Gary's political leanings started to change. As the semester break approached, Gary grew excited about going home and discussing his newfound philosophy with his parents. Although Gary had yet to take his first economics course, he felt he had become quite aware of what was happening in the world, and he was all set to convince his parents of the folly of their conservative thinking. When he did start talking with his parents, however, he soon was convinced that his liberalism was a mistake and he once again changed his views. Gary returned to college determined to use his parents' arguments to change his liberal friends, but was unsuccessful and once again was persuaded that being liberal was the way to go. This flip-flop of feelings really started to disturb Gary who had always considered himself to be fairly intelligent and able to make up his own mind. What was wrong, he wondered? Was he as stupid as he felt?

Actually, Gary is typical of many people lacking the expertise to successfully analyze important issues and arguments, who instead tend to be convinced--not by the merits of an argument--but rather by how the argument is presented. As a beginning economics student, you will probably encounter this problem when reading articles involving economic issues, especially since many of them contain statements by politicians who are adept at presenting their side of an issue. Consequently, it will be important for you to be able to separate logical arguments from arguments based primarily on debating techniques. To help you in this task, the concepts section will list several questions which you should ask yourself when analyzing articles or arguments. Then, in the articles section, you will be shown how these questions can be used to help you determine whether or not a proposition is based upon sound logic.

CHECKLIST

Definitions of New Terms

1. Normative--a normative statement makes a value judgment of what "ought to be," that is, it discusses "norms."
2. Positive--a positive statement discusses only those relationships which are true or presumed to be true.
3. Analogy--when similarities or some correspondence are discovered to exist between two separate events.
4. Opportunity Cost--the value of the best alternative that must be foregone when doing something else.
5. Projection--the prediction of future events based on current or past data.

Concepts

1. When analyzing an article or argument you should be aware that there are many techniques which can be used to convince you of a proposition which may not actually be true. In order to avoid falling prey to these techniques you should ask yourself the following questions:
   A. Is an appeal to facts, to an authority, and/or to past history legitimate? That is, are the facts correct and well-documented; are the authorities knowledgeable on the subject being discussed; and does history tell us what the arguer claims it does?
   B. Is an argument based upon the association of two people or groups of people, and is such an association applicable to the argument?
   C. Is a cause and effect argument based upon the timing of two events which are not actually related to each other?
   D. Are any extraneous arguments being made?
   E. Are normative statements used to support an argument?
   F. Have the opportunity costs of the different alternatives been considered?
   G. Are the analogies used appropriately?
   H. Are statistical projections being made from inconsistent, incomplete, or irrelevant data?
   I. Has the arguer limited his argument to two alternatives when there may be more?
   J. Has there been a generalization based from one person's experiences or from a very small sample?
   K. Are any preconceived biases found in the argument?

GUIDE TO ANALYZING ARTICLES

1. If the article is long, make a list of all the arguments presented.
2. Before accepting an argument, ask yourself the questions in the concept section.

Articles

Generally this section of the text contains three articles
obtained from magazines or newspapers. Since, however, your
orientation to economic theory has barely begun, we'd like to
break from our usual presentation of articles containing economic
analysis in this first chapter. Instead we will present a series
of three paragraphs written by the authors for the purpose of
helping you distinguish those arguments which are legitimate from
those arguments which are not. These paragraphs will be treated
as if each series were separate articles and will be examined in
the manner described above.

AN ANALYZED ARTICLE

PARAGRAPHS FROM THE AUTHORS--PART I

Below are several paragraphs containing at least one deceptive
argument. Underneath each paragraph is a short explanation of
what may be erroneous. After each explanation is a letter(s)
which refers back to the questions in the concept section.

1. "The reason we are having so much unemployment is fairly clear
    if one examines past history. Every civilization which has
    stopped backing its currency with gold has suffered the same
    problem. Therefore, if we want to decrease the unemployment
    rate, we should start backing our dollar with gold."

    The speaker is appealing to past history, but is not giving
    any specific examples to prove his point. He is also
    leaving out of his argument any instances of countries
    which did not back their currency with gold and did not
    have high unemployment rates. (A)

2. "I sure hope the equal rights amendment doesn't pass. Since
    the states have started voting on it, prostitution has gone up
    by 6%. If this is equal rights, I want no part of it."

    Just because prostitution has gone up at the same time as
    the voting has taken place, it doesn't mean that the two
    are related. We also do not know whether the 6% rise is
    larger than normal. And finally, we do not know how these
    statistics were gathered. (C,A)

3. "I'm going to vote for John Ellis because he is a Democrat."

    Just because someone is in the favored political party does
    not mean that he has the same views as the speaker. After
    all, some Democrats are conservative while others are
    liberal. (B)

4. "The American welfare system is a disgrace. Just go down to Fourth Street where many of the welfare recipients live, and you will see at least three Cadillacs. Why is my money being used to keep these people in luxury, when I have to work for a living?

This person is using his own experience to make a general statement about all welfare recipients. Just because the people with Cadillacs live near the welfare recipients is not proof that they are on welfare. We also do not know whether welfare payments are being used to buy these cars. (J,B)

5. "There is no question that Burt Reynolds was the best actor of 1977 because more people saw his movies than any other actor's."

The speaker is citing a fact without giving its source. Then he is implying that the most popular actor is the best actor. (A,D)

6. "Don't vote for Harris. He is going to raise taxes and drive all our big industry out of the city."

Only two possible alternatives are given when there may be many more. The speaker also does not discuss the opportunity cost of not raising taxes. (I,F)

7. "Have you seen what has been happening to the price of houses in the city? According to the newspaper, housing prices have gone up by 25% in the past two years. At this rate, no one will be able to afford to buy a house."

A projection has been made on what will happen to the price of houses on only two years' data. Is this enough data to generate an accurate prediction? Also there is no projection for what has been happening to incomes during this period. Such a projection is important because one's ability to buy a house in the future depends on future income as well as future prices. (H)

AN ARTICLE WITH QUESTIONS

PARAGRAPHS FROM THE AUTHORS--PART II

What is deceptive about the following arguments?

1. "No less than six Nobel prize winners say that marijuana is harmful and that is good enough for me to favor its illegality." (A)
2. "Our economy needs war to survive. During the 1930s we had a depression which was only ended by World War II. In the 1960s and 1970s we had our most prosperous years while fighting in

Vietnam. And when that war ended, the result was rising prices and rising unemployment. Thus past history tends to support this thesis." (C,A)

3. "Of course Harry smokes marijuana; he's got a beard and long hair, doesn't he?" (B)
4. "Have you been to the unemployment office lately? I was there yesterday and you should have seen the line. Boy, the economy must be in terrible shape." (J)
5. "Television networks are not serving the public good. Just look at the scheduling. Most of the shows are either sporting events, police shows, or situation comedies. You rarely see any documentaries, operas, or science shows." (K)
6. "I don't understand why you can't do these math problems. Math is just like reading except that numbers are used instead of letters, and you can read, can't you?" (G)
7. "We ought to be able to afford a hockey team at this college. Just look at how much money they collect for tuition." (F)

(Answers are in the back of the book)

AN ARTICLE FOR STUDENT ANALYSIS:

PARAGRAPHS FROM THE AUTHOR--PART III OVERVIEW

Following are several more statements, each based upon some form of faulty reasoning. You should not have too much trouble determining what is wrong with each statement, but if you do, ask yourself the questions listed in the Guide to Analyzing Articles. What is deceptive about the following paragraphs?

1. "Son, you have to go to college or you'll never succeed."
2. "Why is marijuana illegal? Alcohol is harmful and there are no laws prohibiting drinking it."
3. "87 percent of the people feel we should have cheaper bus fares. Therefore, as city councilman, I am going to recommend an increase in the subsidy paid to the bus company so they can lower their prices."
4. "If you don't think we are becoming a socialist country, look at the size of the government's budget. In the past ten years it has doubled in size. At this rate the government will own everything."
5. "The fifty-five mile-per-hour speed limit makes little sense. I drove all the way home at 70 miles-per-hour and no one got hurt."
6. "Finish your dinner, Billy; people are starving in India."
7. "Why would you want to marry Joe? His family is from the poor side of town, and he will never amount to anything."
8. "If you knew anything about the first law of thermodynamics, you'd realize that the bad weather we have been having is caused by the space program."

Supply and Demand

Mr. and Mrs. Novak were becoming dismayed one evening while discussing the family finances. The prices they were paying for food, clothing, and rent were constantly rising, while at the same time the Novaks were receiving only slight increases in the price they received for their labor (their wages). This caused them to wonder how these prices were determined in the first place and why some prices changed more than others. To answer questions such as these, economists look at what is happening in the various market places in the economy. A market place occurs whenever buyers and sellers get together to exchange goods, services, and/or resources for money. There are a very large number of markets in the economy including markets for goods such as clothes, for resources such as capital and labor, for services such as legal and medical, and for financial assets such as stocks and bonds. Markets make a capitalistic economy operate successfully in that the interaction of buyers and sellers taking place in these markets determines the quantities of all goods, services, and resources bought and sold and the prices which they will command.

Because of their importance economists spend a lot of time studying markets. In doing so, they try to predict not only what will happen if buyers and sellers are left alone to determine prices and quantities, but also what will happen if there is government intervention in a market place. The tool the economist uses in this analysis is called supply and demand analysis. If the Novaks had been familiar with supply and demand analysis they could have answered their own questions, and many other economic events they read about would have been more understandable.

CHECKLIST

Definitions of New Terms

1. Demand--a schedule showing the quantity that buyers are

willing and able to purchase at each and every price, all other factors remaining unchanged.

2. Demand Curve--a graphical presentation of the demand schedule.
3. Tastes--one's subjective feeling about a good or service.
4. Expectations--predictions.
5. Complement--a good is a complement to good X if it is used along with good X.
6. Substitute--a good is a substitute to good X if it can be used in place of good X.
7. Normal Good--a good is normal if the demand for it rises as income rises.
8. Inferior Good--a good is inferior if the demand for it falls as income rises.
9. Supply--a schedule showing the quantity that sellers are willing and able to sell at each and every price, all other factors remaining unchanged.
10. Supply Curve--a graphical presentation of the supply schedule.
11. Costs of Production--the total costs of the resources used by a firm to produce a good. Some costs require immediate money payments; others do not.
12. Equilibrium--the price-quantity combinations such that the market is stable and there are no incentives for price and quantity to change.
13. Surplus--the amount by which the quantity supplied is greater than the quantity demanded. Surpluses occur when the price is above the equilibrium price.
14. Shortage--the amount by which the quantity demanded is greater than the quantity supplied. Shortages occur when the price is below the equilibrium price.
15. Price Ceiling (maximum price)--a price ceiling occurs when a regulation stops the price from rising above a given price.
16. Price Floor (minimum price)--a price floor occurs when a regulation stops the price from falling below a given price.

Concepts

1. The demand curve slopes downward to the right showing that as price rises a lower quantity will be demanded and as price falls a higher quantity will be demanded.
2. The supply curve slopes upward to the right showing that as price rises a larger quantity will be supplied and as price falls a lower quantity will be supplied.
3. A change in price will only cause a movement along the demand and supply curves and will not cause either of these curves to shift.
4. Among the economic variables that will shift the demand curve are changes in tastes, incomes, expectations, prices of other goods, and the number of buyers.
5. Among the economic variables that will shift the supply curve are changes in costs, expectations, and the number of sellers.
6. Changes in the equilibrium price and quantity will occur when the demand and/or supply curves shift. These changes are as follows:
   A. An increase in demand yields a price increase and a quantity increase.

B. A decrease in demand yields a price decrease and a quantity decrease.
C. An increase in supply yields a price decrease and a quantity increase.
D. A decrease in supply yields a price increase and a quantity decrease.

GUIDE TO ANALYZING ARTICLES

1. Make a list of all the economic variables that are changing in the article and determine whether each change affects buyers and/or sellers. Things that affect buyers could shift the demand curve; things that affect sellers could shift the supply curve.
2. If only price is changing, there will be a movement back to equilibrium unless prices are being changed and held at non-equilibrium levels by nonmarket institutions. If this is the case there will be a permanent shortage or surplus and we can proceed no further with our analysis.
3. If influences other than prices are changing, determine which curve or curves are being shifted and the direction of the shifts.
4. Diagram each shift and note its effect on the equilibrium price and quantity.
5. Compare the effects of the shifts to see if anything conclusive can be said about the new equilibrium price and quantity. (If more than one curve is shifting, the change in at least one of the variables will be indeterminant unless one can estimate how much each of the curves have shifted.)

Articles

AN ANALYZED ARTICLE: OVERVIEW

This article was written at a time when a new minimum wage law had
just gone into effect. The new minimum wage law provided for a 30¢
increase in the previous minimum wage of $2.35 per hour (par. 2).
It also included corresponding wage increases to those workers
whose salaries were based primarily on tips (par. 7). President
Carter supported and signed this law because he felt that the law
would put money "into the hands of those who need it to buy the
necessities of life" (par. 4). Our analysis should tell us whether
in fact such a law helped the working poor as Carter had suggested.

Minimum Hourly Wage Raises Today

Buffalo Courier-Express *(Jan. 1, 1976). Reprinted with
permission, courtesy of* The Associated Press.

1. WASHINGTON (AP)—Millions of America's lowest-
paid workers, many of them working on farms, in
department stores and behind fast-food counters, are
getting a pay raise with the new year.

2. Under legislation approved earlier this year, the
hourly minimum wage goes to $2.65 today, an
increase of 35 cents. The increase affects 4.5 million
workers and will pump an estimated $2.2 billion into the
nation's economy.

3. The legislation also provides for annual raises each
Jan. 1 through 1981, when the minimum wage will go
to $3.35, or almost $7,000 a year. The Labor
Department says the increases eventually will affect the pay
of 5.4 million workers and be good to the economy for
about $8.5 billion.

4. President Carter, who signed the minimum wage
legislation in November, said it would put money
"into the hands of those who need it to buy the

necessities of life."

5. Congress agreed to a change, however, that will mean
that an estimated 650,000 employees who would
have been covered under the old law will no longer
necessarily receive the minimum wage.

6. Under the current law, businesses with annual gross
sales of $250,000 are not required to pay the
minimum wage. The level goes to $275,000 as of July
1; $325,000 on July 1, 1980; and $362,500 after Dec. 31,
1981.

7. The law also will raise the wages of waiters, waitresses
and bartenders, but will keep them substantially
below the minimum wage on the theory that tips
make up the difference. Under current law, employers may
pay such workers a minimum of 50 percent of the
minimum wage. The figure will drop to 45 percent on Jan.
1, 1979 and 40 percent, or $2.01, 12 months later.

Analysis

For the sake of convenience, let's start our analysis at an equilibrium with the equilibrium wage being $2.35 per hour and the
equilibrium quantity of workers equaling 4.5 million (Par. 2).
This is shown in Figure 1.

Next we have an increase in wages because of the new law. This
results in a movement along both the demand and supply curves
because the wage rate is just the price of labor. At the new wage
of $2.65 per hour, the quantity of labor demanded will be less
than the quantity of labor supplied and a surplus of labor will
occur. Surpluses normally cause a movement back to the
equilibrium, but in this case, a non-market institution (the

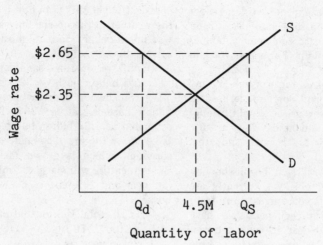

Figure 1

government) has entered the labor market and has stopped the wage
from returning to the equilibrium wage of $2.35. Thus the surplus
of labor has been perpetuated by the government fixing the minimum
wage at $2.65. Since the quantity of labor demanded is less than
the 4.5 million workers previously employed, and since firms
cannot be forced to hire workers they don't want, 4.5-Q_D
workers wil be unemployed by the new minimum wage law. Therefore
an important result of the new minimum wage law is an increase in
unemployment.

Which workers will be fired? The workers fired will most likely
be those workers who are not producing enough revenue for their
employers to warrant being paid $2.65 per hour. These are
society's less productive workers, and are probably those very
same people who are finding it difficult to purchase the "necessities of life." Therefore, our analysis indicates that the
poorest of workers will probably find themselves in worse shape
after the minimum wage law has gone into effect. Thus, if
President Carter signed this law in order to help these poor
people, he must have received some poor economic advice. (He
might have had other reasons for signing this law. What might
some of these reasons be?)

AN ARTICLE WITH QUESTIONS

Largest U.S. Harvest in History Threatens
To Drive Prices Down, Cut Farmers' Income

By FRANCIS L. PARTSCH
Staff Reporter of *The Wall Street Journal*

1. There's bad news on the farm this fall: The harvest
promises to be the largest in history.
That may sound like a paradox, but it isn't. This

2. year's crops of such major commodities as corn,
wheat and grain sorghum are so abundant that they
have driven farmers' prices far below expectations. The

resulting impact on farm income is expected to force more farmers out of business and weaken the economies of rural communities across the nation. It also could put a damper on President Nixon's hopes of holding Farm Belt votes in the 1972 election.

3. The big harvest isn't bad news for everyone by any means. Much corn, wheat and sorghum is used as animal feed, and their lower prices should prompt breeders to increase their flocks and herds. This, in turn, would mean lower consumer prices for meats and other animal products.

4. Some of these bargains have already begun showing up in supermarkets. Broiler chickens currently are selling for 23 cents a pound in some areas, down from 29 cents a pound a year ago. Lower feeding costs also have sent the price of eggs plunging to near 40 cents a dozen from 60 cents as recently as July. The price reductions have been so marked that trade groups are calling on producers to stem output by trimming their flocks.

5. Retail prices of beef and pork won't be affected for about a year because it takes at least that long to raise cattle and pigs to market weight, compared to a few months for chickens, but the new abundance of feed should eventually be felt here, too.

A Damper On Increases

6. "Pork prices at this time next year should be about where they are now, and the same goes for beef," predicts Dennis B. Sharpe, economist for the Federal Reserve Bank of Chicago. "If the harvest would have come in at last year's level, we would have expected price increases on both those products."

7. In addition, even some farmers who are hauling in record crops stand to benefit. That's particularly true of soybean growers. Despite the fact that this year's harvest is estimated at 1.18 billion bushels, up slightly from last year's peak, the price of soybeans has risen to about $3.15 a bushel, from $2.95 a year ago. The increase reflects the growing world demand for the versatile vegetable as a high-protein food supplement.

8. Many other farmers, however, see mostly troubles in the huge quantities of grain they are bringing in from their fields. The reason for their huge harvests is the almost total absence this year of Southern corn leaf blight, a disease that destroyed some 15% of the nation's corn crop in 1970.

9. The spores that caused the blight survived the winter and were expected to strike again this year, so at the recommendation of the U.S. Department of Agriculture corn farmers sharply increased their planting this spring to compensate for the looked-for losses. Growers of wheat and sorghum did likewise, expecting that their commodities would be in strong demand if corn failed again.

10. But instead, growing conditions this summer were nearly perfect all across the country. Spring came early, allowing farmers to plant almost two weeks earlier than usual. There was plenty of rain in May and June, getting the young plants off to a good start. Southern corn leaf blight thrives in hot, humid weather, but this year the weather in the crucial July and August growing period was unseasonably cool in most places. The blight didn't survive; the corn did.

11. As a result, this year's corn crop has been pegged at 5.4 billion bushels, 32% higher than last year's and 13% higher than the previous U.S. record of 4.76 billion bushels, set in 1967. The total wheat harvest is estimated at 1.63 billion bushels, 18% above last year and 0.5% above the previous high year of 1968. Production of sorghum, which is grown mostly in the West to feed Western cattle, will reach 892 million bushels, up 28% from last year and 19% above the 1967 mark of 755.6 million bushels.

12. In all, total U.S. output of food and fiber is expected to top 1970 by 12%, the biggest one-year jump in a dozen years.

Brunt Of Price Declines

13. The brunt of the price declines following in the wake of the big harvest has fallen on farmers whose main cash crop is corn; they make up approximately half of the nation's 2.9 million farm owners and operators. Last year, corn delivered in Chicago was selling for about $1.40 a bushel, and that rose to $1.62 a bushel this June, when it was still believed that blight damage would be heavy. From there, though, the drop has been sharp, with recent Chicago quotes hovering around $1.10 a bushel. In parts of the rural Midwest, corn farmers are being offered as little as 90 cents a bushel for their output. This is well below the average $1.05 a bushel that the government will loan farmers on their crop through support programs.

14. Many farmers would like to hold their crops off the market for the time being in hopes of getting a better price later, but the effect of the big harvest on storage space is expected to make this difficult. Some areas have adequate storage capacity, but other don't. For instance, in McLean County in Central Illinois, which claims to be the most fertile corn-growing region in the nation, there is only space to store about 30 million bushels of a 50-million-bushel crop. "We'd planned to build more bins this year, but we didn't because we expected a small crop," says Paul Anderson, president of Hasen Winkle Grain Co., a storage firm in Bloomington, the McLean County seat. "Now it looks like a lot of corn here will be stored on the ground."

A Cruel Dilemma

15. Corn stored on the ground commonly deteriorates and loses part of its market value.

16. All this poses a cruel dilemma for farmers. "The situation now gives me a sinking feeling—I'm stuck if I sell or if I hold," says Iven Britt, who farms 200 acres in McLean County. He says that his fields this year are yielding 135 bushels of corn an acre compared to just 92 bushels last year, but he adds that "it didn't pay to have such a good crop. I'd rather get 100 bushels an acre and get

something for it on the market. It was bad last year, seeing the blight kill my corn, but this isn't much better."

17. Wheat farmers, who comprise about 25% of the farming population, aren't as bad off as corn growers, but their outlook isn't rosy. Instead of the sizable price increase they looked for this fall, the current Chicago quote of $1.55 a bushel for their crop is down from the June 1971 high of $1.67.

18. Furthermore, that price could well drop in the months ahead. A large portion of the U.S. wheat crop has been exported in recent years, but the Agriculture Department recently estimated that the current shipping strike and increased competition from other nations would cut U.S. exports by 15% in the year ending next June 30.

19. Canada, whose wheat production this year is expected to soar to 500 million bushels from 338 million bushels in 1970, looms as an especially tough competitor in foreign markets. So do Australia, Brazil and Argentina, all of which are expected to produce bumper feed grain crops this year.

20. Sorghum farmers likewise are feeling the big-harvest pinch. Current prices of $1.85 a hundred pounds for the grain are down from the year-ago $2 a hundredweight and $2.65 earlier in 1971.

21. The income of wheat and sorghum farmers probably won't be off this year, but it won't rise much, either. "And with retail prices going up the way they have, this amounts to a loss of real income," points out an official of one farmers' group.

22. Overall, though, farmers' income is expected to decline to a total of $15.5 billion in 1971 from $15.7 billion in 1970, one top USDA official predicts privately. This drop isn't large, but then neither is the $11,200 that the average farm family earned last year.

Increased Subsidies

23. The atmosphere of gloom on the farm would be heightened if some leaders' predictions of increased farm failures come true. "You're going to see a lot of farm sales this winter," warns Walter Goeppinger, president of the National Corn Growers Association, a farmers' group. "The price drops have been especially hard on younger fellows who borrowed heavily to get started and now are having difficulty paying off their loans."

24. And the farmers' woes don't bode well for the Nixon administration. Last Monday, Agriculture Secretary Clifford Hardin moved to try to buoy farmer's income by increasing subsidies his department will pay to farmers who reduce the acreage they plant with corn next year, but the full impact of that move won't be felt until next fall. More recently, top Agriculture Department officials have been considering a plan to boost prices by buying corn on the open market.

25. Meantime, "farmers tend to blame the party in power when things go wrong," says Mr. Goeppinger. "And right now, things are going wrong."

Questions

1. What seems to be the problem in the agricultural sector of the economy? (Par. 2,3 and headline)
2. What four products are being highlighted in the article?
3. What should our analysis tell us?
4. List seven things that are affecting these four goods (Par. 2,7,9,10,14,18).
5. What is happening to the supply of corn? (Par. 2,9,10,14)
6. What is happening to the supply of sorghum? (Par. 2,9.10)
7. What is happening to the supply of wheat? (Par. 2,7,9,10)
8. What is happening to the supply of soybeans? (Par. 7,10)
9. What is happening to the demand for wheat? (Par. 18)
10. What is happening to the demand for soybeans? (Par. 7)
11. Why aren't there changes in the demand for corn and the demand for sorghum?
12. Draw the old and new supply and demand curves for each product and determine what is happening to each product's equilibrium price and quantity.
13. Using any further information given in the article, try to find out whether some of the indeterminant solutions in no. 12 (above) can be eliminated.
14. Does this analysis indicate why there is trouble in the agricultural sector of the economy?

AN ARTICLE FOR STUDENT ANALYSIS: OVERVIEW

This article was written in the spring of 1977 when the country was experiencing rapid increases in the price of coffee. These price increases affected several other markets including, as indicated in this article, the market for tea. The analysis presented in this article is not very difficult, but it points out very clearly how changes in the price of one product can affect the price of another product.

Steep Increase in Tea Price Brewing as Coffee Revolt Spurs Demand

By THE ASSOCIATED PRESS

Buffalo Evening News *(March 9, 1977). Reprinted by permission, courtesy of* The Associated Press.

1. Coffee drinkers who switched to tea to save money will soon find the cost of the substitute rising.

2. London dealers said Tuesday that the price of tea is about to soar all over the world, and a cup in Britain may cost twice as much this summer as it does now. They said a key reason is that many consumers are

3. turning from increasingly expensive coffee to cheaper beverages, particularly tea.

4. London auction prices rose from $1.20 a kilogram (2.2 pounds) on Feb. 28, 1976, to $2.57 a kilo on the same day this year. At Monday's auction the price hit $2.90 a kilo.

5. Brooke Bond, one of Britain's largest tea wholesalers, said American and Canadian buying at recent auctions in the Near East and London caused a shortage in a market that until a few months ago was burdened with a glut.

6. "I can't remember any time before when there actually hasn't been enough tea at an auction to meet the trade's demands, but that is what is happening now," another dealer said.

7. The impact on the tea drinker has not been immediate because it takes several months for price increases to work their way through the distribution pipeline.

8. A "brew-up" is still inexpensive for Britons, who drink more tea per capita than any other nation. An average cup of tea made at home from loose tea leaves costs about seven-tenths of a cent, milk and sugar included. It costs 4.27 cents to make a cup of instant coffee at home in Britain.

9. "Coffee has become so expensive that people have switched to tea, and that's happened even more in the United States, where President Carter has joined the tea set," said a leading London tea broker.

10. Mr. Carter sipped tea during his first televised fireside chat and during last weekend's radio call-in show. He explained that he was trying to avoid drinking coffee.

3

Elasticity

One day at a business lunch Mr. Olson, an automobile dealer, was telling Mr. Winslow, a clothing store owner, about his latest marketing plan. Mr. Olson found that when he decreased the price of his cars by $5, he could sell ten more cars a month and increase his total revenue. Mr. Winslow, always responsive to a good marketing idea, decided to lower the price of his shirts by $5. When his sales increased by 10 shirts, Winslow was happy--until he found out that his total revenue had unexpectedly declined. This confused Mr. Winslow because his plan had the same numerical results as Olson's, yet his total revenue had declined while Mr. Olson's had increased. Mr. Winslow decided to consult his economist who told him that the auto and shirt industries were not comparable. After all, the economist pointed out, a $5 decrease in price represents a very small percentage decrease in the price of cars, but a very large percentage decrease in the price of shirts. Likewise, the volume of cars sold increased by a much larger percentage than the volume of shirts sold. Therefore, Mr. Winslow should have expected his total revenue to decline when he received the results of his price change.

   Mr. Winslow learned the hard way what many economists have known for some time. That is, whenever examining changes in two economic variables, it is often more useful to compare percentage changes rather than absolute changes. One tool economists use to make this comparison is called elasticity. Many mistakes in economic analysis stem from a lack of knowledge about this concept, while at the same time, elasticity is at the heart of many of the most controversial issues in economics. Therefore elasticity can be a valuable concept to understand.

CHECKLIST

Definitions of New Terms

1. Elasticity (E)--a measurement which compares the percentage

change in one variable to the percentage change in another by dividing the first percentage change by the second.
2. Inelastic--when the elasticity is less than 1, it is said to inelastic.
3. Elastic--when the elasticity is greater than 1, it is said to be elastic.
4. Unitary Elastic--when the elasticity equals 1, it is said to be unitary elastic.

Concepts

1. The formula for calculating the elasticity between two variables (A & B) equals

$$E = \frac{\% \Delta \text{ in A}}{\% \Delta \text{ in B}} = \frac{A_1 - A_2 \Big/ \dfrac{A_1 + A_2}{2}}{B_1 - B_2 \Big/ \dfrac{B_1 + B_2}{2}}$$

2. The elasticity measurement is interpreted as follows:
   A. If $E > 1$, the percentage change of the variable in the numerator is greater than the percentage change of the variable in the denominator.
   B. If E 1, the percentage change of the variable in the numerator is less than the percentage change of the variable in the denominator.
   C. If $E = 1$, the percentage change of the variable in the numerator is equal to the percentage change of the variable in the denominator.

3. Some specific elasticities and their uses
   A. The price elasticity of demand = $\% \Delta$ in quantity demanded/ $\% \Delta$ in price
      i. determines the effect of a change in price on total revenue (TR).
         a. If $E > 1$, a rise in price lowers TR, a fall in price raises TR.
         b. if $E < 1$, a rise in price raises TR, a fall in price lowers TR.
         c. If $E = 1$, total revenue is at its highest.
         d. Since E rises as you go up the demand curve, TR rises as you go up the demand curve until $E = 1$ after which TR will decrease.
      ii. determines how much of an increase in costs can be shifted onto the consumers of a product
      iii. determines whether an excise tax can be used to change consumers' behavior
   B. The price elasticity of supply = $\% \Delta$ in quantity supplied/$\% \Delta$ in price
      i. determines the effect on the quantity of labor employed when wages rise

C. Cross elasticity = $\%\Delta$ in $Q_{D,A}/\%\Delta$ in P_B
    i. determines whether two goods are complements or substitutes
D. Income elasticity = $\%\Delta$ in $Q_{D,A}/\%\Delta$ in income
    i. determines whether a good is normal or inferior
E. Elasticity of investment with respect to interest rates = $\%\Delta$ in investment/$\%\Delta$ in interest rates
    i. determines whether policies used to change interest rates will be effective in changing economy activity

GUIDE TO ANALYZING ARTICLES

1. If an elasticity(s) is given in the article:
   A. Make sure you know which variable is in the numerator and which variable is in the denominator;
   B. Determine whether its size is consistent with the data given;
   C. Determine whether the article's conclusions are consistent with the elasticity(s);
   D. If no conclusions are made, use the given elasticity(s) to formulate your own conclusions.
2. If no elasticity(s) is given in the article:
   A. List the variables changing in the article;
   B. From this list, determine which elasticity(s) is appropriate for analyzing the article;
   C. Calculate or estimate the appropriate elasticity(s);
   D. Determine whether the article's conclusions are consistent with the elasticity(s);
   E. If no conclusions are made, use your elasticity calculations to formulate yor own conclusions.

Articles

AN ANALYZED ARTICLE: OVERVIEW

This article was written during a crisis period for New York
taxi drivers. Apparently, the latest price increase did not
increase total revenue as much as the taxi industry had hoped.
Consequently, the industry asked for another increase in taxi
fares. Our analysis should tell us why the industry was disappointed and whether their new rate increases will be successful.

Despite Fare Rise, Taxi Fleets Report New Losses Again

The New York Times *(Mar. 24, 1975). © by The New York
Times Company. Reprinted by permission.*

1. The City's taxi fleets have found the fare increase granted last fall inadequate and are preparing to seek a new increase, according to Taxi News, the industry's paper.

2. The 17.5 percent fare increase that went into effect in November has produced only about a 10 to 11 percent increase in gross revenues rather than the 17.5 percent that the Taxi and Limousine Commission had predicted, the paper said. As a result, the paper said, the possibility of operational profit has been wiped out and losses are building up again, because "operating costs have continued to inflate."

3. The industry's paper said that the Metropolitan Taxicab Board of Trade, representing the city's 60 fleet owners, would probably demand that the Taxi Commission "live up to its commitment to give them the fare increase that will provide the 17.5 percent increase in gross revenue.

4. "According to industry accountants, that can only be done by reshaping the fare upward to the 25 percent schedule they originally submitted," the paper added.

5. The Taxi News also suggested that the industry was expected to put forward a plan to offset the rising costs of gasoline. This might take the form of charging passengers 1 cent for each 2 cents per gallon of increased gasoline costs, the paper said. If gasoline costs dropped, it said, the procedure would be reversed, and 1 cent would be taken off the trip cost for each 2-cent reduction in the cost of gasoline.

6. The Metropolitan Taxicab Board of Trade has called a news conference for this morning to announce details of its plans and to document the fleet industry's needs, a spokesman said.

Analysis

According to paragraph 2, taxi drivers increased their price by
17.5 percent in November and expected their gross or total revenue
to rise by 17.5 percent as well. For this to have occurred, the
quantity demanded could not have fallen when the price rose. Such
a situation would have required a perfectly inelastic (E=0) demand
curve. Of course this is where the taxi industry made its mistake
since it should not have expected such a demand curve, especially
because of the many substitutes for taxis.

Well, if the price elasticity of demand is not equal to zero,
than what is it? Although we can not know for sure since we do
not know what exactly happened to quantity, there is enough data
in paragraph 2 to estimate the elasticity. The two variables we
find changing are price and total revenue. Price rose by 17.5
percent while total revenue rose by 10 or 11 percent. For this to
have occurred, the percentage change in quantity must have been
less than the percentage change in price and, according to our

concepts section, the price elasticity of demand must have been less than one.

Now that we have estimated the elasticity, we now must ask ourselves if we can use this information to analyze whether further price increases would yield the revenue increases the taxi industry hoped for. The answer is yes. According to the concepts section, increases in prices lead to increases in total revenue whenever the price elasticity of demand is less than 1. Therefore it would appear that the taxi industry correctly analyzed the situation when they recommended further price increases. It must also be remembered, however, that as prices are raised and one moves up the demand curve, the price elasticity of demand will eventually equal one. After this occurs further price increases will lower total revenue rather than raise it. Therefore, the taxi industry must be very careful to make sure it does not raise price too much.

30-Cent Gasoline Tax Hike Studied

By THE L.A. TIMES-WASHINGTON POST SERVICE

Buffalo Evening News (April 12, 1977). *Reprinted by permission, courtesy of L.A. Times-Washington Post Service.*

U. S. Might Retain 10¢ Annual Boost Up To 50-Cent Lid

1. WASHINGTON, April 12—The Carter administration is considering a proposal that would add 10 cents a gallon to gasoline taxes in each of the next three years if U.S. gasoline consumption continues rising above this year's level.

2. The current federal tax is 4 cents a gallon. The Carter plan also calls for continuing the 10-cent tax increase unless Americans reduce their gasoline consumption from 1977 levels by 2 percent a year between 1981 and 1985. The cumulative tax, if enacted, would not exceed 50 cents a gallon, according to one proposal.

3. A 10-cent-a-gallon tax would net the federal government approximately $10 billion which, in turn, could be used to lower social security taxes or state sales taxes to reduce the burden on consumers, administration sources said.

4. U. S. Gasoline prices have risen 53 percent since the 1973 Arab oil embargo and now average 61.8 cents a gallon. Compared with prices in other industrialized countries, U. S. gasoline prices are among the lowest.

5. Last year Americans consumed 7 million barrels of gasoline a day.

6. A "standby" gasoline tax, President Carter's planners hope, would reduce gasoline consumptioand further ease political opposition he would undoubtedly face if he called for an immediate increase in gasoline taxes.

7. Administration officials said Monday that specifics of the standby gasoline tax and other energy proposals are "moving targets" and are still being analyzed in top level administration meetings.

8. Mr. Carter has said he will announce his energy policy proposals April 20.

* * *

* * *

Questions

1. What is the main problem confronting the Carter administration in this article? (Par. 1, 5, 6)
2. What solution is being proposed by the Carter administration? (Par. 1,2)
3. What are the goals of this policy? (Par. 2,3)
4. What are the economic variables that will be changing if this policy is enacted? (Par. 1,2,3)
5. Which elasticity should be determined?

6. What must this elasticity be if the proposed policy is to work? (Par. 1,2,4)
7. Can we reasonably expect this elasticity to be present?
8. Do you think the Carter administration has suggested a workable policy?

AN ARTICLE FOR STUDENT ANALYSIS: OVERVIEW

This article comes from a weekly column on wine that appears in the Buffalo Evening News. The headline clearly shows that the concept of elasticity is applicable because both price and total revenue (sales) are mentioned. You probably do not have enough information to calculate the elasticities, but try to estimate the elasticities for both foreign and domestic wines. Then, using these elasiticities, try to make some conclusions concerning the wine pricing policies of these restaurants.

Price Policy Triples Restaurant's Sales

By WILLIAM MURRAY

Buffalo Evening News *(Nov. 22, 1976). Reprinted by permission.*

1. You've read about those old prospectors who dig away for years without striking gold when suddenly ... Now *Wine Almanac* feels the same way about the long time it has been trying to get restaurants to charge reasonable prices for wine.

2. Last week came a letter from David P. Shearer of Greenstreets Cafe, telling how he had reduced prices on his wine list and had reaped tripling of his wine sales as the result.

3. This is exactly what has happened in many other parts of the country. When restauranteurs stop doubling the retail price of wine—or worse—they find their customers start ordering more wine with their meals.

* * *

4. This rests on the basic logic that wine is food, not merely an intoxicant like hard liquor. The theory of many restaurant owners that profits depend on liquor sales is an old one—and one which has not kept bad restaurants from going out of business despite liquor sales.

5. A restaurant makes money because it serves good food at a reasonable price. The owner should no more charge double the retail price for wine than he should for a slice of bread or a glass of milk.

6. Along with his letter, Dave Shearer sent copies of his old and new wine lists. His new list carries a preface for the diner: "Our wines are priced about $1 and 50 cents a half bottle over retail stores prices, therefore enabling you to enhance your meal by drinking wine. May I suggest a full bottle with your dinner, or perhaps a half bottle with your appetizer, and a different half bottle with your entree."

* * *

7. A quick look at the two wine lists shows some interesting changes, ones which certainly should inspire the diner to order wine. Bottles and half bottles of imported wines dropped from $1.50 to $2 in several cases.

8. Shearer also has been careful to carry a cosmopolitan choice of wines, offering French, German, Italian, Portuguese and Spanish wines as well as American vintages and aperitifs.

9. Earlier I received similar information from Robert Lenz, innkeeper at Asa Ransom House in Clarence. He also noted that he had followed the suggestion in Wine Almanac to offer reasonable wine prices. Although he sticks closer to American wines, he offers his patrons a wide selection at very tempting prices.

10. The Turgeon Brothers' restaurants have followed a similar policy for several years, although inflation has chipped away a bit at the $1 difference in retail and restaurant prices.

* * *

11. Mastrantonio's La Galleria and several other restaurants follow the policy of considering wine as part of the meal, rather than a chance to sock the customer. It is impossible to know the many others who might do the

same. Wine Almanac would be interested in getting reaction from some of these because there is no intent to overlook any restaurant trying to please wine lovers.

12. This policy should cover all wines, not just a few selected ones to merely give the impression of offering reasonable price.

13. Remember that the restaurant already receives the same profit margin as a liquor store when it purchases its wine. Any extra charge should be added only to cover storage and service costs, plus a slight profit.

Introduction to Microeconomics

Jill checks the breadbox--no bread. Next the refrigerator--no milk. Without a thought, Jill gets some money, goes to the nearest store, and finds bread and milk readily available. Jill, like most other people, takes this ready availability of the things she needs for granted: the sun rises every morning; the nearest store has bread and milk.

Do you every wonder who decided that a certain amount of land should be used for grazing dairy herds whereas some other amount should be sown into wheat? Who told dairy farmers and wheat farmers where and how they should produce their products? Moreover, how was it decided that Jill should have a certain amount of income, an amount which determines her share of total output?

The answers to the questions raised above are not found in nature. Instead, they are the result of choices each society must make. These choices involve three specific problems: 1. how to allocate resources; 2. how to organize production; and 3. how to distribute products. Since these problems deal with specific economic units such as consumers and firms, they are called microeconomic problems.

In the U.S., most microeconomic problems are solved through the use of markets. The Soviet Union and China, on the other hand, prefer central planning. Other countries use some combination of markets and central planning.

In this chapter, you will learn how to distinguish between allocation, production, and distribution problems and you will examine some situations where microeconomic decisions are being made.

CHECKLIST

Definitions of New Terms

1. <u>Microeconomics</u>--the study of individual units of an economic system, such as consumers, resource owners, and firms, rather than aggregate economic activity.
2. <u>Allocation of resources</u>--the process of determining what specific products should be produced from the economy's scarce resources.
3. <u>Organization of production</u>--the process of establishing facilities for production and coordinating all productive activity.
4. <u>Distribution of products</u>--the process of dividing the economy's output among the various consuming units.
5. <u>Market economy</u>--an economic system in which all allocation, production, and distribution decisions are made by individual economic units reacting to market-determined prices.
6. <u>Centrally planned economy</u>--an economic system in which state planning agencies make all economic decisions.
7. <u>Mixed economy</u>--an economic system which uses some combination of markets and central planning.

Concepts

1. <u>Allocative efficiency</u>--occurs when the type and quantity of products produced from scarce resources conform to the priorities established by the economic system. In a market economy, consumer demand determines the priorities. In a centrally planned economy, a state agency assigns the priorities.
2. <u>Productive efficiency</u>--when the productive units in an economic system produce at lowest possible cost per unit. To accomplish this, things such as the plant size, input mix, and output level must be appropriate.
3. <u>Distributional equity</u>--when a socially acceptable income distribution is achieved. Without making value judgments, an economist can only 1. present data on the existing distribution of income, and 2. predict the redistributive effects of economic policy.

GUIDE FOR ANALYZING ARTICLES

1. Determine if the discussion is about an allocation, production, or distribution situation. In general, you will find:
   A. an allocation situation when changes in an industry's output and/or consumers' tastes are being discussed;
   B. a production situation when some aspect of a firm's productive activity is being discussed;
   C. a distributive situation when the income of some individuals is changing relative to that of other individuals.
2. In an allocative situation, determine if the specific amount

of each type of product is consistent with the:
A. market demand of consumers in a market economy;
B. priorities of planners in a centrally planned economy.
3. In a production situation, determine what is being done to assure that products are being produced at lowest cost.
4. In a distributive situation, determine:
A. the reason for differences in income among individuals;
B. if relative incomes are changing.

Articles

AN ANALYZED ARTICLE: OVERVIEW

In this article we have the opportunity to discuss all three microeconomic problems, namely, allocation, production, and distribution. Since China's economy is centrally planned, you will be able to see how the state is solving some problems in each of these three areas. While reading this article, give some thought to how these problems are solved in the U.S. economy.

China's New Economic Policy

By ROBERT KEATLEY
Mr. Keatley, who covers foreign affairs in the Journal's
Washington bureau, recently made his sixth visit to China.

Reprinted by permission of The Wall Street Journal,
(Sept. 22, 1977), © *Dow Jones & Company Inc., 1977.*
All rights reserved.

1. China's new leaders, most of them actually retreads or survivors of purges under the late Chairman Mao Tse-tung, have some old-fashioned ideas about how to solve their country's grave economic and social problems.

2. "There must be less empty talk and more hard work," insists Communist Party vice chairman and government Deputy Premier Teng Hsiao-ping, the feisty twice-purged politician who has reemerged as, in effect, China's general manager of almost everything.

3. If any single sentence sums up Peking's policies in the Post-Mao period, that statement does. After 11 years of confusing and often ludicrous internal disputes, which not only ignored but often aggravated basic national problems, the men now in charge have set a new course. They are abandoning the noisiest rhetoric of the later Mao era and are moving back to policies that often got them into trouble with the old Chairman. The new leaders worry less about abstract idological purity and more about producing additional goods for their people—who number awesomely close to one billion.

4. They need to. Though China isn't near collapse, as some enemies might wish, the late Chairman's final decade of life was one of much disorder and even chaos in China. The economy has suffered and social problems have increased; change is needed, the new leaders agree.

*
*
*

5. "Hua is aware that without economic achievements he can't consolidate and keep his power in years to come," explains a Peking-based diplomat, who says that's why Vice Chairman Teng has been put in charge of the economy. "The Chinese people now expect miracles from a miracle man (Mr. Teng) who has had a miracle career."

6. Well, there won't be any miracles; China doesn't have the resources or technology to produce sudden prosperity. In fact, the new policies will continue to stress agriculture, light industry and heavy industry—in that order. But important changes, all designed to improve efficiency, are in the works. Among them:

Capital Allocation

7. A basic and contentious issue has long been where to spend China's limited investment funds. Not only do military men want more money to upgrade their dated weapons, but civilian planners debate how to invest what's left over. It appears that rail transportation, coal, iron and steel and oil will get special stress-particularly projects that eliminate bottlenecks. For example, iron ore mining and steel processing will be expanded to permit better use of existing steel production capacity. China now imports steel products it should make for itself.

Consumer Demand

8. China plans to raise factory workers' wages by 15% to 20% in October, according to a dispatch yesterday by the Japanese news agency Kyodo. Managers, technicians, store clerks, school teachers and other relatively highly paid personnel also will receive boosts, according to Kyodo. If true—the reports couldn't be confirmed in the U.S.—the wage increase would be the first major boost in about 14 years. Also, the government in some places has been giving workers movie tickets, vacation opportunities and even cash bonuses for extra effort.

9. A wage rise, however, would cut into funds available for investment, another priority of the new leadership. And another problem will be to prevent a

27

further widening of the gap between city and country living standards, already a source of social tension. One guess is that television will be spread across the land, perhaps by an official TV set or two for every village or neighborhood, as a visible sign of affluence.

Management

10. Central and regional planning are being tightened to reduce waste and duplication, a reinstatement of a Teng policy repudiated by his now-vanquished foes. But within such guidelines, local managers will get more leeway about organizing production. Factory profits are now desirable and not attacked as signs of a capitalist mentality.

Agriculture

11. This remains the central problem. The nation must feed four times the U.S. population from only 60% as much arable land. Crop increases have matched population growth over the past 20 years, but U.S. experts think an adverse trend is developing. Thus, modernization is needed—more chemical fertilizers, better seeds, mechanization. But this will be ponderous and expensive, with weather still a major and uncontrollable factor. That's why China is spending $1.5 billion to import farm products, money which it would rather spend on modernization.

Trade And Technology

12. Here too a reversal is underway. Mr. Teng previously was deposed in part because he favored the "capitulationist policy of worshipping and toadying to foreign countries and selling out our national resources," the official press complained only last fall. Now such things as exporting oil to buy factories, which Mr. Teng had wanted to do, are approved. China wants "to learn from other countries and introduce their advanced technology to meet our needs . . . to increase our ability to develop our national economy and achieve modernization independently," according to the official People's Daily.

13. Officials hint commerce will rise even though Sino-American political relations aren't showing much progress.

14. None of this means that Chinese society is being radically revised, or that it will be Chairman Mao's basic concepts remain in force, and liberalization—which is occurring in the intellectual sphere as well as the economic—will be carefully controlled; today's leaders, like those they ousted, consider too much relaxation both costly and dangerous. But the move away from the late Chairman's more radical legacy is clear and likely to persist, largely because of China's pressing need for economic growth and modernization.

15. "They can now praise Mao forever and also depart from his teachings in the name of Mao," says a diplomat in Peking. And if the result means a bit more stability and affluence, that would suit Washington just fine—for a benign China, concerned mostly with its own problems, will help all Asia remain calm.

Analysis

You might have had a difficult time determining from this article that China has a centrally planned economic system if you had not already known so. However, you were given a big hint when you read that "Vice Chairman Teng has been put in charge of the economy" (par. 5). Later, additional evidence of direct government involvement in resource allocation, production, and distribution is given. (Is anyone in the U.S. "put in charge" of the economy?)

The specific material on resource allocation is found in paragraphs 6 and 7. Agriculture, light industry, and heavy industry, respectively, have been given priority status in the economy, however, these sectors must compete with the military for China's scarce resources. Moving to specific industries, we find that rail transportation, coal, iron and steel, and oil will receive additional resources. Since China has few new resources, these industries will receive additional resources only by taking resources away from other industries. Chairman Hua hopes these reallocations will achieve economic growth because he believes his political future depends upon such growth. (Does the political future of American presidents depend upon their ability to reallocate resources and achieve economic growth? How would an American president reallocate resources?)

A second means of providing additional growth is through

improved productive efficiency. One way the Chinese expect to accomplish this is by granting "local managers more leeway in organizing production" (par. 10). Those production units which are most efficient should earn profits, which will earn rewards for their managers and workers (par. 10,8). (Does this method of improving productive efficiency resemble anything done in a market economy?)

Although the Chinese would also like to make agricultural production more efficient, little improvement is expected because modernization would be "ponderous and expensive" (par. 11). On the other hand, China may be able to improve its industrial productivity by using the proceeds from oil exports to import factories, which would immediately provide them with advanced technology (par. 12).

Chinese planners are also redistributing income in their new economic policy. Three observations can be made about the redistributive effects of this policy. First, it appears that city workers' income will increase relative to that of farm workers (par. 8). Second, one may infer that city factory workers will receive a larger increase in income than other city workers. This inference is derived from the statement that city factory workers will receive a 15 percent to 20 percent increase whereas other types of city workers will simply receive "boosts" (par. 8). (Remember, this is just a hunch.) Finally, those workers who exert "extra effort" will be entitled to extra consumer goods (par. 8).

In conclusion, we have seen that the Chinese are reallocating resources according to their growth objectives; they are improving productive efficiency by changes in management and technology; and they are redistributing income. (Will the new income distribution be more equitable? Why?)

AN ARTICLE WITH QUESTIONS

National Interest Is Energy Priority

By GEORGE F. WILL
Mr. Will this week won the Pulitzer Prize
for commentary, a tribute to the general
caliber of his nationally syndicated column.

Buffalo Evening News *(April 20, 1977). Reprinted by permission of the Washington Post Writers Group.*

1. It is a tale of two cities. Detroit, says Tom Murphy, provides "what people want," but Washington is telling people, in effect, "You're not smart enough to know what's best for the country, so we've got to decide for you"

2. Murphy, chairman of General Motors Corp., is understandably unhappy that henceforth the kinds of cars marketed will be determined more by government than by consumers. He is worried that Washington may impose stiff taxes on large cars. And he is alarmed by the law which stipulates that by 1985 each manufacturer's "fleet average" must be 27.5 miles per gallon.

★ ★ ★

3. The effect of that will be to establish a small quota for the large cars the public emphatically prefers. A manufacturer might have to sell four subcompacts in

29

order to keep its "fleet average" in balance and earn the right to sell another large car.

4. If Americans become unhappy about the size of new cars, they may start maintaining their 100 million old cars rather than trading them. But cut new-car sales by even 10 percent and you will have an earthquake in the automotive and related industries such as steel, rubber, glass and rugs.

5. Since 1974, GM's fuel efficiency has improved nearly 50 percent, and this year its big cars shrank a foot without sacrificing interior space. But there are limits to what engineering ingenuity can do in preserving dimensions while increasing efficiency.

6. Fuel efficiency is needed because no politically possible increase in the price of gasoline will cut demand substantially. Even at 60 cents a gallon, the average driver of a big car would save only $100 a year in gasoline costs by switching to a compact. So the key to substantial conservation is not trying to get people to drive less. It is getting them into more efficient cars.

7. But Murphy's question echoes across the land: What entitles government to censor consumer preferences?

The answer in part, is this:

8. Government exists not merely to serve individuals' immediate preferences, but to achieve collective purposes for an ongoing nation. Government, unlike the free market, has a duty to look far down the road and consider the interests of citizens yet unborn and energy needs of the future.

9. Unfortunately, many citizens today think of themselves primarily as consumers, and think government's primary duty is to facilitate enjoyable consumption.

★ ★ ★

10. So liberals advocate a "consumer protection agency." Conservatives champion "consumer sovereignty."

11. God (according to Jefferson) endowed mankind with an inalienable right to pursue happiness.

12. Neither Detroit nor Washington is recognizably the City of God. But Washington is the city of government and is responsible for stipulating the national nterest. So, increasingly, it will discourage some ways of pursuing happiness.

Questions

1. What would have made you choose this article for this chapter?
2. Is an allocative, production, or distribution problem discussed in this article? How did you determine this?
3. What is the nature of the microeconomic problems? (See paragraphs 3 and 8.)
4. Do you agree with the argument presented in paragraph 8?

AN ARTICLE FOR STUDENT ANALYSIS: OVERVIEW

Although he is a syndicated columnist and not an economist, Nicholas Von Hoffman's article contains a provocative discussion of why he favors an economic policy of direct redistribution of income from taxpayers to unemployed steelworkers rather than helping them by limiting steel imports.

This article not only presents Von Hoffman's attitude about distributive equity for steelworkers, but it also reveals his views about why the U.S. steel industry is less productive than the Japanese.

Inefficiency, Not Foreign Imports, Held Responsible for Steel Woes

By NICHOLAS VON HOFFMAN

Buffalo Courier-Express *(Oct. 9, 1977). © King Features Syndicate, Inc. 1977.*

1. The steel industry, union and management both, are orchestrating a campaign to push the American government away from free trade and toward the economic isolationism of the 1930s. The thousands of workers being laid off at the big steel plant in Youngstown, Ohio, must disturb us all, and anger those of us who fall for the malarkey that it was those crafty, paternaturally energetic Nips who have done this awful thing to our fellow citizens.

2. Nevertheless the real plight of the workers and communities like Youngstown should not be a reason for helping either management or the union. It will take new legislation, but we can save Youngstown without saving the Youngstown Sheet and Tube Co. which is closing its plant and ending 5,000 jobs in that Mahoning Valley city. Just as we have special programs of aid when natural disasters hit a community, so we could declare Youngstown an economic disaster area. Under such a program the laid-off workers would continue to receive a weekly pay check equivalent to the one they had been receiving from the steel company.

3. Ordinary unemployment compensation won't be enough. The purchasing power in the area has to be maintained until new industry paying similar wages can be brought in or people and businesses can gradually be moved away. The key word is gradual. The moving also requires significant help for the smaller businesses affected as well as for the dislocated workers.

4. This could be a reemployment program that works. We're not dealing with demoralized center city youth who've never held a job and don't know how. These are good workers with all the right habits and values to fit in wherever there may be a need.

5. If this sounds expensive, it's not nearly so as slapping import quotas and tariffs on foreign steel. Helping the workers and the community directly will cost hundreds of millions, maybe even several billions for a few years; helping the workers by helping the management and the union, however, will cost tens of billions indefinitely.

6. No matter how much steel executives deny it, the reason they're in the soup doesn't have anything to do with crazy little yellow men working for inhumanly low wages or unfair help to the Japanese steel industry by its government. Our government is every bit as assiduous in helping our export industries as the Japanese, the German or the French.

7. The Japanese are simply more efficient. In 1975 it took 9.2 hours of labor in Japan to produce a ton of steel; it took 10.9 hours of labor here. That isn't a reflection on the American working man, but on his boss and the tools the boss has provided his workers with.

8. Eighty percent of Japan's steel is made with new basic oxygen furnaces as opposed to 63 percent of America's, which also trails West Germany and France in this regard. The Japanese are so far ahead of us in the technology of the new, super-huge blast furnaces that Inland Steel had to hire Nippon Kokan, Japan's second-biggest steel maker, to provide expert advice. "We simply didn't have the experience to design a furnace that will eventually produce 10,000 tons of iron a day," an Inland official was quoted as saying.

9. The same kind of thing holds true for introduction of the new continuous casting process for rolling steel. Again, American steel companies are well behind all three of their principal competitors. How inefficient domestic steel producers are is seen by the fact the Japanese can buy West Virginia coking coal, as important in steel manufacture as iron ore, ship it 12,000 miles to Yokohama, make steel out of it, ship it back to the United States and undersell steel made 75 miles from West Virginia with some of the same raw material.

10. Some steel men say the new investments weren't made because the Justice Department refused to permit mergers that would have allowed raising the necessary capital. As long as foreign steel can compete here, no reason exists to block mergers of domestic companies, but that doesn't explain the failure of the industry giants to stay competitive. Over the years they've been given billions of dollars in tax write-offs for equipment depreciation. They were supposed to spend the money on new plants, and they didn't.

11. American firms buying foreign-made steel say they do so for reasons other than price. Often, they say, the product is higher quality and the service is better and quicker.

12. Twenty-five years ago Great Britain, another "mature" industrial society, chose to save jobs by subsidizing obsolescence. Need more be said?

Consumer Behavior

Among Douglas's birthday presents was a crisp dollar bill from his Grandfather. An accompanying note said, "Spend this for candy." As soon as his guests had left, Douglas ran to the nearest store and carefully picked out candies: six candy kisses @ 2¢ each, five gumballs @ 2¢ each, one chocolate bar @ 20¢ each, etc. He paid for his selections and left, clutching his sack of sugary delights, a smile of total satisfaction on his face.

If you had read this chapter and then observed Douglas making his purchases, you could have told Douglas he just maximized his satisfaction by following the Law of Equal Marginal Utilities Per Dollar when he made his selections. Moreover, you could have referred to the Law of Diminishing Marginal Utility and predicted that Douglas will probably not get as much additional satisfaction from his second kiss as he gets from the first kiss. (But, despite all you will know about consumer behavior when you finish this chapter, you will not learn how to get as much satisfaction from a dollar as Douglas just got!)

Economists have developed several theories of consumer behavior to provide some background information for the Law of Demand. In this chapter, we will learn about some of these theories before seeing how they apply to several specific demand situations.

CHECKLIST

Definitions of New Terms

1. Utility--another word for satisfaction. Although economists often refer to units of utility, sometimes called utils, this is always done in either a conceptual or a relative sense since they cannot measure satisfaction on a unit basis.
2. Marginal Utility--the additional utility provided by another unit of a product.

3. Law of Diminishing Marginal Utility--for most consumers and most products, the increase in total utility from consuming additional units of a product becomes smaller and smaller. For example, a youngster would undoubtly prefer two candy kisses to one (more total utility), but the second kiss would be less satisfying than the first.

4. Interpersonal Consumption Effects--when one individual's utility is being affected by the attitudes or consuming habits of others. When present, these effects may alter the laws of consumer behavior.

5. Conspicuous Consumption--a type of interpersonal consumption effect whereby a consumer's utility is increased when others are impressed with the consumer's purchases. This effect may cause a consumer to buy more units of a product when its price increases.

6. Addictive Consumption Effects--if a consumer is addicted to a product, marginal utility may increase as more units are consumed.

Concepts

1. Law of Equal Marginal Utility Per Dollar--to maximize satisfaction, consumers allocate their income among products so that the marginal utility per dollar (that is, marginal utility divided by price) of each product is equal. Or, to state it in equation form, $MU_a/P_a = MU_b/P_b$. Using this and the Law of Diminishing Marginal Utility, we can show that when the price of one product, say P_b, increases, the consumer will buy less of "b" in order to raise the marginal utility of "b" proportionate to the rise in the price of "b." We have just shown one reason why consumers buy fewer units at higher prices. (Another reason is that higher prices reduce real income.) It is relatively easy to derive a downsloping demand curve by using the procedure described above.

GUIDE TO ANALYZING ARTICLES

1. Determine if you can find suffcient price and quantity information to generalize about the nature of the demand curve for the products being discussed.
   A. Be sure to refer back to the chapter on supply and demand and the chapter on elasticity.
2. Try to use the information on demand to make observations about marginal utility.
   A. Does the Law of Diminishing Marginal Utility seem to apply?
   B. Are interpersonal or addictive effects present?
3. Determine if the Law of Equal Marginal Utilities Per Dollar is applicable.
   A. Remember this Law can frequently be used when two or more products are being consumed and the price of one product is changing.
4. Use your analysis to explain and predict consumer behavior.

Articles

AN ANALYZED ARTICLE: OVERVIEW

Hairdresser Jon Goodman sells a service that seems to defy the Law of Demand--the higher his price, the greater the number of customers. The article does not explain why this phenomenon occurs, but it provides enough information for us to apply our theories of consumer behavior and provide one explanation for the apparent upward-sloping demand curve.

They Wait in Line for His $200 Haircuts

By PATRICIA SHELTON
Chicago Daily News Service

Chicago Daily News, *by Patricia Shelton. Reprinted by permission from Field Enterprises, Inc. (Reprinted in* The Buffalo Evening News, *(Sept. 24, 1975).*

1. CHICAGO—Ever since Jon Goodman raised his price for haircuts from 25 to 50 cents when he was a kid in Summetville, Ind., people have been telling him he's going to price himself right out of his scissors.

2. But the higher he goes—and he very possibly is the highest-priced hairdresser in the world today—the bigger and more ardent his loyal coterie of clients becomes.

3. Goodman, style director and manager of the beauty salon at Chicago's Bonwit Teller, figures that if he doesn't value his work, nobody else will. He now values it to the tune of $200 for your first time in his chair, and a minimum of $50 for each visit thereafter.

4. Besides, on your visit he'll tell you bluntly that it may take four or five times to get your look exactly right.

5. And don't tell him what you want. If you know, you don't need to pay his prices.

* * *

6. "I'm no good unless I have complete control," said Goodman. Obviously, plenty of women and a considerable number of men are willing to give him free reign, because it usually takes two to three weeks to get an appointment.

7. Although Goodman is first of all a hairstylist for women, he's picking up a growing following of male clients—most successful executives.

8. What you're entitled to for your first $200 is anything Goodman thinks needs to be done to you, including a new makeup job and excluding hand-streaking of hair. The streaking could cost you another $100.

9. The $50 for each subsequent visit entitles you to a shampoo, set and cut.

10. Many of his customers are rich. But others actually have to scrimp and save to pay their tab. It's not uncommon for both kinds of customers to ask his advice about their clothes—or their lives in general.

* * *

11. He couldn't care less what hair style trend-setters such as Alexandre of Rome, and Vidal Sasson are pushing. "The important thing is to bring out the individual, not that you can't tint it and tamper with it," he said.

Analysis

We find two types of data in this article. First, we learn that Jon Goodman's prices have increased from 25¢, when he was a kid, to $200 today. Despite this increase in price, he has more customers today than ever before. Consequently, even if we adjust for inflation, higher consumer income, and improvements in Jon's skill, we are still left with an apparent upward-sloping demand curve.

One way to explain this unusual situation is to divide Jon's services into two separate products. The $200 price that Jon charges for a first visit will apply to Jon's first product, which we will label "being a Jon Goodman client." It is this product that appears to have an upward-sloping demand since higher prices seem to cause an increase in quantity demanded.

Jon also sells a second product--we will call this one "repeat visits"--which sells for a minimum of $50 (par. 3). Therefore, customers will pay $200 for the first visit but only $50 for a second visit; this is the type of behavior we would expect from a downward-sloping demand curve.

Now that we have found an upward-sloping demand for one product and a downward sloping demand for another, what generalizations can we make about the marginal utility of Jon's products? First, let us examine the service we called "being a Jon Goodman client." Let us begin by assuming that Jon is a good hairdresser. So are a lot of other hairdressers in Chicago! Why are Jon's clients willing to pay so much more for their first visit? One explanation is that the difference between other prices and Jon's price represents the utility his customers get from the envy of friends who cannot afford Jon's prices. Jon offers a service that can be conspicuously consumed: everyone who is "anyone" must pay his $200 price. Moreover, those clients who can afford Jon's prices derive even more marginal utility from higher prices.

What is the marginal utility of a second trip to Jon's after one is known as "being a Jon Goodman client?" Probably considerably less than the marginal utility of the first visit. If so, we have a case of diminishing marginal utility for "repeat visits."

We have offered one explanation for the consumer behavior found in this article. This explanation was based upon marginal utility analysis. Although our analysis does not prove that there is increasing marginal utility for one product and decreasing marginal utility for another, we were able to explain an unusual demand situation by making these assumptions.

AN ARTICLE WITH QUESTIONS

Carey Tilts to Economy at Expense of Environment

By LINDA GREENHOUSE
Special to *The New York Times*

1. ALBANY, Feb. 5—Governor Carey's decision to stress economic recovery, even at the expense of some of the recent gains of the environmental movement, reflects not only a belief that strict environmental regulations are bad for business, but also a political judgment that the environmental movement has run its course and that most people are not more interested in such issues as jobs and taxes.

2. This change of priorities has rapidly emerged as a major theme of the Carey administration's second year. "We must regulate no more than necessary," he told the Legislature in his State of the State message a month ago.

3. Since then, Mr. Carey has publicly sided with his Commerce Commissioner, John S. Dyson, rather than his Environmental Commissioner, Ogden R. Reid, on the question of how quickly the General Electric Company should be forced to stop discharging the industrial chemical polychlorinated biphenyl into the Hudson River.

4. The Governor's economic message to the Legislature, due next week, is expected to provide much greater detail on the new direction. It is likely that the Governor will back Mr. Dyson against Mr. Reid on another key issue and will ask the Legislature for an 18-month delay in the implementation of the state's new Economic Quality Review Act.

5. The spectacle of two of the Governor's cabinet members airing their differences in public, as Mr. Reid and Mr. Dyson have been doing in the last month, is unmatched in recent memory here. But there are indications that the unusual public dispute in not at all the embarrassment to the Governor that many people assume it to be.

6. To the contrary, some Carey advisors hint strongly that in publicly taking on Mr. Reid, Mr. Dyson is doing exactly what he was told to do when he was shifted from the Department of Agriculture and Markets into Commerce two months ago.

7. While Mr. Carey is convinced that the public mood has turned away from strict adherence to the tenets of the environmental movement, one aide said "we may be six-term Congressman and one-time gubernatorial candidate who is widely assumed to have ambitions for the United State Senate or other elective office—the risk is minimized when the adversary role is played by Mr. Dyson. Mr. Carey can appear as a moderate mediator between the two, gradually tilting toward Mr. Dyson's position.

8. Mr. Dyson is clearly a rising star in the administration. Mr. Carey brought the boyish-looking, 32-year-old former newspaper publisher with him to a gathering of maritime union leaders. It was a unlikely setting for a Commerce Commissioner—who is traditionally the cabinet's liaison with employers, not employees—but the Governor said he wanted to dramatize what he called a "new alliance of labor, government and business."

9. It was at that labor meeting that Governor Carey, declaring that "it will do little good if we rescue our environment at the cost of our economy," made an unmistakable reference to Mr. Reid, "Anyone who doesn't agree with that principle," Mr. Carey said "won't be working in this government.

10. Much of the Governor's dissatisfaction with Mr. Reid has stemmed from the P.C.B. issue, although there are other problems as well. Mr. Reid has asked the General Electric Company to end all discharges of the toxic chemical by next September, a goal the company has said is unfeasible and could cause it to close the two Hudson River plants in question.

11. Current Federal standards allow a P.C.B. discharge of 3.5 ounces a day beginning in June, 1977. There is a proposed Federal amendment that would bring the discharge to zero, but the Governor's feeling is that as long as the Federal standard is 3.5, the state should be no more stringent than other states. Since General Electric discharged 30 pounds of the chemical every day for years, and is now discharging between two and three pounds daily, the Governor sees the difference between zero and 3.5 ounces—which company has said it can live with—as largely symbolic, the kind of strict adherence to environmental purity at the expense of business that he wants to end.

12. The evolution of the Governor's policy is being watched closely here, and many of Mr. Carey's fellow politicians believe that his political judgment is correct. "I'd play this thing the same way Carey has," one top Republican aide closely familiar with the environmental movement said today. "Reid has overplayed his hand. The public wants everyone to stop clowning around and get back to the bread and butter."

13. Still, Mr. Carey's course is scarcely risk-free. With his "new alliance" of business and labor—inherently a tenuous union at best—Mr. Carey is treading new ground for a Democratic Governor. He too, could overplay his hand.

14. In turning the Environmental Quality Review back to the Legislature for reworking, for example, Mr. Carey risks ending up with a totally gutted law and could emerge looking like the Governor who fought for the forces of pollution. While the public may applaud environmental laissez-faire, its desire to actually see the clock turned back is far from certain.

15. From all accounts, it is a risk the Governor understands and one he is obviously willing to take.

Questions

1. What is being consumed in this article? (Remember, be flexible.)
2. Can you find any information that relates to the demand for the product being consumed? (Hint: you should be able to find some information about changes in the amount being consumed in paragraph 11.)
3. Can you use the information in the article to make generalizations about the marginal utility of consumers for this product? (Hint: in this situation, the consumers are citizens of New York and their Governor is speaking for them.)
4. Can you apply the Law of Equal Marginal Utilities Per Dollar to the situation?
5. What generalizations or predictions can you make about demand?

AN ARTICLE FOR STUDENT ANALYSIS: OVERVIEW

Hamburger sales have increased as hamburger-orientated, fast-food
establishments have become popular with American consumers.
Moreover, further increases in hamburger sales are predicted once
the price of steak becomes relatively more expensive. This comparison of hamburger and steak consumption can be analyzed by
using the Law of Equal Marginal Utility Per Dollar equation. When
using this equation, be sure to include changes in tastes as well
as changes in prices.

Like It or Not, We're Part of "Hamburger Society"

By DAN MORGAN
L.A. Times-Washington Post Service

Buffalo Evening News *(Feb. 8, 1977). Reprinted by
permission, courtesy of the L.A. Times-Washington Post
Service.*

1. WASHINGTON—Americans are now devouring hamburgers at the rate of 50 billion a year.

2. Hamburgers have become the people's food: the
equivalent of the Italian's spaghetti, the Indian's
curry or the Russian's borscht.

3. Americans spend more than $25 billion a year for
beef, and a substantial amount of that money is for
hamburgers.

4. If any proof of the entrenched position of the
hamburger in the country's diet is needed, Mc-
Donald's restaurants can give it. The chain, with 23
billion sold already, will open about one new outlet a day
for the next 10 years.

* * *

5. The steak, that other great national symbol, has not
yet been relegated to the scrap heap of history but
economic developments are eclipsing the steak, altering the
tastes of consumers and changing the structure of the beef
industry.

6. The preference of Americans for meals and snacks in
restaurants and fast food stores shows no signs of
letting up. Consumer Reports magazine predicts that
by 1980 half the meals eaten in this country will be away
from home, if present trends continue.

7. While many restaurant chains are expanding their
menus and offering more salad, seafood, pizza and
Mexican recipes, hamburgers are still the staple of the
fast food industry.

* * *

8. The other development that seems destined to speed
up the evolution of the country into a hamburger
society is economic. Sometime soon—if not this year,
then surely in 1978 and 1979—the price of beef is going to
rise, possibly sharply.

9. The stage for this already has been set on the nation's
ranges, farms and cattle fattening yards, and there is
no changing it. The size of the country's beef herd is
now being rapidly reduced, as ranchers suffer some of their
worst losses since the 1930s. So the supply of beef is bound
to drop and prices are going to rise.

10. The Livestock Business Advisory Services Inc., of
Kansas City, Mo., predicts that a porterhouse steak
that averaged $2.39 a pound in 1976 will cost as
much as $2.50 this year and $2.70 in 1978.

* * *

11. Most of the steaks that Americans eat are carved from
steers that have grown fat from substantial quantities
of corn—as much as a ton of the grain, and sometimes
more.

12. Corn prices are now the lowest they have been since
1972, but they are still high enough to substantially
increase the price of raising choice grain-fattened
animals. As the price of that kind of meat increases, more
consumers are likely to switch to cheaper hamburger meat,
economists say.

13. "After 1977, steaks are going to be something we eat
only on special occasions—on those evenings when we
say, 'Let's get out the Lowenbrau,'" said an economist.

* * *

14. In this changing situation, hamburger has a special
role to play in the beef economy.

15. Unlike choice steaks, hamburger can be made from
ground up dairy cows, imported boneless beef, or
from older breeding cows of the beef herd that have
been fed mostly grass.

16. Hamburger prices haven't varied much since January
1974. The average price nationwide has never gone

over $1.05 a pound and has usually been considerably lower.

17. The price of sirloin steak also is about what it was three years ago, too, except that there was a sudden 50 cents-a-pound jump in early 1975. The average price hit $2.25 on July 4 of that year before sliding down again.

* * *

18. The large supply of beef now coming to market has cushioned American consumers against economic blows that have hit the beef industry in the last three years.

19. But the time is coming when consumers will feel the impact of higher corn, fertilizer, fuel and farm machinery prices.

20. "It's set in concrete," said Howard Madsen, economist with the American Meat Institute.

21. Many shoppers are expected to switch from steak to hamburger to save money but the hamburger society also is almost sure to feel the impact of what has happened.

* * *

22. The American Meat Institute estimates that only 8 million cows will be killed in 1980—30 percent fewer than in 1975.

23. By that time, the expansion of the fast food industry will mean strong bidding for the available supply of hamburger. The number of fast food outlets is expected to increase from 28,000 to 43,000 by then.

24. Some nutritionists feel that a sharp increase in the price of both steak and hamburger would not be such a bad thing. They argue it might encourage people to eat more balanced meals.

25. Even though most hamburger meat comes from ground-up cows whose meat is lean, hamburger makers add substantial amounts of pure fat to give juiciness and bond the meat together.

6

Costs of Production

Dan calls his friend Don to ask for a ride to school. Don says, jokingly, "I can't afford to pick you up anymore. I just read the results of a government study and learned it costs me over 18¢ a mile to drive my car."

"The trouble with you is you can't figure out anything for yourself," retorts Dan. The figures you read were probably for a tank! Look, if you get 20 m.p.g. and gas costs 60¢ a gallon, you can drive a mile for 3¢. Your car might ride like a tank, but it is a lot cheaper to drive. So when you bill me for the ride you're going to give me in about 5 minutes, be sure to use 3¢, not 18¢."

Can you help settle the argument? Who is right?

Both are right, depending upon how the argument is phrased. If computing only the cost of driving one more mile, which is the additional or marginal cost, then 3¢ a mile is the correct cost. But, when computing the total cost of driving a mile for someone who drives 10,000 miles a year, then the average cost per mile is 18.73¢. (This was the figure given in a government study of 1976 costs.)

Average and marginal costs are only two of a variety of cost concepts that must be understood when analyzing costs of production. In this chapter, you will learn about some of the most widely used cost concepts before using these concepts to analyze the production costs of actual firms.

CHECKLIST

Definitions of New Terms

1. Short-Run--the production situation where the firm's operations are restricted by one or more inputs that are fixed in size. For example, in the short run a firm must confine its operations to a building of a certain size.

2. Long-Run--when the firm has the opportunity to vary the size of all its inputs. For example, the firm may build or rent any size building in the long-run.
3. Fixed Costs--are costs which the firm incurs whether or not it operates during the period. An example is property taxes.
4. Variable Costs--those costs which increase with each additional unit produced. Workers' wages is an example.
5. Accounting Costs--those costs which require payments to others.
6. Economic Costs--when all costs of using resources to produce some output are included. This usually requires adding some implicit resource costs to accounting costs. For example, if a building is owned by the firm, rent expense is not an accounting cost, but it must be included as an economic cost.
7. Opportunity Cost--is a cost figure determined by considering what a resource would be worth if it were being used in its next best alternative. Opportunity costs should be used to compute the true economic costs of production.
8. Total Cost--total fixed cost plus total variable cost.
9. Average Fixed Cost--total fixed cost divided by output.
10. Average Variable Cost--total variable cost divided by output.
11. Average Total Cost--total cost divided by output.
12. Marginal Cost--the additional cost required to produce another unit of output.
13. Diminishing Marginal Returns--when an additional unit of an input adds less to total output than a previously added input. When this occurs, marginal costs will begin increasing.
14. Economies of Scale--when a larger scale plant produces output at a lower unit cost. These economies can be attributed to specialization and technological advantages.
15. Diseconomies of Scale--when a larger size plant produces output at a higher unit cost. Problems of coordination are usually blamed for diseconomies.
16. Physical Plant Capacity--that output level when no more output can be produced from a given sized plant.
17. Economic Capacity--that output level where short-run average costs are minimized. This frequently occurs before physical capacity is reached.

Concepts

1. Short-Run Total Costs: Figure 1 shows the relationship of the three short-run total costs to output. The dotted lines show the two major components of total costs: total variable cost (TVC) and total fixed cost (TFC). Total cost (TC) is the summation of these two costs. As you can see, all variations in total cost are caused by variations in total variable cost. The total cost curve in Figure 1 is drawn to show traditional assumptions about production cost behavior. Total costs first increase at a decreasing rate (increasing returns) and then increase at an increasing rate (diminishing returns). Whereas the TFC of an actual firm would be exactly like that shown in Figure 1, TVC and TC might have considerably different shapes. (However, regardless of shape, TVC and TC must be higher at each higher output.)

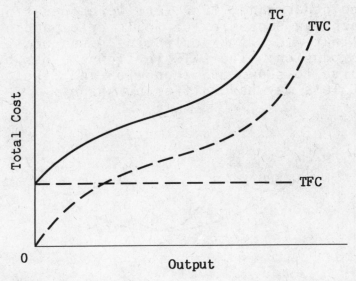

Figure 1

2. Short-Run Average and Marginal Costs: Figure 2 shows the
    relationship of the two major short-run costs--average total
    cost (ATC) and marginal cost (MC)--to output. The shape of
    the marginal cost curve corresponds to the assumptions of
    increasing and diminishing returns that were made when drawing
    TVC and TC in Figure 1. Diminishing returns occurs at output
    OA. Average total cost falls until it equals marginal cost;
    it is then pulled up by increasing marginal costs. Output AB,
    where minimum ATC occurs, is economic capacity. Output OC,
    where no more additional output can be produced, is physical
    capacity.

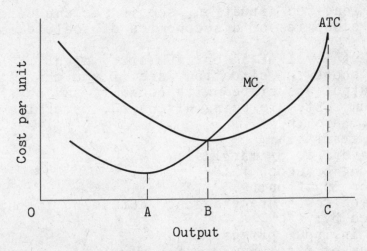

Figure 2

3. Long-Run Average Cost Curve: Figure 3 shows a long-run cost
    curve (LATC) with three selected short-run average total cost
    curves; each shows a different sized plant. The LATC is really
    a planning curve which shows the lowest cost of producing with
    different sized plants. ATC_2 shows the optimal plant size
    for this firm; no other plant size can produce at a lower cost

per unit. On the other hand, if a firm were operating with
ATC_1, it could achieve economies of scale by expanding.
Finally, we see that ATC_3 is experiencing diseconomies of
scale from overexpansion. The LATC in Figure 3 has been drawn
as a U-shaped curve to show both economies and diseconomies of
scale. Actual LATC's may have different shapes.

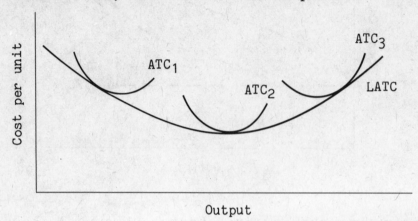

Figure 3

GUIDE FOR ANLAYZING ARTICLES

1. Determine if the discussion is about a short- or long-run
    situation.
    A. If the firm is producing with a specific plant size, it is
       a short-run situation.
    B. If the firm is expanding or contracting its plant size, it
       is a long-run situation.
2. If it is a long-run situation, see if you can determine:
    A. whether economies of diseconomies of scale exist in the
       industry;
    B. the output level of an optimum-sized plant.
3. If it is a short-run situation, see if you can determine the
    level of output associated with economic and physical capacity.
4. If short-run costs are being discussed, determine their type
    and nature. Are they:
    A. fixed or variable;
    B. total, average, or marginal;
    C. accounting or economic;
    D. actual or opportunity.
5. If production costs are changing, determine if the changes are
    being caused by:
    A. changes in input prices;
    B. economies or diseconomies of scale;
    C. technological changes.
6. What can you conclude about the nature of production costs for
    the firm and/or the industry?

Articles

AN ANALYZED ARTICLE: OVERVIEW

Anheuser-Busch and Schlitz, two major brewing firms, each brew their beer by different production techniques and each incurs different costs. This article compares their techniques and input costs and also provides some information on economies of scale in the brewing industry. You should be able to apply a variety of cost concepts in your analysis of this article and, in doing so, be able to explain why Schlitz's costs are lower.

Gussie Busch's Bitter Brew

Reprinted by permission of Forbes *Magazine from the June 1, 1974 issue.*

Does It Pay To Build Quality Into A Product If Most Of The Consumers Don't Care? Anheuser-Busch Has One Answer To The Problem. Schlitz Seems To Have A More Successful Answer.

1. In most businesses it is hard to be No. Two. The big prizes go to No. One. In electrical equipment for example, General Electric consistently has better profit margins than Westinghouse, and in automobiles, General Motors has always come well ahead of Ford. But suddenly it is different in the beer business. Anheuser-Busch is No. One by a huge margin. Its net sales were better than $1.1 billion last year, comfortably ahead of Jos. Schlitz's $700 million. Profits are another matter. When it comes to the bottom line, Schlitz is way ahead. Schlitz last year earned 7.6% on sales and 21% on stockholders' equity; Anheuser's figures were 5.9% and 13.8%. In beer, No. Two is No. One.

2. This year the numbers will be even more decisively in Schlitz's favor. It will be the third year of declining profitability for Anheuser-Busch; Schlitz's trend has been straight up for over a decade.

3. This is bitter brew indeed for Anheuser-Busch and its boss, August A. Busch Jr. In the past year Anheuser-Busch stock has dropped 40%, while Schlitz is down only 22%. Today the Busch family's 15% holdings have a market value of only $242 million, while the Uihleins, who own 80% of Schlitz, own stock worth a resounding $1.2 billion.

4. How can a company so unmistakably No. One in sales be a poor No. Two in profits? The answer lies not so much in the numbers themselves as in matters of style and of taste. Brewing is a family business. The Busches of St. Louis run Anheuser-Busch almost like a private company. So do the Uihleins of Milwaukee, who run Schlitz. But the styles are very different. And so are the products—for A-B, Michelob, Budweiser and Busch Bavarian beers; for Schlitz, Schlitz and Old Mikwaukee beers and Schlitz Malt Liquor.

5. At 75, August A. Busch Jr. is a big, affable man deeply steeped in the traditions of the beer business. He is still boss at Anheuser, although he has made his son, 37-year-old August A. Busch III, president. The two Busches, "Gussie" and "Augie," as they are known respectively, control 15% of the company's stock.

6. Tired of being a playboy and worried about his company's declining fortunes, Gussie Busch grabbed the wheel in the mid-Fifties at the company his grandfather had founded, and pushed it ahead of its longtime rivel Schlitz. He did so by building a brilliant executive team and borrowing heavily, pouring money into building new, big, automated breweries. He traveled tirelessly to the four corners of the U.S., pumping hands and mending fences. With that brilliant top team, he showed the beer world what flair and flamboyance could do for sales. Gussie did such a thorough job that even today, his rival, Schlitz boss Rober Uihlein, concedes: "There's no way we'll pass Busch in sales in the foreseeable future."

7. Uihlein, aged 58, is the fourth-generation heir to a German immigrant's brewing fortune. In 1961, six years after Gussie Busch settled down to business, Bobby Uihlein did the same, putting away his polo ponies and going to work getting Schlitz back into the brewing race.

8. It so happened that about the time Uihlein was getting seriously into the race, Gussie Busch was slowing down. Since then Schlitz has gone from no debt as recently as 1968 to $65 million, while Anheuser by the end of 1973 had cut its debt by $50 million, to $93 million. With the borrowed money Schlitz has increased its brewing capacity by 85% while Anheuser's has grown 80%.

9. At present, Schlitz has 23 million barrels of brewing capacity. Anheuser has 34 million. Over the next three to four years, Schlitz will add 12 million, Anheuser only 7 million. Thus, by early 1978, the gap in capacity will be considerably narrowed.

10. Because of his growing caution, in 1968 Gussie Busch lost his company's marketing genius, Vice President

Ed Vogel, the man who put modern marketing into A-B and is now a consultant to the brewing and soft drink industries. He told *Forbes:* "Gus has become more interested in his debt-to-equity ratio and in keeping control of the company than in expanding. If he had followed my advice and built bigger breweries, Anheuser-Busch would have had 50% of the market today." As it is, Anheuser has 24%, up from 10.4% ten years ago.

11. However, this difference in the pace of expansion doesn't explain the *profit* difference. Why did Schlitz net 7.6% on sales, Anheuser only 5.9% last year? The surprising answer is that it costs Schlitz less to produce a can or a bottle of beer than it costs Anheuser. Schlitz would argue that this is because it is more efficient, Anheuser claims that Schlitz cuts corners. But, corner-cutting or not, the customers don't seem to care: Schlitz's sales rose 15% last year and went up another 21% in the first quarter of 1974. Like Anheuser, Schlitz today can sell every ounce of beer its breweries can produce.

12. *Why* does it cost Schlitz less? One answer is: bigger breweries. Schlitz has built or is building three breweries of 4-million-barrel initial capacity; Anheuser-Busch none. In modern brewing methods, a big brewery requires no more labor than a smaller one. As Bobby Uihlein point out: "In the brewhouse in our old Milwaukee brewery we have 24 men on a shift. In our big new Winston-Salem or Memphis plants there are two." Yet the three plants are roughly equal in capacity. The story is in the figures: Schlitz's sales per employee last year were close to $110,000. Anheuser's were closer to $90,000.

13. But there is much more to the cost picture than merely the size and age of breweries. Schlitz's brewing methods are less labor-intensive. Much of this is due to changes that Uihlein has wrought in the past few years. Uihlein took his biggest chances, and is reaping his greatest dollar rewards in the changes he made in the brewing process itself. All brewing starts with malted barley, which is barley grain, steeped in water and allowed to germinate to prepare it for fermentation. Today, that's about the only part of the brewing cycle where Schlitz and Anheuser-Busch see eye-to-eye. Each uses different materials. In the U.S., all brewers add either corn or rice, called brewing adjuncts, to be fermented along with the malt barley; and they all add some kind of hops, for their particular aroma and bitter flavor.

14. Schlitz once used corn grits as its adjunct, but has now switched to a far cheaper corn syrup in some locations; A-B still uses rice, except for its Busch Bavarian beer, where it uses corn. A-B uses natural hops, with some imported hops added; Schlitz has been using the cheaper hop extract and is switching to still more economical hop pellets. All these changes mean that Schlitz tastes different, very different, from A-B beers and may taste different in different areas of the country. (How different? See the box opposite.)

15. Anheuser has always paid more for its raw materials than Schlitz has, principally because rice is more expensive than corn. Thus last year, while both companies raised sales by about 15%, Anheuser's profit fell while Schlitz's rose; A-B was clobbered by rice costs, which climbed from $6.75 a hundredweight to $12, up 78%.

16. Corn prices rose, too, but Schlitz bought almost 60% of its 1973 corn ahead—in 1972 at $4.50 a cwt—and watched prices climb to over $8. A-B, which didn't hedge, took it on the chin. Commodity prices are off those peaks now, but over the long run A-B is likely to pay an increasing premium for using rice, which can be planted only in areas with abundant water and just the right climate.

17. The whole commodity problem is serious enough for Augie Busch to have named Patrick T. (Tom) Stokes, 32, vice president of raw materials and transportation. He's trying to get A-B closer to the farmer, help find special strains of rice and especially to contract—as Schlitz had done with corn—for future production. But success to date has been limited. "So far," Stokes admits, "the contracting program isn't supplying a major portion of our requirements."

18. Where Uihlein really put the screws to Busch was in the brewing process itself. Uihlein shortened it—drastically. Where it takes Anheuser-Busch 32 to 40 days to drew beer, it now takes Schlitz 15 to 20. The change was so drastic that David Kendall, head of the Flavor Sciences unit at Arthur D. Little, says: "Today's Schlitz isn't the same product as yesterday's." But the changes did not turn its drinkers away and destroy its market. Instead, Schlitz captured market share, filled its new monster breweries to capacity and recouped a huge reward on its profit statement.

19. Basically, A-B brews a lighter, somewhat sweeter beer, and Schlitz a somewhat more aromatic, bitter brew. A-B says that's an important difference, that theirs is the quality beer, and Schlitz is "less drinkable," according to Augie. That is, heavier beer drinkers can take more Budweiser over a period of time without feeling full. Certainly Budweiser has its loyal drinkers. But so does Schlitz. Since Americans like very cold beer, does taste really matter?

20. Asking Gussie Busch to change the taste of his beer, however, would be like asking the Pope to approve abortion. "The old man would burn the brewery first," is how Joseph DeMarco, A-B wholesaler for New Jersey and part of New York City, summed it up to Forbes. How does son Augie feel? Nobody knows for sure, because at Anheuser-Busch, no one contradicts "The Chief"—even Augie calls his father that.

*
*
*

21. It is hard not to sympathize with Gussie Busch, with his pride in tradition and his product. Yet if the job of management is to make money for its stockholders and to assure the long-term health of the company, it is fair to ask whether Busch should not begin paying more attention to the dollar sign. Will Gus Busch's pride yield to economics? Will he give his son his head to go out and take after Schlitz? The answers aren't in yet. but the beer business will be an interesting arena over the next few years.

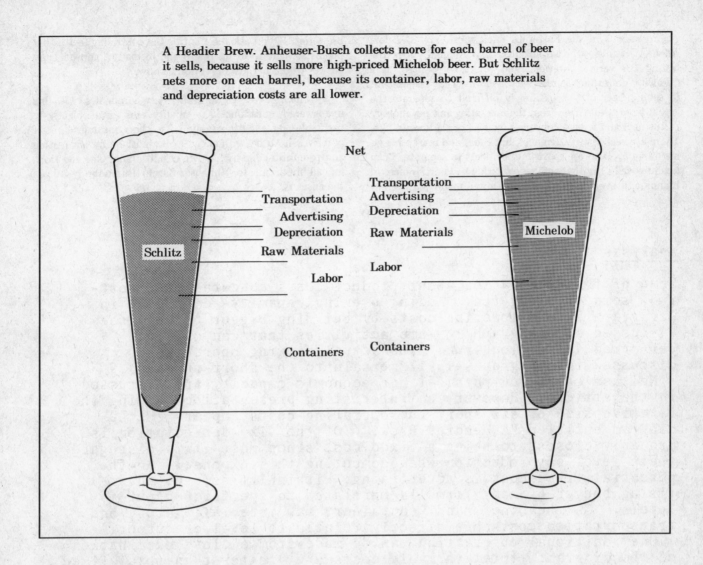

A Headier Brew. Anheuser-Busch collects more for each barrel of beer it sells, because it sells more high-priced Michelob beer. But Schlitz nets more on each barrel, because its container, labor, raw materials and depreciation costs are all lower.

Does Taste Make Waste?

Taste is an elusive quality—in spite of the fact that everyone has strong ideas on it.

In Cambridge, Mass. Arthur D. Little's Flavor Sciences unit, which has been tasting Anheuser-Busch's beers for a dozen years, claims it has the measurement of taste down to a precise practice. David A. Kendall, the group's chief, told FORBES about it: "We break taste down into three categories. First, the basic tastes themselves: sweet, sour, salt and bitter. Second, aroma: In beer such things as hops and yeast impart characteristic aromas. Last, the feelings associated with tastes, like the tingle of carbon dioxide or astringency." Kendall has trained tasters to measure these qualities down to a gnat's eyelash. "We're not allowed to say, I like this beer,'" he points out. "We have to *say why*."

So how important is taste to selling beer? "We came to the conclusion years ago," Kendall notes, "that there are three categories of the consuming public. Those who don't measure flavor at all, those who can tell the differences, but who buy for other reasons, like price. And, finally, those

who are very concerned and discriminating. The public is split about evenly among all three."

Meanwhile, in Philadelphia, the Wharton School is studying beer drinkers. James Emshoff, who heads that study, told FORBES: "It seems that heavier users can tell the difference more than light users." But the study of over 1,000 beer drinkers shows that overall, only 40% to 50% could reliably detect the difference between brands.

Interestingly, *New York* magazine, the lively, taste-setting journal for sophisticated metropolitans, had its own beer-tasting panel in 1971. *New York's experts—admittedly on a highly subjective basis—ranked Budweiser and Schlitz about equally; both were in the third tier in a five-tier taste test.*

All of which seems to prove that one man's preference is another man's *yechh!* There are, it seems, regional taste differences. New Yorkers seem to like a more bitter beer, like Rheingold. Californians go for the lighter Coors. In Texas they serve their beer at a chilling 32 degrees, which tends to mask flavor differences.

What sells beer to the probable majority who can't taste the difference? We turned to Dr. Kurt Konigsbacher.—

vice president of the Foster D. Snell subsidiary of Booz, Allen & Hamilton. Konigsbacher, like Kendall, does the testing for various brewers, and refers to himself as a "brewing consultant guru." We asked him what taste meant in selling beer. "It is extremely difficult to separate the actual taste stimulation from the marketing and psychology of the beer and what a consumer feels he or she should like. There *are* real taste differences, but those and marketing go hand-in-glove and are extremely difficult to separate. I can unequivocally say there are recognizable taste differences in brands and even within the same brand made in different breweries. If you ask me, 'Is this the overriding factor that makes somebody drink one brand instead of another? my answer would have to be, 'I don't know.'"

Which leaves us—and the beer companies—with big unanswered questions: Are quality and taste objectively verifiable? Is quality simply what the consumer himself perceives it to be, influenced as he must be by advertising and promotion and by his own conditioning? The questions are all-important to Anheuser-Busch. But nobody knows the answers.

Analysis

Some of the information about product costs concerns the short-run, some the long-run. Adding brewing capacity--discussed in paragraph 9--and lowering costs by building bigger breweries-- discussed in paragraph 12--are activities that can only be performed in the long-run. The actual brewing operations discussed in paragraphs 13-17 pertain to the short-run.

Neither short-run physical nor economic capacity are discussed in the article. However, an interesting presentation showing the relative size of six short-run operating costs appears in the diagram entitled "A Headier Brew." Of the six, depreciation is probably closest to being a fixed cost since most firms disregard their level of production when computing this expense. Another potential fixed cost is advertising; within limits, the advertising budget of many firms is unrelated to specific output levels. On the other hand, container, raw material, labor, and transportation costs are directly related to level of output.

One additional observation can be made from a close examination of the diagram: total variable costs are greater than total fixed costs.

No specific data on total, average, or marginal costs is provided in the article. However, since "it costs Schlitz less to produce a can or bottle of beer than it costs Anheuser," we know Schlitz's total and average costs are lower (par. 11).

All costs shown in the diagram are accounting costs. There are some obvious implicit costs of brewing beer that are not shown. For example, the cost of using stockholders' capital (or equity) is not shown as a cost of production. In economics, we include this type of item in economic costs and assign it a cost value by using the opportunity cost concept. Although we have no information on the opportunity cost of capital for the brewing industry, we can make one observation: if Anheuser's 13 percent return on stockholders' equity represents a normal return, then the 21 percent return for Schlitz's stockholders represents a return that is greater than the opportunity cost of their capital (par. 1).

Both firms faced changing cost conditions in the industry. Schlitz gained a cost advantage over Anheuser by making three adjustments to these changing costs. First, when faced with rising raw material costs, Schlitz switched to lower-priced materials, namely, brewing adjuncts and hops (par. 14). Of course, as the article points out, these changes would most likely affect product quality (par. 14).

A second cost advantage was gained by Schlitz when it bought 60 percent of its corn needs early at $4.50 a cwt.; Anheuser bought later and had to pay $8 a cwt (par. 16). Finally, when technological changes provided economies of scale for the brewing industry, Schlitz began building three 4-million barrel capacity facilities (par. 12).

We can conclude that brewing requires relatively more variable costs than fixed costs. In addition, we found that Schlitz reduced its variable costs relative to Anheuser by stockpiling and substituting. We also found Schlitz taking advantage of technologically induced economies of scale. These efforts by Schlitz to lower operating costs is one reason for Schlitz's relatively greater profitability. Perhaps you noticed that the analysis avoided the controversy over taste and quality. You may draw your own conclusions after reading the article.

AN ARTICLE WITH QUESTIONS

Another Energy Bill Sleeper

Reprinted by permission of The Wall Street Journal
(Aug. 3, 1977), © *Dow Jones & Company, Inc., 1977.*
All rights reserved.

1. We've tried to enlighten our readers on barbs and fishhooks buried in the energy bill Tip O'Neill is marching through the House of Representatives this week, but it's tough to keep up with all of them. The legislation was conceived and is being enacted in such haste that no one can cope with all the details, any one of which might derail the future production of energy.

2. Take for example subpart 2 of Part E, which threatens to bury every electric utility in the nation in red tape, stopping the expansion of electrical generating capacity. The provision would remake the entire regulatory process for electricity rates, now painfully worked out by commissions in each state. The bill would authorize the Federal Energy Administration to take over a state's powers if it failed to set rates on the basis of "marginal pricing," the exact meaning of which remains to be determined.

3. Marginal pricing is a complicated concept when applied to electricity, but in essence it means that a businessman would be required to pay what it costs the utility to furnish him with the electricity he uses, in the particular way he uses it. In other words, if he happened to use a lot of electricity at peak load hours, thus requiring the utility to maintain excess generating capacity for use only at that time, he would pay more.

4. In principle, of course, this sounds like a good idea. Theoretically, it would encourage energy conservation by encouraging customers to avoid peak load hours, thus enabling utilities to get by with less capacity. But as with a lot of other things in the energy bill, there is a hidden agenda behind this innocent facade.

5. For some time now, Congressmen Dingell and Moffett, who are behind this particular provision, have been trying to use the marginal pricing principle to accomplish two things: (1) Eliminate any competition among states to offer low electricity rates to industry in order to attract jobs; (2) Transfer some of the burden of electric rate increases from residential consumers to industry, hiding some of the cost of electricity to individuals by burying it in the price of goods consumers buy.

6. Now, whatever you might think of the objectives here, the truly gigantic problems arise in implementation. For starters, to comply with the federal law states would apparently have to require installation of a new kind of electric meter that would record not only electricity usage but the hours in which it was used. We wonder what the energy cost will be in producing and installing all those new meters.

7. Joseph C. Swidler, who has probably been involved in electric power regulation longer than anyone else in Washington, raised some other points in his testimony on the bill. He notes, first of all, that the idea of electricity rate competition among states is largely a red herring. Utility rates are one of the least important considerations in plant location decision. Also, with electricity priced marginally and oil and gas still under price controls, the provision would defeat the purpose of the energy act by creating incentives for energy users to use oil and gas.

8. Nobody yet knows for sure how you calculate marginal costs. Mr. Swidler notes that four methods

have been presented in a rate case involving Commonwealth Edison in Chicago. The range of increases to commercial and industrial users under these different methods is from $111 million to $493 million above the amounts now proposed. Since the federal bill also requires that utilities could not have an abnormal return, the excess yields from commercial and industrial customers would be refunded to residential consumers.

9. "There may well be companies where the mix of loads is such that, to dispose of excess revenues from commercial and industrial customers charged on the basis of some of the marginal cost formulas, it would be necessary to pay residential customers to take electricity," Mr. Swidler says.

10. And then the bill has an "antipancaking" provision, prohibiting utilities from filing for a second rate increase while a previous application is pending. Given the time this kind of rate-setting process would consume—several years is not unlikely—it is not hard to imagine utilities getting into serious difficulties in an inflationary period while waiting for a new rate to come through. Mr. Swidler thinks the new bill would "seriously impair the credit and risk the viability" of private electric utilities. All of course, in the name of solving our energy problems.

Questions

1. What aspects of production are discussed in this article? (See Par. 2 and 3.)
2. What is the purpose of the article?
3. Is the discussion about a short- or long-run situation? Or both?
4. Can you determine anything about economies of scale or the size of an optimum-sized plant? (See Par. 2.)
5. Can you determine the level of short-run economic and physical capacity? (Hint: look at the discussion of peak load in Par. 3 and 4.)
6. What type of short-run costs are discussed? Can you determine the nature of these costs?
7. What conclusions about the costs of producing electricity can you draw from this article?

AN ARTICLE FOR STUDENT ANALYSIS: OVERVIEW

This article should be read after reviewing the short- and long-run cost concepts found in Figure 3. Roy Chapin, Chairman of American Motors, provides cost data which can be used to make some generalizations about the shape of the LATC for auto producers. Remember: the LATC is only a planning curve; once a plant is built, the operating costs are short-run costs, (i.e., the ATC in Figure 3.)

"When You Get Beyond a Certain Size, the Economies of Scale Do Not Just Continue"

Reprinted by permission of Forbes *Magazine from the May 15, 1974 issue.*

1. A FEW YEARS AGO the Small Business Administration declared American Motors to be a small business. At the time, AMC had 40,000 employees, ranked as the 100th largest American corporation, and turned out 300,000 cars a year. *Small?* By the standards of its competition—General Motors with $36 billion is sales, Ford with $23 billion—AMC is small. But small on this scale doesn't have to mean inefficient.

2. "We all build cars the same way," says American Motors' Chairman Roy Chapin, "and we know that in the basic assembly structure of our vehicles—between the time the body starts and the time it comes off as a

finished vehicle—our hours per car are *less* than some of our competitors'. Our return on equity is about the same as GM's. We think we've done a more efficient job of organizing our manpower, our tooling, the speeds at which we run our lines."

3. AMC's present prosperity is so impressive as to lend grist to the claims of Senator Philip Hart (Dem., Mich.) and others that medium-sized companies are just as efficient as huge ones and that GM, as a consequence, ought to be split up into as many as 12 independent companies.

4. "The one area where Senator Hart has validity," Chapin says, "is that when you get beyond a certain size, the economies of scale do not just continue *ad infinitum.* You can build a very profitable, viable automobile company on a volume of between 300,000 and 500,000 units a year. At American Motors we really have only two major product categories: the Matador/Ambassador and the Hornet/Gremlin. Both have basically the same tooling and use the same parts, but the vehicles look different and serve somewhat different purposes. If your volume, like ours, runs between 150,000 and 350,000 units in each of those categories, your cost per unit will be just a few dollars more than somebody making twice as many."

5. Which is why AMC now looks like a winner again. With the demand for AMC's small cars booming, the production economics that worked against it when it was producing 300,000 cars a year have now—at 420,000—begun working for it.

6. Here's a quick lesson in automotive economics. You have a big block like this," Chapin says, shaping an invisible square with his hands. "That's your fixed costs. That's me, the building, utilities, amortization of your tooling—all the things that are constant whether you make a car or your don't. What you then have to do is make enough vehicles with enough marginal profit to cover that block. Let's say that marginal profit is $1,000 a vehicle. Once you get above that so-called break-even point, every extra $1,000 goes into your pocket. Since you don't have any additional fixed costs, those extra $1,000s are, in effect free up to a certain point.

7. "At that point you have to build another assembly plant, fill another assembly line, buy another set of tools, put in another set of supervisors, hire more typists to fill out schedules. You have to duplicate almost all of your fixed costs. The trick is to get maximum productivity out of a given set of fixed costs, without having to add another set."

8. How soon those additional costs start paying for themselves depends on volume. "Say we want to build another 200,000 units to keep pace with demand," says Chapin. "Once you pass the 500,000 mark, the first 50,000 are going to cost you money; the next 100,000 will probably not leave you much better off, if any. Until you get to 650,000 you haven't really got your bait back for building all those new facilities. These are not our numbers, by the way, but the principle is correct."

9. Chapin is not simply musing in a vacuum. AMC is already near the half-million-car maximum capability of its existing organization. "We'll make $50 million, let's say, this year on our 400,000 units, but if we went to 700,000 and had to duplicate all this all over again, that $50 million might turn out to be $75 million or something like that." Except that Chapin can't double AMC's sales or production overnight. So in the meantime any increase in size would probably be less efficient.

10. These are very real questions at American Motors these days, not academic questions. AMC with its small-car emphasis is sitting in the catbird seat. To expand or not to expand is the question. "I do think the hysterical emphasis on small cars is diminishing," Chapin cautions. "The big car is not gone, and it's not going to be gone, but the small car is definitely here to stay. Short term, I think we'll benefit, and Ford's going to benefit. Longer than that, it's awfully difficult to say, but I don't think Ford's going to start selling more cars than GM or that we are going to sell more than Ford. We might sell more than Chrysler, but that's another story."

11. Even at its present size, American Motors has some of the same problems that face its bigger competitors. The assembly lines, whether they turn out 600,000 cars or 4 million, remain as boring and repetitive as ever, but Chapin sees no evidence to suggest that the widely reported change in the life-styles and attitudes of its workers is going to make any significant impact on the economics of mass production. What is more, the alternatives that have been suggested—the job enrichment programs like those Volvo has experimented with—do not rise to the challenge and produce a better product. They just cost more.

12. "Whenever we have absenteeism on the line—and it can run as high as 10% on Mondays and Fridays—we move people around. They do half their job and half of another. And you know what? They hate it. There are a lot of rotten jobs in automobile plants. But a great many people do not want a great challenge. They want something they can learn and know and be good at. Obviously you don't attract highly intellectual people.

13. "It's the same old story. The average man in our plant makes $6 an hour—that's the magic word. That $12,000 for a 2,000-hour year, and lots of times he can hardly write his name. We couldn't hire them for $3 an hour. To make that kind of money there's a trade-off, and plenty of people are willing to make that trade-off. The only time we have trouble recruiting people is when everything is booming."

7

Price Setting by the Market

Kathy is studying for her Econ 1 exam with John, a new friend she met in class. After an hour or so, John says, "Don't you think we've done enough? Let's go to a movie."

Kathy protests, "Listen, the instructor marks on a curve. I need an A in this course and I think there will be a high grade distribution. In fact, all my friends back in the dorm are going to study all night."

John thinks for a moment, then exclaims, "Say, let's see if all your friends want to go to the movie with us."

"Look," replies Kathy, "There are over 200 students in that class. Unless you can get all of them to quit studying, I'm staying right here. Now, if supply shifts to the right, what will happen to market price?"

John's problem is that he is in a classroom where real competition exists. The grade distribution established by the class will determine the score Kathy needs to get an A. Although each student's exam score helps determine the grade distribution, in a large class each student's input is so insignificant that from their perspective, the grade is set by some amorphous thing called "the class."

Some firms find themselves in a similar situation. Their product price is set by something like "the class," but in their case it is called "the market." Although each firm's output becomes part of market supply, its contribution to total supply is so insignificant that it does not feel it has any part in determining product price. Nevertheless, if it were not for the output of each firm, there would be no market supply.

Therefore, the market sets product price for each and every firm in a competitive industry. Firms in such an industry are competing--not with each other--but with the market. Moreover, this amorphous thing called "the market" determines their fate: if market price does not cover their costs, they will fail (go bankrupt).

CHECKLIST

Definitions of New Terms

1. <u>Average Revenue (AR)</u>--total revenue divided by units sold. When market determines product price, price (P) = AR.
2. <u>Marginal Revenue (MR)</u>--the additional revenue earned when one more unit is sold. When market determines price, P = AR = MR.
3. Total Revenue--price times the total quantity sold.
4. <u>Economic Profit</u>--total revenue minus economic cost. (Remember, economic cost includes all costs of using resources and is usually greater than accounting costs.)
5. Break-even--in economic theory, this occurs when total revenue equals total economic costs of production. Correspondingly, average revenue will equal average total cost at break-even.

Concepts

1. <u>When a market sets product price, the firm's demand curve, average revenue curve, and marginal revenue curve are all equal to that price</u>
When a market sets product price, all firms in the industry must sell all their output at this price. Consequently, in a graph the demand for each firm's product is a horizontal line beginning at market price. Moreover, if each and every unit is sold at the same price, that price is also the firm's average revenue and marginal revenue. Figure 1(A) shows this for a representative firm when market price is equal to OB.

(A)   REPRESENTATIVE FIRM   (B) MARKET

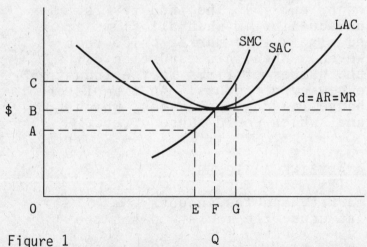
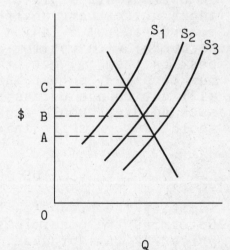

Figure 1

2. <u>Short-run equilibrium and output</u>
A firm's total profits are greatest when it produces an output at which marginal revenue and marginal cost are equal. Therefore, the firm in Figure 1 should produce OG units when price is OC. At this market price, the firm would earn an economic profit equal to the difference between average revenue (AR) and short-run average cost (SAC) times the number of units sold (OG). Moreover, the firm would continue to produce

51

this output so long as market price remains the same. However, if market price falls to OB, the firm will immediately reduce output to OF units. At this price, the firm's revenues just cover its costs. You will notice that, regardless of price, the firm always produces an output at which product price equals the marginal cost of production. When this occurs, the conditions for allocative efficiency are satisfied since consumers' satisfaction (as measured by product price) is just equal to the cost of producing the last unit (as measured by marginal cost). (Refer to Concept 1, Chapter 4.).

3. Entry and exit will shift market supply

If S_1 in Figure 1(B) is the market supply curve, market price will be OC, and the representative firm will earn economic profits. New firms will be attracted into the industry by these profits; the additional output supplied by these new firms will shift market supply to the right until S_2 is reached, at which point all economic profits in the industry are eliminated. On the other hand, if S_3 were the supply curve, a price of OA would exist initially. At this price, economic losses would appear, exit would occur, supply would shift left until S_2 is reached. (Note: if we add that the firm is also producing at economic capacity, it meets the conditions for productive efficiency. (See Concept 2, Chapter 4.))

4. Long-run equilibrium

In the long-run, the representative firm will adjust the size of its plant to achieve all economies of scale and avoid all diseconomies of scale. If we assume this has been accomplished by the firm in Figure 1(A), it will be producing with an optimum-sized plant. (For simplicity, it was assumed that input prices were unaffected by entry.) The industry is considered to be in long-run equilibrium when all firms are producing with optimum-sized plants at a market price that permits them to just break-even. When this condition exits, market price, output, and the number of firms in the industry will not change unless some new event occurs. An example of such an event would be a change in consumer tastes, which would cause a shift in demand, which would cause...,etc.

GUIDE FOR ANALYZING ARTICLES

1. Identify the product, the market, and the industry.
2. Determine the conditions that cause the market to set the price for this product.
3. Determine if product price and/or output has changed or is expected to change.
4. If product price has changed or is expected to change, explain why.
   A. Did market demand shift?
   B. Did market supply shift because:
      i. input prices changed?
     ii. technology changed?
    iii. the number of firms in the industry changed?

5. If output has changed or is expected to change, explain why.
   A. Did market price change?
   B. Did operating costs change because:
      i. input prices changed?
      ii. technology changed?
6. Explain or predict the effect the above changes will have on:
   A. the profitability of firms.
   B. the number and size of firms in the industry.
   C. the output of the industry.

Articles

AN ANALYZED ARTICLE: OVERVIEW

This article explains the price and output changes that occurred in the mink industry during the 1950s and 1960s. The price of pelts, which is set in regional markets, rose during the 1950s and early 1960s, then fell later during the 1960s. These price changes caused significant shifts in the number of firms in the industry. This article is appropriate for this chapter since mink pelts are a fairly uniform product produced by a relatively large number of mink producers.

Mink Farming Is Growing More Scarce As Costs Rise and Fur Demand Declines

By MICHAEL L. GECZI
Staff Reporter of *The Wall Street Journal*

Reprinted by permission of The Wall Street Journal *(Oct. 27, 1975), © Dow Jones & Company, Inc., 1975. All rights reserved.*

1. NEW YORK—Mink farms could well be on the endangered-species list.

2. The animals themselves never have reached an endangered status, but the number of U.S. farms raising the small mammals for their pelts has decreased sharply in recent years. In the industry's peak year, 1966, about 6,000 mink farms were operating in the U.S. Today, there are 1,221 according to the U.S. Agriculture Department.

3. Despite slight increases the past two years, total pelt production last year was 3.1 million, or half of the record 6.2 million pelts produced in 1966. Annual sales at the auction level, where most pelts are sold, were about $54 million in 1974, according to one estimate, down from more than $120 million in the mid-1960s.

4. The smaller operations have been the hardest hit. "The mom and pop outfits and the part-timers were the ones that folded," says an Agriculture Department official. "The bigger farms have kept operating."

5. Some industry officials say a profitable mink farm of any size is rare. "We've been in dire straits for the past four or five years," says Robert Langenfeld, president of Associated Fur Farms Inc., New Holstein, Wis., one of the nation's largest mink farms.

6. The industry's descent has been as rapid as its rise in the 1950s and 1960s, during which time mink grew in popularity as a fashionable status symbol. Growth was aided by the development of new colors (there are currently 13). As producers' feed and labor costs remained relatively stable in the face of strong demand, more people entered the industry.

Unsold Inventories

7. Growth proved to be too rapid, however; large unsold inventories from the record 1966 crop caused a price bust in 1967, and the situation has worsened since. Feed and labor costs have climbed rapidly. Competition from less-expensive foreign pelts has heightened.

8. Perhaps most important, mink has lost much of its prestige. Industry officials say the desire to wear a mink coat has in many instances given way to ecological concerns. Cries from conservationists "caused a mass reaction for the 'poor' animal," says Louis Henry, president of Hudson Bay Fur Sales Inc., The Hudson's Bay Co. unit that handles about two-thirds of the pelts sold at auction in the U.S. annually.

9. Mr. Henry recalls that in 1966 pelts sold at auction for an average of $24 each. The going price today for a mutation (colored) skin is about $14. Dark furs bring a slightly higher price.

10. In the 1960s, a mink producer would net about $5 on a mutation pelt, says Mr. Langenfeld. "Now," he ways, "we're losing about $3 a pelt on our mutations." He says it costs the company $17 to raise a kit, or young mink, and bring its pelt to auctions.

11. Mink farmers breed their animals in March. The kits—usually four to a litter—are born in early May. They're raised for six months before being killed-humanely, producers say—by gas or electocution. The skins then are removed and readied for sale.

12. In most cases they are sent to one of four main U.S. auction centers, in New York City, Seattle, Minneapolis and Milwaukee. Fees received by one of the

two associations that offer the pelts for sale and by the company conducting the acction can take up to 7.75% of the pelt's selling price.

Finicky Animal

13. The price the producers get for their pelts is their reward for raising a finicky animal that prefers only the freshest meat, poultry and fish. Most mink farms have expensive refrigeration, grinding and mixing machines, and also must hire extra help to thaw and feed daily rations to the animals. All this causes the mink's diet to represent more than half of the total cost of raising a mink to pelt-producing size.

14. Mink researchers have been working to develop a dry diet that would be more economical and still satisfy the taste and nutritional requirements of the animal. Some farmers are using the dry diets, but they are far from gaining industry-wide acceptance.

15. U.S. producers are said to produce a high-quality pelt much prized by those who don't mind paying handsomely for a coat or stole. But about half of the six million or so pelts used annually in the U.S. are less-expensive foreign ones produced mainly in Scandinavia. Some industry officials say an increasing number of garments made from these pelts are being sold to people who formerly would have bought the more expensive item made from U.S.-produced pelts.

16. Mr. Henry says the worst may be over, however. "I think it (sales) will stabilize just about where it is," he says. Some observers expect a pickup in business as the recession eases.

17. Will business ever return to the good old days? "I don't know any mink farmers who ever had any good old days," says Mr. Langenfeld.

Analysis

Since the price of mink pelts first rose and then fell, we will begin our analysis by explaining the price rise. To do this, we will assume an equilibrium situation existed in 1950, just prior to the time period discussed in the article, and then proceed to explain the changes that occurred. Therefore, we begin with the demand and supply curves for 1950 (hypothetical) shown in Figure 2(A). These market forces have established a price of P_1 as the price for domestic mink pelts. Turning to Figure 2(B), we see that P_1 is a long-run equilibrium price since the average producer (a representative firm) is operating an optimum-sized plant at its economic capacity and is just breaking even. (Do you see why this firm is just breaking even? If you don't, see footnote[1].)

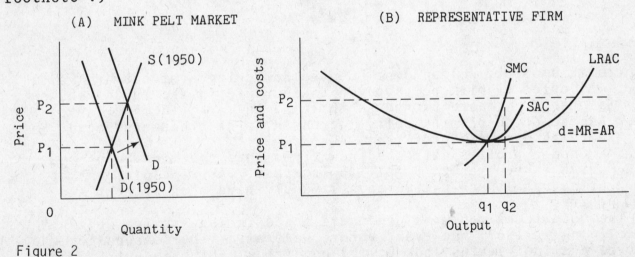

Figure 2

1. The firm would produce where MR = MC, which is Q_1 units. Since AR = SAC at this output, revenue is just covering all economic costs. But remember that all resources are being paid when this occurs.

During the 1950s and 1960s, mink "grew in popularity as a fashionable status symbol" (par. 6). If you can remember what you learned in Chapter 2, you should be able to determine what would happen in the mink market when this change in taste occurs. The answer is shown in Figure 3(A). Demand shifts to the right, causing market price to increase to some higher price, which is P_2 in the diagram.

Turning to the mink industry, we see in Figure 2(B) that the representative firm's demand curve shifts up to P_2. At this higher marginal revenue, the firm increases its output to q_2, and since average revenue is greater than short-run average cost, economic profits now occur.

We know that economic profits attract new firms, and this is exactly what happened in the mink industry (par. 6). Entry causes market supply to shift to the right, as shown in Figure 3(A). By 1966, 6,000 mink farms were producing mink pelts and the price was $24 (par. 2 and 9). As you can see in Figure 3(A), if entry had not occurred, price would have been higher than $24. Do you see what the price would have been?[2]

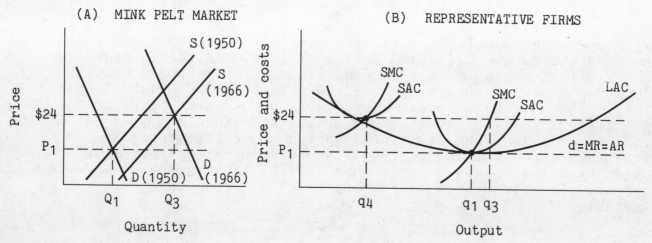

(A) MINK PELT MARKET   (B) REPRESENTATIVE FIRMS

Figure 3

Up to this point, we can conclude the following from our analysis:
1. The price of milk pelts began to increase in the 1950s because a change in taste caused an increase in market demand;
2. As the price of mink pelts increased, mink producers began earning economic profits;
3. Economic profits attracted new firms into the mink industry, which caused market supply to increase. As a result, market price was lower in 1966 than it would have been without the entry.

The good times for mink producers ended in 1966--prices began declining in 1967. However, before we examine the reasons for the price decline, let us look at the condition of the industry just prior to 1967. Although we pointed out earlier that new firms had entered the industry, we neglected to point out that many of these

2. If entry had not occurred, market price would have been determined by the intersection of Supply 1950 and Demand 1966.

firms were either "mom and pop outfits" or "part-timers" (par. 4).
One would assume that these new firms would operate at a much
smaller scale than the representative firm we have been discussing
up to this point. Therefore, we will add a representative "mom
and pop" firm to Figure 3(B). We are assuming that this sub-
optimal firm is just covering its costs of operation at the market
price of $24.

Now to return to 1967. This was the year that consumers changed
their taste for mink: some consumers quit buying mink for ecological reasons; others switched from domestic pelts to lower-
quality, lower-priced foreign imports (par. 8). Figure 4(A) shows
that change in taste caused demand for domestic pelts to shift to
the left, forcing market price down.

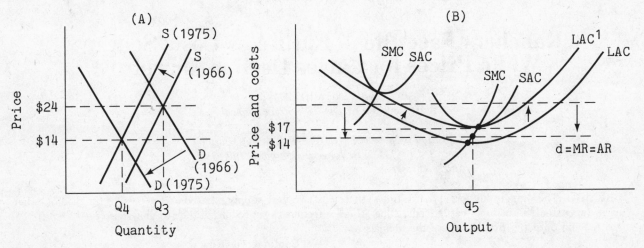

Figure 4

Adding to the financial woes of mink producers were the increased
feed and labor costs (par. 7). These increasing operating costs
combined with falling revenues put a squeeze on the profits of
mink producers. This squeeze effect can be seen in Figure 4(B):
the average revenue curve is shifting down while the cost curves
are shifting up.

After studying Figure 4(B), can you predict what would happen?
Compare average revenue with short-run average cost for the "mom
and pop" producers. Once you do this, it should come as no
surprise to read in paragraph 4 that "the mon and pop outfits were
the ones that folded."

With firms leaving the industry, market supply begins moving
back to the left, and market price begins to increase from the
level that the falling demand had caused. By 1975, only 1,221 of
the original 6,000 mink farms were still operating (par. 2). Market price had fallen from $24 in 1966 to $14 in 1975. (Do you see
how much market price would have fallen if no exit had occurred?[3]

However, even with exit, market price was still not high enough
to cover operating costs in the industry. According to paragraph
10, it costs $17 to produce a mink pelt in 1975.

3.   Find the intersection of Supply 1966 and Demand 1975.

The second half of our analysis has provided us with the following conclusions:
1. The price of domestic milk pelts fell after 1966 because a change in consumer taste caused demand to decrease;
2. As the price of pelts fell and operating costs increased, economic losses began to appear in the industry;
3. Economic losses caused exit. Market supply shifted to the left, increasing market price to a higher level than would have existed otherwise. However, economic losses were still occurring in the mink industry in 1975, so more exit will probably occur.

AN ARTICLE WITH QUESTIONS

Ranchers Face Bleak Future as Costs Soar While Prices for Calves Decline Sharply

By GENE MEYER
Staff Reporter of *The Wall Street Journal*

1. CHICAGO—The much publicized hard times that have devastated the nation's cattle-feedlot operators are moving onto the prairies where the animals are born.

2. Ranchers say their production costs have about doubled in the past year, while the price at which they sell their calves to feedlot operators has been cut by more than half. The ranchers see even bleaker prospects ahead.

3. The American National Cattlemen's Association says the nation's about 500,000 "cow-calf operators"— ranchers and farmers who raise the calves bought by feeders to fatten for market—could lose more than $1 billion by next summer. This would wipe out some ranchers and hurt many others for years to come, an association spokesman says.

4. The loss would crimp retail business tied to the farm in more than 40 states where, according to the Agriculture Department, beef cattle are among the top four agriculture money makers. It also would mean tighter beef supplies and higher retail prices a few years hence, because the ranchers are cutting production to halt their losses—thus reducing the primary source of the beef which the rest of us eat.

5. Cattle feeders—who sell live grain-fed steers to meat packers—and ranchers have been taking their worst financial drubbing in more than 20 years recently. While the worst may be over for the country's 140,000 feeders, troubles are just beginning for the ranchers, says Ed Uvacek, livestock economist at Texas A&M University. He estimates that ranchers had about 50 million calves, roughly a two-year supply, started on the path to the feedlots when feeders began to curtail their buying sharply.

Will Continue To Grow

6. Furthermore, these numbers will continue to grow even while feedlots fill only to 75% of last year's levels. That's because a rancher is committed to consequences of a production decision made nearly three years earlier, explains William O. Helming, president of Livestock Business Advisory Services Inc., a Kansas City, Mo., consulting concern. The rancher's income comes from calves that are born nine months after the cows are bred, then sold 18 to 24 months later when they are big enough to enter feedlots.

7. Thus the national cattle herd, which has been increasing to its current record size by more than 5% a year for the past two decades, will continue growing about that fast for two or more years due to this biological momentum. In addition, pork and poultry producers are going through a similar but shorter-lived experience and their competing products are hitting the market at the same time as beef.

8. The beef animals also are more expensive than ever to raise. It now costs about $190, roughly double a year ago, to keep a cow healthy and productive and grow her calf to feedlot weight. Prices for hay, feed supplement and grain are all up sharply, as are fuel, fertilizer, labor and other expenses ranchers must incur to stay in business.

9. Meantime, the price for feeder calves ready for the feedlot has tumbled to $25 a hundredweight from

58

last year's record $70 or more. Livestock economists say feeder-calf prices at best will remain at present levels for the next two years and might even decline futher.

10. The ranchers are trying to beat the squeeze by selling off their animals as quickly as possible. As a result, more than 15% of the cattle being slaughtered now, compared with 3.3% last year, are going straight to the packer from the range.

Still Holding Prices Down

11. Packers will frequently pay a little more than feeders for the ranchers' cattle. Mr. Helming says, but the glut is still holding prices down. Indeed, prices for older cows, which become stew meat, sausage and other processed meats, have fallen to about $8 a hundredweight at the ranch, their lowest price in more than 20 years.

12. Livestock economists generally see only one possible way for ranchers to escape their present-bind—feed their calves to market weight themselves in hopes that cattle prices strengthen during the extra time that takes. But, with record cattle numbers and high-priced grain, success is far from assured, the experts caution.

13. Kenneth Monfort, president of Monfort of Colorado, the country's largest feedlot operator (and thus, the largest feeder-calf buyer), takes a gloomier view. "It will be a disaster," he says. "Ranchers could lose billions of dollars, their equity, their lifetime work, their land, their homes."

14. Consumers may feel the loss as soon as 1976, he continues, when lower beef supplies force per-capita meat consumption down to the 1960 level of about 90 pounds from the current 115. Other observers expect per-capita consumption to rise to about 130 pounds over the next four years before supplies start dropping sharply.

15. Nearly everyone agrees that the shortage will last longer than it did during the beef-price freeze in the summer of 1973. Cattle then were ready for market, but were held off. Next time around, industry observers say, we'll have to wait while the animals grow.

Questions

1. Identify the product, market, and industry.
2. Why does a market set the price in this particular situation?
3. What price and output changes have occurred?
4. Why did product price change?
   A. Draw a diagram of the market and show the changes that have occurred over the past year (par. 5 and 7).
5. What is happening to the output of ranchers?
   A. Draw a diagram of a representative firm to show how ranchers are reacting (par. 10).
6. Predict the effect the changes described above will have on:
   A. the profitability of firms;
   B. the number and size of firms in the industry;
   C. the output of the industry.

AN ARTICLE FOR STUDENT ANALYSIS: OVERVIEW

This article provides a third example of an industry in which a large number of producers sell their product at prices set for them by a market. You will find a fairly complete description of the shrimp industry including data on the number of producers, product prices, costs of operation, and profitability. With a little work, your analysis should be as complete as those done for the first two articles.

Despite Higher Prices, Shrimpers' Profits Are Hurt by Rising Expenses and Imports

By KAREN L. ARRINGTON
Staff Reporter of *The Wall Street Journal*

Reprinted by permission of The Wall Street Journal
(July 28, 1976), © *Dow Jones & Company, Inc.*
All rights reserved.

1. FREEPORT, Texas—Two years ago, depressed prices, rising costs and import competition rocked the U.S. shrimp-fishing industry, sending many single-boat operators into dry dock.

2. Today, retail shrimp prices have rebounded sharply, up about 50% from a year ago in some cases and more than doubled since 1973, but the folks who net the seafood delicacies are still struggling to make ends meet.

3. To be sure, shrimpers aren't bemoaning the higher prices and their return to marginal profitability, but they do feel they have a long way to go and several problems to overcome before once again becoming a healthy industry. "Prices are satisfactory, and shrimpers have been showing a small profit since about mid-1975," says George Snow, executive director of the Louisiana Shrimp Association. "But this is only allowing most shrimpers to recoup their losses of two years ago."

4. A combination of factors is preventing domestic shrimpers from fully enjoying increased profits that should follow higher prices and strong demand for their catches. Skyrocketing operating costs and a further influx of lower-priced imported shrimp continue to plague U.S. shrimp fishermen. In addition, poor weather and a political hassle over territorial fishing rights in the Gulf of Mexico threaten U.S. shrimpers along the Gulf Coast, the source of this country's most productive and valuable shrimp beds.

Gulf Coast Concentration

5. Shrimping accounts for more than a quarter of the production and annual sales of U.S. seafood industry.

Last year, more than half of the 208 million pounds of shrimp and 79% of its $206 million value came from catches concentrated between Brownsville, Texas, and Key West, Fla. (The Pacific Northwest ranks second, with 39% of the country's shrimp volume, mostly from Alaskan catches). Nearly 8,100 boats, or three-quarters of the total U.S. shrimp fleet, work out of Gulf ports, employing more than 20,000 crewmen.

6. There isn't any estimate of how many shrimp-boat operators were squeezed out of business two years ago, but even those who survived had a scare. "Shrimp prices went down when everything else was going up, and it almost put me out of business," says Eugene Vandergrifft, a Freeport shrimper and president of the Texas Shrimp Association. "In 1974, when the price here was $2.10 a pound, it was costing us $2.40 a pound to produce."

7. Imported shrimp depressed domestic shrimp prices at a time when operating costs were on the rise. As a result, shrimpers showed an average loss of nearly $10,000 a boat in 1974, according to data submitted to the Commerce Department. Last year, their profit was a slim $600 a boat or about 2% of sales, far below the 14% average profit for the three years prior to 1974.

8. Along the Gulf Coast today, shrimp is retailing for as much as $5.40 a pound, with prices hitting $6 or more a pound in New York and $7 in Washington, D.C. "For us to survive, we need the price of shrimp to be up there," contends Julius Collins, a Brownsville shrimp-boat operator.

9. And, although shrimp is rapidly becoming a luxury item on most menus, consumers appear willing to pay the higher prices. Whether fresh, frozen, canned, breaded, boiled, fried or in cocktails, gumbo or jambalaya, Americans are eating more shrimp and resisting any shift to less-expensive substitutes, industry studies show.

Operating Costs Treble

10. Still, the average shrimp-boat operator is finding it difficult to pay his bills. Shrimpers typically are small operators, with half of all U.S. shrimp boats being captain-owned. Larger operators may own several boats. All shrimpers say their operating costs have tripled in the last three years. Wright Gore Jr., vice president of Western Seafood Co., a Freeport wholesaler and operator of 10 boats, says, "Our operating costs have jumped to $20,000 a boat annually from $7,500 in just two years."

11. Fuel costs, for example, now account for a third of a shrimper's operating expenses, compared with only one-tenth three years ago. The price of diesel fuel along the Southeast coast averages 35 cents a gallon, up from 10 cents in 1973 (an average shrimp boat uses 400 to 500 gallons of fuel a day). This expense alone, shrimpers say, has forced them to trawl shorter distances, shrimp fewer days and just keep the boat moored during lean months.

12. Rising insurance rates and crew wages are also taking an increased share of a boat's revenues. Average yearly insurance premiums have doubled in two years to about $5,000 a boat. Inexperienced crewmen are demanding $4 an hour, up from $2 an hour two years ago.

(An average shrimp boat carries a crew of three, including the captain, although larger corporate-owned boats may have five to 10 with each man earning between $8,000 to $10,000 a year.)

13. Shrimpers complain too that imported shrimp is undercutting domestic prices. Fuel and labor costs alone for U.S. Shrimpers are up to four times greater than those of their international counterparts—principally Mexico, India, Pakistan and some South American countries. This enables foreign shrimpers to sell their catches here at prices below those of domestic shrimp, depending on size and quality.

"Dumping Has Hurt"

14. Shrimp-industry spokesmen agree that the country needs imported shrimp to help supply the U.S market, "but dumping (selling the shrimp at below fair market value) in the past by Mexico and India has hurt us," says Western Seafood's Mr. Gore. Increased imports during a good domestic season force U.S. prices down. In 1974, shrimp imports totaled 252 million pounds, up 20% from a year earlier and comfortably more than the 224 million pounds landed by U.S. shrimpers that year. (Shrimp are weighed after their heads have been pinched off, and all weights refer to heads-off weight.)

15. Earlier this year, the U.S. International Trade Commission found that shrimp imports were entering the country in large enough quantities to be "a substantial cause of injury" to the U.S. shrimp industry. Soon afterwards, President Ford ordered trade–adjustment assistance for the industry and its employees, offering low-interest loans to those shrimpers who bailed out during the recent slump.

16. But that didn't solve the present problems of Gulf Coast shrimpers. Above-average rainfall and unseasonably cold weather in the last two years have contributed to reduced supplies. "Fresh water from heavy rains and unusually low temperatures in April annd May killed many of the susceptible young shrimp maturing in the estuaries," says Gary Graham, a marine fisheries specialist with the Texas Agricultural Extension Service.

17. Some shrimp-boat captains along the Gulf Coast also stand to lose one of their prime fishing areas. The U.S. and Mexico are continuing negotiations over fishing rights off the Mexican coast. Beginning next month, Mexico proposes to prohibit all but its own boats from fishing within 200 miles of its coast. If that proposal takes effect, U.S. shrimpers will lose about 10 million pounds of shrimp annually, some sources estimate.

Prices Could Go Higher

18. In addition, if the 600 boats that normally fish the Mexican waters are forced to compete for supplies inside the Gulf waters from Texas to Florida, prices of these supplies will probably go even higher. If this country is denied rights to Mexican waters, legislation sponsored by Texas Democratic Sen. Lloyd Bentsen, and passed earlier this year, would prohibit Mexico from exporting 80 million pounds of shrimp annually to the U.S. (Shrimp is Mexico's third largest export, and the U.S. is its principal market.)

19. "If they (Mexico) can push us out and if our government doesn't put a high tariff on Mexican shrimp, then we don't have much of a government left," says J. W. Beatty, a Cameron, La., shrimp boat owner-operator.

20. For different reasons, shrimpers in Maine, New Hampshire and Massachusetts have had their coasts closed off to them since April. "There just aren't any shrimp," says Jack Mahoney with the National Marine Fisheries Service in Gloucester, Mass. "All fish supplies are in a depletive state here, especially shrimp." Too much fishing shrunk the supplies, officials say. State biologists say they will monitor shrimp breeding this fall, but no date has been set to reopen shrimping in New England.

8

Price Setting by the Government: Minimum Prices

Henry, a farmer, is visiting his brother, Fred, who is an auto worker. During one of their conversations, Fred says, "I hear you farmers want the government to guarantee your prices. You have always said you believe in free enterprise; how can you believe in free enterprise and at the same time ask the government to step in and set prices? The government doesn't set auto prices and it shouldn't set agricultural prices either."

"You're right, Fred, the government doesn't set auto prices; the Big Three take care of that themselves. Look, the firms I buy my equipment from set their prices to cover costs. But the market sets my prices. If my costs increase, I can't simply raise the price of my products. If I'm going to survive in this system, I need the government to make sure my prices increase whenever my costs increase."

Most agricultural products are produced under conditions which facilitate market-determined product prices. However, for a variety of economic, social, and political reasons, government has used a variety of policies over the years to alter the market forces of some agricultural markets.

In this chapter, we will first learn the economic basis of these various agricultural policies and then examine some current and proposed agricultural policies.

CHECKLIST

Definitions of New Terms

1. Price Supports--a system which government uses to prevent the prices of certain agricultural products from falling below a predetermined level.
2. Parity--providing a price for products which guarantees the

same purchasing power per unit sold relative to what the sale of those units would have afforded in some earlier period.
3. Target Price--a price set by government for certain agricultural products. If the market price falls below the target price, the government pays farmers the difference.

Concepts

1. Supporting agricultural prices by maintaining market prices at a government determined level
   A. Output restriction plans: The government either assigns production allotments, which proportionally reduce each producer's output, or pays producers to take resources out of production. In either case, market supply is shifted to the left, as shown in Figure 1, and market price is increased up to the support level, P_2. Output is reduced from Q_1 to Q_2 units. The economic effect of output restriction plans will be to:
   i. increase product price for consumers;
   ii. take productive resources out of use.

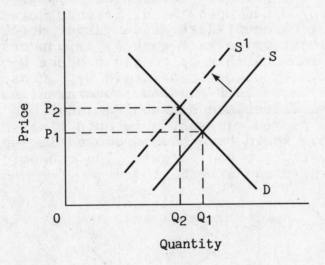

Figure 1

   B. Government purchase plans. The government maintains the support price by agreeing to buy all output at that price. Thus, in order to maintain the support price, P_2, in Figure 2, the government will purchase the surplus, Q_1-Q_2 units. The government must now store its purchases and eventually dispose of them. (NOTE: The government may maintain the support price by simply granting loans based on quantity stored.) The economic effect of government purchase plans will be to:
   i. increase product price for consumers;
   ii. employ more resources;
   iii. spend taxpayers' money for purchases;
   iv. spend taxpayers' money for storage and disposal costs.

63

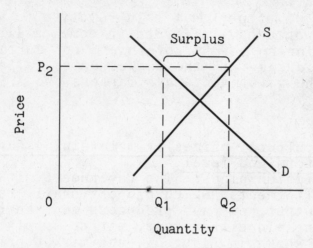

Figure 2

2. <u>Supporting agricultural producers by paying a direct subsidy based on market prices</u>

A. <u>Direct subsidy plan</u>. The government pays producers a direct subsidy based upon the difference between market price and a government-determined target price. Assume P_2 is the target price in Figure 3. Producers base their output decisions on this price and produce Q_2. Consumers will only buy output Q_2 if price is P_1. Consequently, market price falls to P_1 and the government must pay producers the difference between P_2 and P_1 on all Q_2 units sold. As you can see, more output was produced under this plan than would have been produced if supply and demand had set price and output. The economic effect of direct subsidy plans will be to:

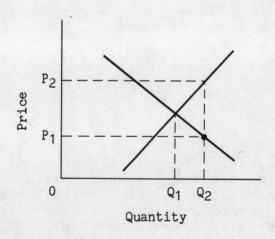

Figure 3

   i. employ more resources;
  ii. lower prices for consumers;
 iii. spend taxpayers' money to pay producers the difference between the market price and the target price.

GUIDE FOR ANALYZING ARTICLES

1. Identify the products, producers, and industries that are affected or will be affected by the government policy.
2. Determine the type of policy being used or being proposed.
3. Explain or predict the economic effect of the policy on:
   A. product price;
   B. output;
   C. total resources used;
   D. government purchases and total government cost;
   E. consumer purchases and total government cost;
   F. profitability of producers.
4. Explain or predict the long-run implications of the policy on the industry.
   A. Will entry or exit occur?
   B. Will the situation created lead to arguments for a change in policy?

Articles

AN ANALYZED ARTICLE: OVERVIEW

Prior to the time this article was written, the government had been supporting fluid milk prices at $8.26 per hundred pounds; it has increased its support price to $9.00. This increase in support price is expected to increase milk production, government purchases of dairy products, and consumer milk prices.

Boost of 9% in Milk-Price Supports to Increase Retail Costs, Output

Reprinted by permission of The Wall Street Journal
(April 5, 1977), © Dow Jones & Company, Inc., 1977.
All rights reserved.

1. Its back to the drawing boards for dairy-industry analysts pondering the likely implications of the government's recent 9% boost in milk-price supports. The analysts say a few things are relatively easy to

2. forecast. Lifting the supports to $9 per hundred pounds of fluid milk from $8.26 means retail prices for dairy products probably will rise.

3. That's already happening in many parts of the country, observers say. Moreover, consumers might grumble, but not balk, at paying those higher prices because "rightly or wrongly, other food prices are rising also," says Truman F. Graf, a University of Wisconsin milk-market economist.

4. Another easy forecast is that the higher support prices will encourage increased production. "We're going to get more milk," declares Judd Mason, a National Milk Producers Federation economist, and the government probably will buy the major share of the extra output. But the experts aren't sure exactly how much more milk there will be.

5. Dairy specialists say the added funds farmers receive for the milk will encourage increased feeding of more expensive high-protein feeds and feed supplements. The high-protein diet in turn will improve cows' milk-producing capabilities, they say.

6. "We're dealing with one variable—output per cow," says Hollis Hatfield, a dairy economist for the American Farm Bureau Federation. The higher milk prices "enhance the milk-to-feed price ratio" beyond earlier expectations, he says, and "production will surge" as a result.

While individual forecasts vary, dairy experts foresee

7. a possible rise of 3% or more in milk production this year to about 124 billion pounds. The added output is about double the increase that was projected before the higher price supports were announced.

8. Critics of the big boost argue that dairy-product supplies were mounting even before price supports were raised. Indeed, the government bought more milk under the program during January and February of this year than during all of 1976. Market sources say some farmers fear the $9 support price will become a ceiling price if government-held surpluses continue to build.

9. "The administration's decision might be historic," Mr. Hatfield says. "Usually the support price isn't high enough," but "this time it's too high." Smaller support increases presumably would have tempered the production surge and encouraged consumers, rather than the government, to buy more of the extra output. That, in turn, would leave future milk prices less at the mercy of later price-support moves, which could be lower as easily as higher, the critics argue.

10. Government purchases during the current marketing year, which began last Friday, are expected to total $740 million, compared with less than $330 million last year. Butter purchases under the program are expected to more than double this year to 265 million pounds while those of cheese will rise 80% to 180 million pounds. The Agriculture Department concedes it has no "projected use" or no outlet at this time for almost half that combined amount of butter and cheese.

11. The increased milk-price supports "will bring on more dairy products than we've got demand for," Mr. Hatfield asserts.

Analysis

The policy being used by the government is aimed primarily at raw fluid milk, a product produced by dairy farmers operating in the dairy industry. However, some products produced from raw milk are also affected by the policy being discussed; among these products are retail fluid milk, butter, and cheese.

Raw milk prices are being supported by a government purchase plan. However, since raw milk cannot be stored, the government buys storable dairy products, such as cheese and butter, as a means of increasing the demand for raw milk.

In order to help explain and predict the various economic effects of this government purchase policy, we will use Figure 4. Figure 4(A) shows that in the absence of government purchases, consumer demand (D) and producer supply (S) will set a market price of OA in the dairy products market. At this price, quantity OE will be purchased. Correspondingly, Figure 4(B) shows that in the absence of government purchases of dairy products, the raw milk price will be OH and quantity purchased will be OI[1].

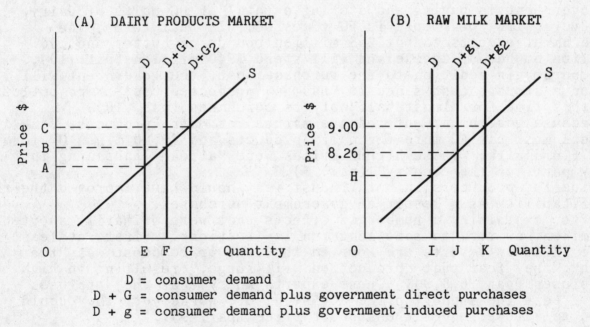

(A) DAIRY PRODUCTS MARKET   (B) RAW MILK MARKET

D = consumer demand
D + G = consumer demand plus government direct purchases
D + g = consumer demand plus government induced purchases

Figure 4

Now that we have set the stage for our analysis, we will introduce government. We will begin by noting that prior to the current boost in support prices, the government was supporting raw milk prices at $8.26 per hundredweight. To do this, it bought EF units of dairy produces (for example, cheese and butter). These direct purchases by government caused an increase in market demand (from D to D + G_1) in the dairy products market, thereby increasing quantity supplied from OE to OF units. In order to produce these additional units, producers of dairy products buy

---

1. Note: demand is shown as a perfectly inelastic curve in both markets in order to simplify the analysis.

more raw milk. The government-induced purchases of raw milk shifts demand from D to D + g_1, increasing market price to $8.26, which is the level desired by government.

Having followed this series of events through the two markets, you should be able to explain what government must do to boost the price of raw milk up to the current support price of $9.00 per hundredweight. In short, government buys FG more units of dairy products, which causes producers to buy JK more units of raw milk. Presto--a $9.00 price for raw milk.

Now that we have gone through the analysis, we can summarize the economic effects of this purchase policy.

We will begin with the effect of this policy on product price. As Figure 4 shows, the direct effect of government purchases was an increase in the price of dairy products from OA to OC; the indirect effect was an increase in the price of raw milk from OH to $9.00

As for the effect on output, more dairy products and more raw milk are being produced. Consequently, more resources are being used by both industries.

Government is buying and storing a total of EG units of dairy products; its total cost is EG times OC. In real terms, the government expects to buy 265 million pounds of butter and 180 million pounds of cheese and will spend $740 million (par. 10). Of course, in addition to the purchase cost, the government will incur a storage cost since it "has no 'projected use' or no outlet at this time for almost half" of its purchases (par. 10).

Because government entered the market for dairy products, consumers must pay AC more for dairy products and $9.00 minus OH more for fluid milk. These higher prices were "already happening in many parts of the country" (par. 3).

Finally, producers in both industries should have improved their profitability as a result of government purchases.

After explaining a number of effects that were primarily short-term, we now turn to some long-run implications. First, at least some industry experts are worried that the price boost was "too high"; they fear that "production will surge," resulting in high surpluses (par. 6,8,9). These experts worry that the surpluses may freeze the support price at $9.00, or, worse yet, they could lead to a lowering of the support price (par. 9).

Finally, will consumers complain loudly enough to get this government support policy changed? Our milk-market economist does not think so; he feels "consumers might grumble, but not balk" at the higher prices (par. 3).

AN ARTICLE WITH QUESTIONS

Striking Farmers Demand Law for Minimum Prices

By WILLIAM ROBBINS
Special to *The New York Times*

1. KANSAS CITY, Kan., Jan. 16—Leaders of the national farm strike movement, given their first opportunity to present their case at a Congressional hearing, said here today that they were going bankrupt because of current agricultural prices and demanded minimum-price legislation that would assure them a profit.

2. "If farmers go down the drain, we'll take the rest of this country down with us," said Rodney W. Shay of St. Francis, Kan., who warned that the problems of agriculture could have serious repercussions throughout the national economy.

3. The witnesses, representing the American Agriculture Movement, the loose-knit organization that is leading the farm strike, gave their testimony at a field hearing conducted by Senator Robert Dole, Republican of Kansas, representing the Senate Agriculture Committee. The Senator said he would present the record of the hearing along with a report of his own to the full committee.

4. Supporting the farmers' warnings, Senator Dole said, "The ripple effect of the farmers' plight has now occurred and is adversely affecting farm communities."

5. About 300 farmers attending the hearing at the Soldiers and Sailors Memorial Hall, a big brick municipal auditorium here, punctuated the Senator's remarks and the testimony with applause.

Would Enforce 100% Parity

6. In the most systematic presentation of the legislative program they are proposing, Greg Suhler, leading witness on a panel of strike leaders, said that a proposed new law should contain these words, "It will be illegal for anyone to buy, sell or trade any agricultural product at less than 100 percent of parity."

7. As long used in agricultural legislation, parity is a term intended to convey the idea of fairness to farmers. Full parity would give their products the same buying power it had in the period from 1910 to 1914. Thus if the price of a bushel of wheat would buy a pair of shoes in 1914, at parity, the wheat price would pay for a pair of shoes today.

8. "How much would that cost the Government?" Senator Dole asked.

"How much does the minimum wage for labor cost 9. the Government?" responded Gerald McCatherin of Hereford, Tex., one of the panel members. "We're not asking for a subsidy."

10. Although such a law would not require a subsidy, the Agriculture Department has estimated that it would result in sharp increases in food prices. The current average of all farm prices is now 66 percent of parity.

11. To make the program work, the panel proposed that a national board of agricultural producers be set up within the Agriculture Department to establish annual targets for production and that selling rights be allocated to individual farmers.

Critics Fear Regimentation

12. Critics of the proposal have protested that it would lead to excessive regulation and regimentation of farmers.

13. The plan would mean a radical departure from the present farm program, which provides for price support loans and target prices. Under the loan program, farmers can borrow from the Government and store their commodities as collateral. The target prices are income guarantees providing for subsidy payments to make up the difference when market prices fall below the targets.

14. "We have presented you with sufficient proposals to set the wheels in motion to save our agricultural community and in doing so to save our nation from depression," said Wayne Eakin of Greenwood, Del., the panel's concluding speaker.

15. Witnesses from several farm organizations, including the National Farmers Union, the National Grange, the National Farmers Organization and the American Farm Bureau Federation, testified in support of the strikers' income goals without dealing with the means for achieving them.

16. Later this week, the strike leaders will shift their activities to Washington, where they will seek to get the attention of lawmakers through tractor parades, picketing and lobbying.

17. Thus far, their enthusiasm and vigor seem undimmed by the fact that the withholding action on farm products they called for when their strike began a month ago appears to have had little impact on commodity markets.

1. Identify products, producers, and the industry which will be affected by the policy being proposed.
2. What policy is being proposed and who is proposing it?
3. Predict the economic effects of this policy.
    A. Draw a diagram showing the effects of this policy.
4. Predict the long-run implications of this policy.

AN ARTICLE FOR STUDENT ANALYSIS: OVERVIEW

A variety of plans to provide more income for grain and cotton growers are discussed in this article. The 1977 Farm Act is the only congressional policy that applies to farm crops now that the emergency farm bill proposed by Senator Dole was defeated. However, the Carter Administration may use certain policy initiatives without Congressional approval. Review Figures 1 and 3 before beginning your analysis; you will need both concepts to explain the operation of each plan.

Farmers and Subsidies

By SETH S. KING
Special to *The New York Times*

The New York Times *(April 17, 1978).* © *by The New York Times Company. Reprinted by permission.*

1. WASHINGTON—The house having killed the emergency farm bill last week, farmers will again be more dependent on the weather and foreign buyers than on the Government for their living.

2. Grain and cotton growers still have the Carter farm program to fall back on, of course. But what it offers them in terms of cash, compared with what they could get in the free market with larger plantings, raises considerable doubt in Washington about how many will utilize it.

3. As Agriculture Secretary Bob Bergland frequently notes, wheat and corn prices have been edging upward since January, to levels where the President's subsidy payment rates could mean little to grain farmers and the reward in his proposal for setting aside additional acres of feed grains and cotton would be dubious.

• • •

4. The emergency bill would have guaranteed farmers $5.04 a bushel for wheat, $3.45 a bushel for corn and 84 cents a pound for cotton if they idled at least a third of the acreage they planted this year. Those prices would have been close to the ones of the glory years of 1973 and 1974.

5. In their campaign against the bill—introduced by Senator Robert Dole, Republican of Kansas—Administration officials argued that it not only was inflationary and budget-busting but also was not needed since the Carter farm program was working and farm income was improving.

6. Mr. Bergland went so far as to predict that with livestock prices again at a profitable level and with enough grain farmers embracing the Administration's new paid set-aside plan, net farm income in 1978 could rise by as much as $4 billion, to a total of $24 billion. That would compare with the 1973 record of $29.9 billion and would be the third highest in history.

• • •

7. The Carter Administration's "initiatives," which Mr. Bergland can grant without Congressional approval would pay corn farmers 20 cents a bushel on their normal yield if they idle 10 percent of their planted acreage in addition to the 10 percent they must now set aside to be eligible for subsidies and supports. Cotton farmers would get 2 cents a pound. And wheat farmers, three-fourths of whom have already planted their 1978 crops, would be offered 50 cents a bushel if they grazed cattle on 40 percent of what they have planted or cut it for hay instead of harvesting it. The payment is contingent on their already setting aside 20 percent of their normal planting to be eligible for subsidies and supports.

8. Under the subsidy scale in the 1977 Farm Act, which will apply to the 1978 crops, the wheat subsidy level

will be $3 a bushel or $3.05 if the harvest does not exceed 1.8 billion bushels.

• • •

9. Next fall, if the free market should average $2.80 a bushel for winter wheat, as it is doing now, a wheat farmer eligible for subsidies could get about 25 cents a bushel added to that market price. If he went for the additional paid set-aside, he would get another $15 an acre on the paid set-aside plus any rentals or proceeds from hay sales. At current market prices he would get about $84 an acre plus the subsidy.

10. If the corn market averages $2.20 a bushel next fall, as it is doing now a corn farmer would get no subsidy payments because these are pegged at $2.20. If he went into the paid set-aside, he would get about $20 an acre on the 10 percent of land that was idled but a total of about $220 an acre in the marketplace compared with planting costs of at least $200 an acre.

11. In the opinion of some observers in Washington, neither set of figures looks very attractive.

• • •

12. April 1 planting intentions, announced last week, indicated that the total winter and spring wheat plantings would be at least 12 percent less than last year's, meaning that many wheat farmers would be eligible for subsidies, loans and disaster payments by setting aside 20 percent.

13. However, the Administration's offer of the additional paid set-aside had been made before the intentions survey was taken.

14. Corn farmers indicated they would plant only 3 percent fewer acres than they did last year when they raised a record crop. Cotton farmers indicated a 6 percent cut in their acreage. But the Corn Belt is still wet, and planting has been delayed there. If the soil remains wet, many farmers will have to divert corn land to soybeans or leave 10 percent of it idle for a paid set-aside.

• • •

15. Although the Dole bill was defeated and the President was spared the stigma of vetoing it as he had promised, Washington may not be entirely through with the farmers.

16. Mr. Carter has said he would approve Congressional action to raise the wheat subsidy level to $3.40 a bushel. Senator Dole has already introduced a bill to raise it to $3.50. Senator Dick Clark, Democrat of Iowa, has also introduced legislation to raise wheat, corn, and cotton subsidies above their current levels.

17. Both plans have a chance of passage. Whether Mr. Carter would sign them is now known.

71

9

Price Setting by the Government: Maximum Prices

Mabel just called her friend, Hilda, for their daily chat. Mabel has been paying bills, and she tells Hilda, "You know, I don't know how that phone company can get away with it. Rates went up again. And what are we supposed to do if we don't like it--we either pay those crooks, or we will be forced to write letters to keep in touch with our friends."

"I know what you mean about the bills, Mabel. But we own some stock--just a share or two--in the phone company, and Harry said if our dividends don't increase, he is going to get rid of the stuff. He said we could earn a lot more on other stocks. Anyway, I'm glad you decided to pay your phone bill, because wait until you hear what Ann told about Corrine!"

As is frequently the case, there are at least two sides to every complaint. Consumers believe that utilities take advantage of their monopoly position and overcharge for their services so they can earn big profits. On the other side, stockholders--the group that should benefit from the profits--complain that their returns are inadequate. In addition, management complains that it does not have enough money to run the business properly.

All these complaints are directed to the regulatory commission, which must consider all the various arguments and set a price that pleases everyone. (Would you like to be on that commission?)

Regulated firms are unique public/private producers. They have very high fixed costs, both on an absolute and a relative basis. In addition, they produce services considered vital to the public interest. Consequently, government has decided that competition would be either inefficient or unworkable, and has granted these firms exclusive rights to service the public. However, to prevent these firms (called public utilities) from using their monopoly power to overcharge for their products, the government transfers price-setting authority to regulatory agencies.

In order to understand the economic role of a regulatory commission, it's necessary to understand the theory of monopoly--

that is, the theory of price setting by firms that have market power. To facilitate this, we will begin with a brief explanation of how firms determine price and output when they have sufficient market power to set their own prices. We will then learn about the economic role of a regulatory commission. And, finally, we will examine some actual regulatory situations.

CHECKLIST

Definitions of New Terms

1. Monopoly--a firm that produces a product for which there are no substitutes.
2. Natural Monopoly--exists when the lowest per unit cost of production is achieved when only one firm produces for the entire market. This situation is usually due to large economies of scale.
3. Public Utility--a firm, usually a natural monopoly, which has been granted an exclusive franchise to produce in an area because competition is either impossible or not in the public interest. A utility's prices and products are regulated by a regulatory commission.
4. Rate Base--the value of the stockholders' investment in plant and equipment.
5. Rate of Return Regulation--a type of regulation in which a regulatory commission establishs a price that will provide a fair return for stockholders.
6. Regulatory Commission--an appointed group legally authorized to set prices, quality of service, etc. for the utilities in their jurisdiction. These commissions operate at both the state and federal levels.

Concepts

1. A firm producing a unique product sets its own product price.
   A. A firm with a unique product--as opposed to a uniform or standardized product--has its own customers, its own market demand curve, and, consequently, sets its own product price. Every firm with its own customers always has some degree of market power.
   B. A firm with market power first determines its most profitable output; then sells this output at the highest price it can charge customers. Figure 1 provides an illustration of this price setting procedure.
   The most profitable output is always that quantity at which MR = SMC, or OG in Figure 1[1]. The maximum price that

---

1. Marginal revenue will always be lower than price when firms set their own price and then sell all output at that price. We can see this best with an example. Suppose price must be lowered from 50¢ to 49¢ to increase sales from 30 to 31 units. The firm gains 49¢ from selling one more unit, but loses 1¢ on each of the 30 units that could have been sold at 50¢. So whereas the new price is 49¢, marginal revenue is only 19¢ (49¢ - (30 x 1¢) = 19¢).

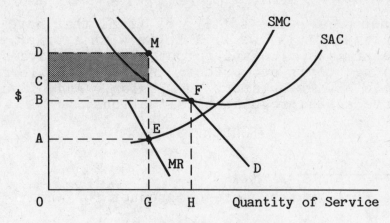

Point M = monopoly price level
Point F = fair price
          (break-even or normal profits)
Point E - efficient price level

Figure 1

customers will pay for a total of OG units is OD. Since
average revenue is greater than average cost (SAC) at this
price and output, an economic profit (see shaded area) is
earned by the firm.[2].

2. Short-run equilibrium price and output. In the short run, the
    firm in Figure 1 will continue to sell OG units at price OD,
    and earn the economic profit shown by the shaded area. Notice
    that the selling price, OD, is greater than the marginal cost,
    OA. This disparity, which indicates that resources are not
    efficiently allocated, will always exist when a firm has some
    degree of market power.

3. Long-run equilibrium price and output. In the long run, a
    firm will seek the most profitable plant size. When a market
    set price, this plant size was located at the lowest point on
    the long-run average cost curve (refer to Figure 1, Chapter 7).
    However, when the firm has some degree of market power, its
    most profitable plant size may not be located at the low point
    of LAC[3]. Consequently, firms with market power are neither
    forced to use an optimum plant size, nor are they forced to
    operate at economic capacity. Both conditions imply produc-
    tive inefficiency. Also, firms with market power may continue
    to earn economic profits, which means some resource owners are
    earning more than their opportunity costs. This may be
    considered to be a distributional inequity.

4. Government sets maximum (and minimum) product price for firms
    with market power when they provide a public service and (A)

---

2. Average revenue is always equal to price, so AR is shown by
    demand.

3. The location of the most profitable plant size will depend
    upon the location of the firm's demand.

they are a natural monopoly, or (B) they might engage in
destructive competition.
   A. Natural monopoly (no competition). If a product can be
      produced most inexpensively by one firm, the government may
      grant the firm exclusive selling rights by making it a
      public utility. In exchange for the exclusive selling
      rights, the government takes away the firm's right to set
      its product price. Figure 1 shows this situation. Given
      its own choice, a firm with exclusive selling rights would
      charge OD and earn maximum economic profits. One choice
      the regulatory commission has is to reduce price to OB;
      this would eliminate all economic profits. Another choice
      would be to set price at OA, which would make price equal
      to marginal cost--resources would be allocated efficiently
      at this price. However, as you can see, if price were OA,
      the firm would suffer an economic loss and would require a
      subsidy.
   B. Potential destructive competition. Certain industries with
      only a few large firms, relatively high fixed costs, and
      significant economies of scale have a propensity for price
      wars. Moreover, these price wars tend to be very
      destructive. Consequently, if such an industry is pro-
      viding a vital public service, the government may decide it
      is in the public interest to prevent these price wars and
      it takes away their pricing perogative. Another reason why
      government may set prices for such firms is because they
      may have monopoly power in some of the market areas they
      serve. An example of an industry that meets both criteria
      is the air passenger industry. This industry faces some
      competition in certain markets; very little in others. The
      Civil Aeronautics Board sets fares and routes for this
      industry.
5. In practice, regulatory commissions usually set a price that
   provides a normal return for stockholders.
   A. To provide a normal return for the utility's stockholders,
      the commission should set price OB in Figure 1. However,
      the practical problems of determining that price include
      the problem of deciding:
      i. what are legitimate operating costs and how much will
         they increase;
     ii. what is the correct value of plant and equipment;
    iii. what is a normal rate of return for this firm.

                  GUIDE FOR ANALYZING ARTICLES

1. Determine the product, the producer(s), and the market area
   being served.
2. Identify the regulatory agency and the nature of regulation
   (i.e., constraining the prices of a natural monopolist or
   preventing destructive competition).
3. In general, indicate the nature of the arguments being
   presented by the various parties.
4. Explain the arguments being presented by the producer to

support its request, if any. Is the producer able to show
that:
   A. its operating costs have increased or are increasing;
   B. its rate base has increased;
   C. its rate of return is inadequate.
5. Explain the position of any parties opposed to the producer's
    request.
6. Explain the agency's position, and, if available, its decision.
7. Predict the economic consequences of the agency's decision.

Articles

AN ANALYZED ARTICLE: OVERVIEW

New York Telephone wants to charge its customers $393 million more; the Public Service Commission staff wants to reduce their proposal to zero. This article explains why the PSC decided to grant the company $232 million instead.

How the Picture Grew Rosier for New York Telephone Rate Boost

By ANN PODD
Courier-Express Staff Reporter

Buffalo Courier-Express *(Dec. 4, 1977). Reprinted by permission.*

1. New York Telephone Co. wanted $393 million more a year from its customers. The staff of the Public Service Commission said the phone firm deserved nothing.

2. The hearing officer on the rate case thought $245 million should do the trick. But the PSC finally decided that the phone company deserved an annual increase of $232 million.

3. According to Charles A. Zielinski, the PSC's acting chairman, it really is not unusual for the different parties to have suggested such diverse amounts.

4. Some facts given to one group may have changed by the time another party was reviewing the rate increase request, "after all," he said, "these rate hearings last about 11 months."

5. The different suggested increases may also reflect the stand the party is taking on rate increases. The PSC staff is supposed to check to see that the consumers' best interests are being served. So they are to try to decide on the "lowest reasonable amount" the utility should receive," Zielinski explained.

6. While the phone company has its own special interests Zielinski explained the following differences between the staff's recommendation and what the PSC eventually awarded the telephone company:

Wages —

7. The staff argued that New York Telephone was already paying its employes much higher than the average wages for similar positions in the same geographic areas. So, they said, New York Telephone should get none of the $90 million they requested for additional wages and fringe benefits costs.

8. But, the PSC noted that the average wages that staff compared the telephone wages to included non-union labor. "When you pull these out, there is almost no difference" Zielinski noted.

9. "If union activity at New York Telephone produces wages comparable to those paid by other unionized firms then it is difficult to conclude that they are in any sense 'to high' simply because they exceed non-union wages," the PSC said in allowing the wage and benefit costs.

Depreciation —

10. The staff argued that the company should not be able to recover any more depreciation costs. However, by the time the PSC was making its decision on the rate request, the federal government had set new standards for depreciation rates. The PSC noted the new rules and allowed the company to recover an additional $40 million in depreciation expenses.

Productivity —

11. When the staff calculated a productivity adjustment—that is the amount of work that can be accomplished by each employe—they used faulty data supplied by the company. The staff recognized this mistake and $16 million more was given to New York Telephone.

12. Zielinski noted that errors in such large and complex rate cases are not unusual. "Besides, how can I fault my staff for the error when the figures supplied by the company were wrong?" he asked.

Taxes —

13. The staff said it predicts changes in the state and municipal tax laws so that the utility's taxes will go down. Zielinski said, "That's a fine argument and we wish it would happen, but we can't close our eyes to reality." Because the PSC could not know for sure that the tax rates would change, it allowed the phone firm $17 million to pay additional taxes.

Growth Allowance —

14. The company said it would grow at a rate less than one percent a year. This means it can't expect as much revenue from new customers as in the past, it said. The staff tried to figure out what the growth rate would be by using a computer. They came up with a three percent growth rate.

15. The PSC settled on a 2 percent rate based on the average growth rate for the last five years. The PSC rejected the staff's recommendation because there were some false assumptions filed as data into the computer.

16. "This was something new that the staff tried," Zielinski explained.

17. "I can't criticize them for trying new things. That's the way we make progress."

18. The telephone company was granted $38 million under this category.

Rate Of Return —

19. The company, staff and PSC all disagreed on what is the proper rate of return on equity. But the PSC had more up to date stock market information when it decided on a 11.5 percent rate of return. This allowed the company to raise rates for another $12 million.

Others —

20. Other disagreements between staff and PSC figures came on smaller amounts on a variety of subjects, such as additional costs for advertising and payments to American Telephone & Telegraph for services rendered to New York Telephone. The PSC decided the company could add $20 million more to its rates annually.

Analysis

The New York Telephone Company provides a variety of phone services for consumers in New York State. This company, which is the sole producer of these services for residents of New York State, has its rates set by the New York State Public Service Commission (PSC).

The company is requesting a $393 million annual increase in revenue to meet increased costs and to pay stockholders a fair return. On the other hand, the PSC staff, the consumers' advocate in these matters, argues that no increase is warranted. The hearing officer for this proposal arrived at a figure of $245 million. Then, when all this information was given to the commissioners, they sifted through it and decided to grant an increase of $232 million.

At this point, it would probably be easiest if we summarized the position of each party about whom we have the most complete information: the company, the PSC staff, and the PSC commissioners. Since we have only one item of information for the hearing officer, we will disregard him for the remainder of this analysis. Refer to Table 1 for this summary.

Items (A) through (D) are operating costs. Regulatory commissions grant rate increases to cover increased operating costs; however, it is the commission's responsibility to verify the accuracy and legitimacy of the operating cost estimates provided by the company. N.Y. Telephone presented its operating cost estimates to the PSC; after examining this data, the PSC staff arrived at its own estimates. In every case, the staff's estimate was lower than that of the company. These two sets of cost estimates were then turned over to the PSC commissioners, who decided to increase the staff's figures by the amounts shown in

Table 1

Items being considered	Requested by company	Allowed by PSC staff	Adjustment by commissioners
A. Increase for wages	+90	none	+90
B. Depreciation allowance		none	+40
C. Increase for taxes	increase needed	should get less	+17
D. Other expenses			+20
E. Productivity adjustment		none--but erroneous data used	+16
F. Growth allowance	1%	3%	2% = +38
G. Rate of return adjustment			11.5% = +12

Table 1. The reasons given for the commissioners' decisions are adequately presented in the article and will not be repeated here.

The next item, productivity adjustment, may seen unusual. The company is required to lower costs by a factor based upon its improved productivity. In effect, productivity gains are lowering costs while such things as wage increases are raising costs. What happened in this case is that the PSC staff, using erroneous company data, computed too high a figure for the productivity adjustment. Consequently, the company's costs would have been reduced too much for this item if the commissioners had not corrected for the error.

Item (F), growth allowance, is used to compensate for changes in the company's projected sales. If the company's sales only increase by its 1 percent estimate, it will need a much larger rate boost than if it grew by the staff's estimate of 3 percent. Since the commissioners decided sales would grow by 2 percent, they had to add $38 million to the staff's figure.

Finally, the commissioners must determine what stockholders should earn on their investment; this requires considering the earnings on comparable investments. In this case, after looking at current stock market information, the PSC decided upon a 11.5 percent return. In order to provide this return, revenue must be increased by an additional $12 million.

When the commissioners added up all their adjustments, they arrived at an increase of $232 million--about 60 percent of what the company requested, but $232 million more than the staff would have given the company.

At this point, the reader will be left to speculate on the consequences of the PSC's decision. Among the things to consider are whether stockholders are receiving enough to encourage investment, whether the quality of service will deteriorate, and whether point F in Figure 1 (see Concepts section, Concept 1) was reached.

AN ARTICLE WITH QUESTIONS

TWA Attacks American Air's Proposal For Discount New York—California Fares

By WILLIAM M. CARLEY
Staff Reporter of *The Wall Street Journal*

1. NEW YORK—Trans World Airlines filed a complaint, against American Airlines blasting American's proposed "Super-Saver" discount fares as a money-losing proposition for the airlines.

2. American, which began advertising its new fares last week, proposed discounts as deep as 45% in the New York-to-California market. That means a round trip between New York and either San Francisco or Los Angeles would cost only $227; the regular coach fare is $412.

3. American said its low fares would generate so much new traffic that any revenue loses would be more than offset, and American would make money on the operation. But some critics say American has touched off a price-cutting wars that will result in net losses to the airlines, already battered by hard economic times in recent years, and TWA agreed with the critics.

CAB Approval Required

4. The American proposal requires approval by the Civil Aeronautics Board. TWA filed its complaint with the board and asked the agency to suspend and investigate the American proposal. At the same time, TWA said that within 10 days it will file a far more restrictive discount-fare proposal as an alternative. TWA has already said it will match the American fare if the government allows it to go into effect.

5. United Airlines, a unit of UAL Inc., the third transcontinental carrier, hasn't announced its position but has said it would be competitive.

6. The Super-Saver fares are American's response to a new type charter approved by the CAB last October. Unlike earlier charters, the Advanced Booking Charter, or ABC as it is called, carries few restrictions except that it must be purchased 30 days in advance. American feared that its regular passengers would be diverted to the new, low-cost charters, and hence proposed the deep fare discounts.

7. Ironically, industry sources say it is the scheduled airlines themselves, including American, TWA and United, which are providing the planes for charter operations. Under government restrictions, the scheduled airlines can't organize most types of charters themselves but can hire out their planes to charter operators.

Price-Cutting Could Spread

8. The price-cutting war, as least so far, is limited to the New York-California market. It could spread further to other heavily traveled routes such as New York-to-Miami, Fla. But analysts say it's unlikely the price-cutting will cover the nation, if only because low-cost charters to less popular destinations aren't economically feasible.

9. The New York-California market, however, is one of the biggest airline markets in the world, and the way American plans to slash prices will cost the airlines money, some analysts say. TWA, in its complaint, agreed.

10. In its filing, TWA said it supports the idea of low fares on scheduled service, but added that American's Super-Saver fare has such serious flaws that "it would undermine TWA's and the industry's attempt to return to reasonable financial health from the disastrous year of 1975." In that year, TWA and many other major carriers reported large losses on their operations.

11. TWA's first criticism of the American proposal was that it is ill-timed, coming just as the industry is approaching its summer peak. Super-Saver fares would be effective for travel beginning April 24. TWA noted that the industry filled an average of 58% of its seats in the June-August period last year, and 60% in the peak month of August. Assuming a forecast 7% traffic growth and no increase in capacity, the load factor would hit a high of 64% in August, TWA added.

12. "It is this very summer peak period that generates the earnings which must carry the major transcontinental carriers through the remainder of the year," TWA stated. "During 1976, the Big Three (American, TWA and United), earned $142 million in the peak third quarter, while losing $29 million during the remaining nine months of the year. Given this earnings pattern, the industry cannot afford the risk of introducing a very low . . . fare right before the summer peak—just when revenue and earnings must be maximized if the carriers are to rebuild their financial health throughout the rest of the year."

13. TWA noted that American would restrict the seats available for the Super-Saver fare to 35% of the total, thus limiting the revenue loss that would result when a regular-fare passenger switched to the cheaper fare. But this limitation is inadequate, TWA asserted.

14. TWA said the use of available excursion-fare seats in the New York-California market has ranged from 12% to 43%, depending on the day of the week. Hence, "While the (35%) restriction may very well prevent a passenger from traveling on the prime flight of his choice, to suggest that it will preclude diversion from other fares is absurd," TWA argued.

Effect On Future Fares

15. TWA also said the use of Super-Saver discount fares would be used in CAB calculations of industry profits in such a way as to limit future fare increases. In effect, the CAB disallows discount fares when calculating profits, thus boosting theoretical profits and limiting the airlines' fare increases.

16. Passengers also will fly from other cities, such as Boston, Philadelphia and Washington, to take advantage of the Super-Saver fare from New York to California because the total cost would be cheaper, TWA said. And passengers will use the reverse procedure from California cities such as Sacramento and San Diego, flying to San Francisco or Los Angeles and then to New York.

17. TWA's revenue would be diluted $8 million and its profit cut $2.3 million as a result of all these factors, the airline said.

American Air's Estimates

18. In its filing with the CAB, American had said that the Super-Saver fare would be used by 100,000 passengers a year, of whom 43% would be new customers. American said it arrived at this conclusion on the basis of extensive surveys of how passengers responded to discount fares offered in recent years.

19. After calculating additional costs, American said it would still profit by more than $3.5 million as a result of Super-Saver revenue. The airline added that only 35% of Super-Saver passengers needed to be new customers for American to break even. Hence, American's forecast of 43% new passengers would have to be off nearly 25% before the fare would become unprofitable, it added.

20. American has said it won't oppose charters in all markets with Super-Saver fares. The airline said that markets with more sporadic travel, such as Mexico and the Caribbean, are suitable for charters and American itself is participating in charter activities in those areas.

Questions

1. Identify the product, the market, and the producers.
2. Identify the regulatory agency.
3. What is being proposed? By whom?. Who is opposed to the proposal?
4. What arguments are being used to support the proposal?
   A. If this argument is true, what is the price elasticity of demand for this service?
5. There are four major arguments being raised in opposition to the proposal. Explain these arguments (par. 3,11,15,16.)
6. What is the position of the regulatory agency?
7. If you were a member of the regulatory agency, what would be your decision? What would be the economic consequence of your decision?

AN ARTICLE FOR STUDENT ANALYSIS: OVERVIEW

The situation in this article is comparable to that found in the first article: in both cases a utility is asking the New York State Public Service Commission for permission to raise prices.

In the first article, the utility is a telephone company; in the second, it is a gas company. When you finish your analysis of this article, you may find it interesting to compare and contrast the two situations.

NFG Requests a 12.5% Rate Boost

By PHILIP LANGDON

Buffalo Evening News *(Feb. 1, 1978). Reprinted by permission.*

Average Hike For Homes $64 A Year

1. National Fuel Gas Distribution Corp. today asked the state Public Service Commission for a 12.5 percent rate increase that would boost the average residential customer's yearly bill by $64.

2. The rate hike would take effect next Jan. 1 and would boost the company's return on common equity to 15 percent, up from the 12.3 percent that the PSC currently allows the gas company and up from a rate of about 7 percent that the company earned last year in New York State.

3. Gerald C. Miller, National Fuel Gas vice president, said that, if approved, bills would go up by 12.5 percent for homes and industries alike, and he claimed industries would not be upset by the increase.

4. "I think industry is concerned primarily with having a fixed supply of fuel," said Mr. Miller, noting that National Fuel Gas is highly unusual among northeastern utilities in having gas available for industrial expansion.

* * *

5. "Obviously, here will be an impact on low-income people and senior citizens," Mr. Miller said. "We still feel strongly that the answer is energy stamps similar to food stamps."

6. "This was a tough decision to make, to ask for a rate increase of this magnitude," Mr. Miller said.

7. The average residential customer's yearly bill is now $512, the company said. For balanced-billing customers, the increases would amount to slightly over $5 a month.

8. Those who are not on balanced-billing now face an average January bill of $81.29, and that would go up about $10, the company said.

* * *

9. The new rates would give National Fuel Gas about $41 million in additional revenues. The company cited inflation as the major reason for the increase, saying "practically all costs of doing business have spiraled since our last major rate filing."

10. In the last five years National Fuel Gas has asked the Public Service Commission for $80 million in rate increases, and about 37 percent of that amount has been approved.

11. National Fuel Gas blamed the PSC's scaling down of past requests for the size of the increase that is being asked today.

12. National Fuel Gas said the average residential bill in Buffalo currently is in the middle range of rates in 13 major cities that the company surveyed.

* * *

13. Rates elsewhere vary from $61.23 a month for a typical residential customer in Detroit to $120.15 in New York City. The company insisted that its rate request is not "padded" but said it recognized that there will be an outcry against the proposed boost.

14. "It's a political football," Mr. Miller said. "We deal with inflammatory rhetoric,"

15. He said NFG now pays $23 million a year in taxes, up from $19 million in 1976. The cost of operating the system has risen to $52 million from $47 million in 1976. There also have been dramatic increases in bad debts, which amounted to $3.6 million in the past 12 months, the company said.

16. In the past five years, the price that National Fuel Gas has paid for its gas grew about 250 percent, which the company said is the major reason gas bills have risen so dramatically.

17. "This cost will probably continue to rise in the future because the federal government has finally recognized the importance of incentive exploration for gas," Mr. Miller said.

* * *

18. He argued that a higher return for stockholders is important so that the company can acquire the capital to improve its system.

19. He said, "the bulk of our stockholders are elderly people," many of them in Florida, and that they depend on dividends for income.

20. A 2 percent rate increase took effect Jan. 6 and the Citizens Alliance has been organizing resistance to payment of gas bills.

21. Mr. Miller criticized the Citizens Alliance, saying: "This is not a boycott. These people are going to take a service and then refuse to pay for it. I think it's an irresponsible action."

22. He maintained that gas is still the cheapest fuel available in Western New York and noted that the company has drilled more than 1,000 wells and built a plant to manufacture synthetic natural gas.

Price Setting by Firms: Competitive Conditions

Sally Freeland and Bob Bangman, both salespersons at Sears, are eating sandwiches that each brought to work. Sally, seeing that Bob also used whole wheat bread, asks what kind of bread he buys.

"This is Brownberry Ovens Natural Wheat; I just found it," replies Bob. "I used Home Pride before, but I switched to Brownberry even though it costs a few cents more. What do you buy?"

"Oh, I buy my bread at a bakery near where I live. This is a very coarse ground wheat and it is usually baked the day I buy it. I know it costs more, but I couldn't eat any other kind of wheat bread now that I've found this."

"That looks like something I might like too; where is that bakery? Say, since I'll be in the area buying bread, I could easily stop by and see you. Why don't you give me your address too?"

The above story interests us because it introduces a different type of product than we saw in the last three chapters. Although Sally and Bob prefer one wheat bread to another, all wheat breads have some degree of substitutability for one another. Consequently, while bakers find they have sufficient market power to set prices, their power is restricted by the competition of substitute products. Therefore, bakers have less market power than the exclusive producers of Chapter 9, but more than the powerless producers of Chapter 7. It is obvious we need some new concepts to explain how prices are determined when products are unique, yet substitutable. To do this, we will replace the traditional market that set prices in Chapter 7 with a quasi-market that establishes a range of prices. We will then examine the role of competition in industries which produce unique, but substitutable, products. Finally, we will examine some situations which allow us to apply our new concepts.

CHECKLIST

Definitions of New Terms

1. <u>Quasi-Market</u>--a market in which each product has some unique feature(s), but is also at least a partial substitute for other products in the market.
2. <u>Quasi-Market Demand</u>--a composite of the consumer demands for each of the products in the quasi-market. Whereas a traditional market employs a demand curve to show the price that will be paid for any given supply of products, a quasi-market employs a demand parallelogram to show the range of prices that will exist for each level of industry output.
3. <u>Representative Firm's Demand Curve</u>--each producing for a quasi-market will assume the demand for its product is considerably more price elastic than it actually is. This unrealistic view exists because each firm fails to consider the reaction of other firms when it foresees relatively large sales gains from minor price reductions. Much of the expected sales gain will fail to materialize once other firms follow the price cut.

Concepts

1. <u>When a variety of similar, but unique, products are produced in an industry, a quasi-market determines upper and lower product price limits; then each firm sets a product price that fits into these limits.</u> In the three previous chapters, consumer demand was represented by a market demand curve and a common price was established for all products produced by the industry. A common price was appropriate because each industry produced a standardized product. However, in many industries, the product of each producer has features which distinguishes it from the products of other producers. As a consequence, each producer has enough market power to be able to set price. However, since all products in the industry are, to some degree, substitutes for one another, each producer's price-setting power is limited by market forces. In order to examine this type of situation, we will construct a quasi-market in which quasi-market demand determines the upper and lower limits of a firm's price-setting power. This quasi-market is shown in Figure 1(A). If the industry produces OX units, the quasi-market will tolerate a range of prices from OA to OE. Figure 1(B) shows a representative firm that produces for this quasi-market. This firm determines its product price by comparing its costs with its conception of the demand for its product; in this case, this representative firm will produce OF units at a price of OC. (We will assume this is the output at which MR = MC.)
2. <u>Profitable products will attract competition.</u> If a firm is earning economic profits from the sale of its product(s), firms in and outside the industry will attempt to duplicate the profitable product(s). If they are successful, it will cause the demand curve of the firm with the profitable product

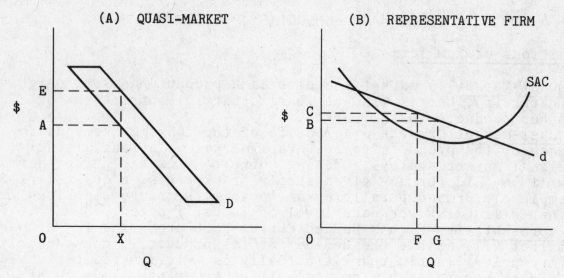

Figure 1

to be shifted to the left. Competition from other firms will
probably continue until all profits have been eliminated.
Such a result is shown in Figure 2. This firm's demand curve
has been shifted to the left until it is just tangent to the
short-run average cost curve. The firm will just break even
at price OA.

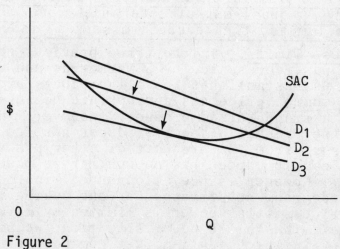

Figure 2

3. Firms in the industry may attempt to increase their market
   share by using either product competition, price competition,
   or both.
   A. Product competition: a firm may attempt to shift its
      demand curve to the right by improving the quality of its
      product, the image of its product, or both.
      i. Improving quality: a firm may attract more customers
         with a better product. Product improvement will defi-
         nitely cost more (SAC will definitely shift rightward).
         On the other hand, customers may or may not like the
         improvement (D may shift rightward). See Figure 3(A).
         Remember, demand must increase relatively more than
         costs for profitable results.

86

ii. Improving image: advertising or other methods may be used to improve a product's image. These methods definitely increase costs (SAC will definitely shift rightward), but their impact on demand will depend upon consumer reaction (D may shift rightward). See Figure 3(B).

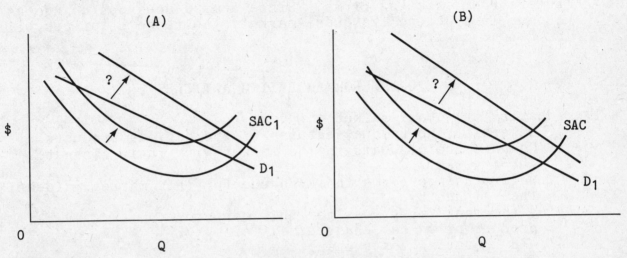

Figure 3

You may now compare the economic implications of these two methods. Both methods will definitely increase the firm's costs, but neither provides any assurance that this expenditure will pay off in increased demand. The major difference between the methods is that when the firm chooses to improve the quality of its product, consumers will probably get more for their money. In other words, if you have to pay more, would you want the producer to improve product quality or product image?

B. Price competition: From each firm's vantage point, it appears that significant sales increases could be achieved by fairly small price-cuts. For example, the firm in Figure 1(B) might believe its demand is very price elastic-- it believes it could increase its sales to OG by lowering price to OB. However, this firm will experience two problems if it tries this tactic. First, some of the new customers will be old customers of other firms; these other firms will probably match the price-cuts and lure some of their old customers back. Second, when this additional output appears on the market, the range of prices set by the quasi-market in Figure 1(A) will be lowered.

4. New firms may enter the industry and compete with existing firms by using product or price competition, or both. The entire discussion of Concept 3 could be repeated here with one difference: when new firms enter, there will definitely be more output produced by the industry. The effect of this new output on the range of prices in the quasi-market will depend upon the products and customers of the entering firms. If a better product is introduced, it may sell above the existing price level. In other words, the demand curve will expand to

the right, increasing the range of prices. On the other hand, the products of entering firms may be comparable to existing products, but they may attract new customers to the industry. In this case, demand will shift to the right and the new output will not change the range of prices. A third possibility is that the new firms are only able to attract customers from existing firms. Since demand does not change as output is added to the quasi-market, the range of prices will be forced down.

GUIDE FOR ANALYZING ARTICLES

1. Identify the quasi-market.
   A. Determine the unique features of the various products.
   B. Compare the products in the market with their closest substitutes.
   C. Determine the firms that produce for this market. Identify their industry.
2. Find the range of prices for this market.
3. If product price has changed, explain why.
   A. Did operating costs change?
   B. Did demand change?
   C. Have new firms entered?
   D. Are any firms attempting to increase their share of the market?
4. Determine if conditions in the industry will lead to competition from existing firms or from new firms. Will product or price competition be used?
5. Predict the economic consequences of competition, either actual or expected, on the:
   A. price, quality, and range of product choices available to consumers;
   B. profitability of firms;
   C. number of firms in the industry;
   D. conditions for entering the industry.

Articles

AN ANALYZED ARTICLE: OVERVIEW

Here we find an example of a new market emerging from an old established market. Running shoes--once a specialty shoe item-- are now a $500 million dollar business. Of all shoes sold to men, 40 percent have a running shoe look. This article provides some interesting information about products and producers found in this market.

Race Is On for Running Shoe Money

By PAMELA G. HOLLIE

The New York Times *(Oct. 24, 1977). © 1977 by The New York Times Company. Reprinted by permission.*

1. Yesterday's New York Marathon, the 26-mile-plus run through the five borroughs to a Central Park finish, was part of a larger, longer race that's just hitting its stride in the market for running shoes. More than a score of companies are competing to serve the sports phenomenon that has grown into a $500-million-a-year business.

2. An estimated 15 million Americans have taken to running. In less than five years, they have stimulated a new and exceptionally lucrative market for high-quality running shoes. And they have inspired an even larger shoe market for people who don't actually run, but like to dress as though they do.

3. Forty percent of all shoes sold to men this year have that running-shoe look, according to Footwear News, a trade publication. Last year, at least 15 million shoes sold looked like running shoes, and another 6 million actually were high quality running shoes.

4. It is a highly competitive market with three reasonably distinct segments. There are the specialist manufacturers—such as Brooks, Nike and New Balance. Just below these top-of-the-line companies are established makers of athletic shoes and sneakers like Converse and Uniroyal, the maker of PRO-Keds, which have expanded and improved their leaisure footwear lines to capitalize on the new vogue.

5. Bringing up the rear are the large department store chains like Sears, J.C. Penney and Montgomery Ward. Their own lines, designed mainly for the non-runners, have done very well but not among shoe buyers willing to pay $25 to $40 a pair, who demand the real thing.

6. This shoe business is not hard to enter, and some observers see a shake-out ahead, hurting for the most part the makers of shoes that lack a reputation for high performance and innovative design. Meanwhile, the race is to the bank.

7. "Business is tremendous," said a spokesman for Blue Ribbon Sports, the Oregon company that makes Nike running shoes. The company began in 1964 with just two Nike styles and about $8,000 in sales. Last year, when Blue Ribbon made 20 styles, revenues hit $27 million.

8. Blue Ribbon, like many of its competitors, is privately held and skittish about discussing profits. "This is such a new market that it is difficult to put profits in perspective," a spokesman said.

9. Reliable figures on shares of market are also hard to come by. Adidas U.S.A. Inc. the American subsidiary of a German company, is the recognized leader and the oldest of the manufacturers of running shoes. With annual sales approaching $199 million, Adidas commands perhaps 30 percent of the market for running shoes.

Challengers To Adidas

10. Among its challengers is New Balance Athletic Shoes of U.S.A. of Alston, Mass., a maker of orthopedic shoes that turned to producing running shoes five years ago. Initial output was 30 pair a day, but the company now produces as many as 2,000 pair a day, and a spokesman said, "We sell all we make."

11. Pony Sports and Leisure Inc. of New York is another newcomer. The company made its first running shoe last year. Now it makes eight styles.

12. Brooks Shoe Manufacturing Company of Hanover, Pa., joined the race three years ago and since then has introduced 22 styles.

13. Puma Sport SchuhFabriken-Rudols Dassler K.G., the German company started by a man whose brother founded Adidas, now produces 20 styles for the American market, and is perhaps one-third the size of Adidas.

Adidas led in the Americanization of running shoes. Its models had been designed mainly for use in Europe, where runners take to forest and parks. Following the 1968 Olympics, however, the company began to adapt to the needs of Americans who tend to run on roads and hard surfaces.

15. Today's high-quality running shoes have a distinctive look—a wide, elevated heel to relieve the strain on the legs and insure stability, and a high toe box to prevent blistering, rubbing or bruising. The cushioning varies, as does the material for the outer and inner soles.

16. Innovations in sole design give runners a variety of choices, from the Nike "waffle" to an odd assortment of nubs and studs that leave distinctive tracks but, according to the experts, make little difference in performance.

17. "One can no longer claim that running is a fad," said an Adidas U.S.A. spokesman. The company says it made track shoes for Jesse Owens, and last year it shod the winner of the Boston Marathon, as well as Olympic games marathon Gold Medalist.

18. Manufacturers take the development of running shoes seriously. The cost of developing a high-quality model may run up to $250,000, from conception to production. It is on developing the "ultimate" running shoe that many specialized shoe comapnies are staking their futures.

19. The two-year-old Pony Company, with the help of Computerized Bio-medical Analysis Inc., a Massachusetts research company that studies the dynamics of human motion, "started from the ground up to build the best possible shoe," said Roberto Muller, its founder, but that may represent only the start.

20. Brooks, relatively unknown before it got into running shoes a few years ago, used the sophisticated model as its springboard into the athletic shoe business. Brooks now relies on running shoes for only 60 percent of its overall volume. Eventually, the company hopes to become a major name in athletic footwear for other sports.

21. "We're trying to protect ourselves," a company spokesman said.

22. Although development cost may be extensive, most running shoes cost relatively little to produce, even the expensive models. Materials cost no more than those in other sports shoes and often less, inasmuch as a running shoe is mostly foam and nylon. Manufacturers' margins run 20 percent to 30 percent, and retailers' margins are still higher.

23. With a good pair of running shoes costing up to $40, leisure shoe makers are encouraged to upgrade their lines with a little foam and a wider heel to get into the business.

24. "That's why the industry has grown so," said a manufacturer of so-called imitators. "Except for the status label and the 'performance' claim, Sears, Penney and Montgomery Ward make shoes just as handsome as Adidas." Given that most people who wear running does don't actually run in them, "it's a hell of a market," he said.

25. Many of the hundreds of shoes on the market do look alike. Only the ardent shoe-spotter easily distinguishes the check trademark of the Pony from the sweep of the Nike, or the Spot-Bilt stripe with three holes from the Braun stripe with three triangles.

Analysis

In drawing the relevant boundaries for a quasi-market, it is necessary to find a clear break in the varying degrees of substitutabiliy of products that could be used for some purpose. To be specific, over the years people have run in a wide variety of footwear products. We are therefore faced with the problem of deciding whether the relevant quasi-market is footwear, athletic shoes, or running shoes. After reading the article, it seems clear that footwear not designed specifically for running are a poor substitute for running shoes. Therefore, based upon this break in the degree of substitutability, running shoes constitute a relevant quasi-market.

One important unique feature which distinguishes one running shoe from another is its performance. A shoe's performance is the result of extensive and expensive product development: these development costs "run up to $250,000" (par. 18).

A second feature that differentiates products is the "status label" held by some running shoes (par. 24).

And running shoes differ in appearance. However, "Sears, Penny and Montgomery Ward make shoes just as handsome as Adidas" (par. 24).

Therefore, within the running shoe quasi-market, we find three types of unique features: performance, status, and appearance. The higher-priced shoes emphasize performance whereas the lower-priced shoes are designed to be good-looking shoes that can be used for running. Nevertheless, almost all running shoes are better suited for long distance running on primarily hard surfaces than is any other footwear product.

Running shoes are produced by three types of producers: specialist manufacturers, such as Nike; athletic shoe manufacturers, such as Converse; and just plain shoe manufacturers (par. 4 and 5). The total number of producers is not mentioned in the article, except in the statement that "more than a score of companies are competing" (par. 1). Probably the best industry designation to attach to these producers is the athletic shoe industry; most of the output comes from this type of producer.

It would be appropriate to next discuss product price changes, but the article does not refer to any. Therefore, we will move on to another point and look for conditions which suggest competition from either existing or new firms. All indications point to the probability that entry into this specific quasi-market will continue to take place. The article mentions several producers who entered this market in recent years, but these new entrants have not significantly reduced the profitability of the industry (par. 10,11,12,13). The extent of this profitability is confirmed in the statement that "the race is to the bank" (par. 6).

Because we have predicted continued competition in the quasi-market, Guide Step 4 requires us to determine if firms will use product or price competition. We also need to indicate if this competition will be from existing producers or new producers. To answer these questions, we need only interpret the statement that "leisure shoe makers are encouraged to upgrade their lines with a little foam and a wider heel to get into the business" (par. 23). This means that product competition will occur and it will be from firms now in other areas of the shoe industry.

What will be the economic consequences of competition in the running shoe quasi-market? This question may best be answered by interpretating a statement from the article: "Some observers see a shake-out ahead, hurting for the most part the makers of shoes that lack a reputation for high performance and innovative design" (par. 6). We could interpret this to mean that there will be much price competition among the lower levels of running shoes. Consumers who buy the less expensive running shoes should find some good buys. On the other hand, some producers will escape this price competition by engaging in product competition. They will further improve their products, but they will also make sure their product has an image as a high performance shoe. (How do you think these producers will accomplish the latter?)

The quote from paragraph 6 also implies that some producers may suffer losses; this may force some firms out of the quasi-market.

Razor Fighting

By LYNN LANGWAY with TONY FULLER in Boston
and PAMELA ELLIS SIMONS in New York

Newsweek *(Nov. 22, 1976). Copyright 1976 by Newsweek,*
Inc. All rights reserved. Reprinted by permission.

1. They flicked their disposable lighter and flaunted their disposable pen. Now the scrappy folks at the Bic Pen Corp. are trying the ultimate in throwaway cheek: in a duel with the Gillette Co., Bic has introduced into the U.S. a flyweight razor that can be discarded after five or so shaves. With a metal blade embedded in the plastic razor, the whole thing weighs under half an ounce and sells for 25 cents—less than some conventional blades alone. "We're out to change the shaving business," vows Bic marketing director Bernard Trueblood. "It's a no-holds-barred fight."

2. That it is. The shaving business has long been dominated by Boston-based Gillette, which controls 60 percent of the $400 million razor-blade market (its closest rival, Schick, has about 25 percent). Gillette has used bargain-priced razors to coax consumers into buying more blades—but the throwaway combo Bic brought forth in Europe two years ago threatens that profitable balance. So early this year, Gillette brought out its own throwaway razor, Good News, in anticipation of Bic's U.S. entry, the Bic Shaver.

Cutting

3. The marketing war could create something of a dilemma for Gillette. At 25 cents, Gillette's throwaway undercuts its own Trac II baldes, which are listed at 30 cents—and the company is thus competing against itself as well as Bic. The same problem faces Schick, which is now marketing throwaways in Greece, and Wilkinson, which introduced them in the U.S. last month. Only Bic has no such conflict. Perhaps as a result, Gillette is looking for a limited market. "We certainly don't consider this a major product," says Joseph A. Marino, Gillette vice president for marketing. "You know, it's for trips and locker rooms, for the guy who forgets his razor." But some industry analysts say Gillette has a problem either way. "If they don't compete strongly and there is a greater market than they think, then they risk losing the market," says Louis Rusitzky, an anlyst for Adams, Harkness & Hill, a Boston brokerage firm. "But if they push it too much, they lose some of their margin on Trac II."

4. All told says analyst John Reidy of Drexel Burnham, the best solution for Gillette might be that the disposable razor never really catches on. On top of everying else, he notes, "Gillete has been given a run for its money by Bic twice"—and Bic has come out on top. Its clear plastic ballpoint pens, priced from 25 cents up, have won 68 percent of the retail market, partly at the expense of Gillette's Paper Mate. And Bic's butane lighters, flashily promoted by "Flick your Bic" ads, have almost caught up with Gillette's Cricket; analysts estimate that Gillette has 42 percent of the lighter market, with Bic garnering 38 percent.

5. Bic runs hard. A partly owned subsidary of Société Bic of Paris, the company came to the U.S. in 1958, when French millionaire Marcel Bich (he drops the "h" to aid pronunciation) bought the Waterman Pen Co. of Milford, Conn. "We work with less overhead, less management," says Robert Adler, Bic president. "We're a young kid on the block who can move." Bic likes to move big volumes of products that are non-refillable—products that can be stamped out quickly and inexpensively on its highspeed plastic molding machines and pumped through existing distribution channels with massive advertising. On its shaver, for example, Bic is spending an estimated $9 million for promotion. Gillette is spending less than $6 million.

Cover-Up

6. Bic has certainly blundered at times. Its "fanny-hose"—pantyhose with an expandable rear—snagged no significant market share, while its Bic Banana failed to outpace Gillette's Flair felt pen despite catchy ads. But analysts say that Bic can more easily cover its mistakes. "If in a year the disposable razor is a bust," says John Jensen of White, Weld, "Bic just calls Europe and says, 'Don't send us any more.'"

7. The new razors may prove an iffy product. Some users complain about the medicine-chest clutter of multi-razors instead of blades, while others say the flyweight razors make shaving more hazardous. And some environmentally conscious consumers question the wisdom of pitching away even more petroleum-based plastic in these energy-thirsty times. Still, the Bic formula has worked before and it may hold good again: what Bic proposes, man disposes.

Questions

1. Identify the market and describe the unique features of the various products found in this market.
2. What close substitutes are available?
3. Who are the producers? Do they all belong to the same industry?
4. Although each of the products has a unique design and a different brand name, there appears to be no price difference. Why?
5. Has there been competition in this market? Is competition expected in the future?
6. What type of competition, product or price, is used and/or will be used in this market?
7. What will be the economic consequences of competition?
   A. What benefits will the consumer receive, if any?
   B. What will be the effect on the producers?
   C. What will be the overall economic effect?

AN ARTICLE FOR STUDENT ANALYSIS: OVERVIEW

This article describes how a relatively stable quasi-market situation became chaotic and unprofitable for producers when a product innovation was introduced. What was the product innovation and why did it lead to problems for C.B. producers?

Over and Out? Citizens' Band Radio Industry Is Sinking Deep Into Debt; Many Predict a Shakeout

By JANICE C. SIMPSON
Staff Reporter of *The Wall Street Journal*

1. Makers of citizens' band radios, struggling to recover from last winter's switch to radios that receive 40 channels from 23-channel models, are sinking into even deeper trouble. Any worthwhile improvement in business isn't expected until the second half of next year, they say, and that could be too late for some companies on the brink of being forced out of business.

2. Sales this year will plunge to between six million and eight million radios from last year's 10 million, the companies estimate. At least half of those sales will be of the cheaper, 23-channel radios. The 40-channel models that can be sold are being heavily discounted—some as much as 50%. And these prices could drop further as some companies, unable to survive the pricing pressure, begin to liquidate and dump their goods on the market.

3. "I don't see the market back to a stable position before mid-1978," says Carl Insel, president of Johnson American Inc., the CB-radio unit of E. F. Johnson Co. and the biggest U.S. maker of CBs. "I don't see anyone reporting a profit before then," he adds. For the third quarter, E. F. Johnson posted a loss of $4.4 million on sales of $10.3 million. The loss would have been greater without earnings from other divisions, Mr. Insel says.

4. Yet only 18 months ago, CB radios were the glamour product of the electronics industry. "They couldn't get enough in the stores—they were going like hot cakes," remembers Jon Gruber, an analyst with the San Francisco brokerage firm of Robertson, Colman, Siebel & Weisel.

Scramble For Radios

5. Distributors eager to supply the stores scrambled to find new manufacturers and foreign suppliers. Then, the Federal Communications Commission announced

its plan to add 17 citizens' band channels. The industry assumed that consumers would prefer new models that could handle this number of channels, so the companies sharply discounted the 23-channel radios to clear their shelves. But consumers didn't switch. The discounted 23-channel radios, some selling as low as $33.95, seemed too good a buy to resist.

6. Earnings began to sag, but the industry remained optimistic. Companies reasoned that as soon as the two million or so 23-channel models in inventory were exhausted, probably during the first half of 1977, consumers would switch to the higher priced 40-channel radios, and the companies would recoup their losses.

7. That didn't happen either. The industry had underestimated its inventories. There were "at least two million more (23-channel models) out there than anyone thought," says one company official. Discounting of 40-channel radios severely squeezed profit margins, and production was cut back.

8. SBE Inc., which imports all its radios, has slashed its force of sales, administrative and packaging workers to 35 from 145 at the end of 1976. Reflecting the problems of its CB unit, E. F. Johnson has dropped 1,200 employes from its 1,800-member workforce. Last month, it announced plans to close its Clear Lake, Iowa, CB plant, laying off another 300 or so workers. Most companies have been forced to borrow to keep operations going.

Rising Bank Debts

9. "All the money that was earned in the two years of the boom was lost this last year," says Paul Robichaux, vice president and general manager of SBE. "The only measure of success in the CB indsutry right now is how small your bank debt is." SBE lost $1.6 million on revenue of $3.6 million in its fiscal third quarter, ended July 31; its debt totals $1.9 million. Another CB company, Hy-Gain Electronics Corp., has seen its debt climb to $25.3 million from nothing two years ago.

10. There are a few exceptions to this dismal picture. The automotive-products division of Motorola Corp. has managed to turn a modest profit, though "certainly not the kind of money we'd like to make," says Thomas Carroll, national sales manager. And Tandy Corp., which imports CBs for its Radio Shack retail chain, sold "significantly more radios in fiscal 1977 (ended June 30) than we did in fiscal 1976," says Garland P. Asher, director of financial planning. "We didn't sell them at full price," he concedes, "but we didn't lose money."

11. Few companies, however, have the support of a big concern like Motorola, or the advantage that Tandy has of being both an importer and retailer. In April, Gladding Co., maker of Pearce-Simpson brand CBs, filed for protection under Chapter 11 of the federal Bankruptcy Act, citing problems caused by the switchover to 40-channel models. Under Chapter 11, a company gets court protection from its creditors while it tries to refinance its debt.

12. It is the smaller companies that are most likely to disappear if the widely expected industry shakeout occurs. "The major (CB) companies are prepared to weather the storm, but I see RCA and GE and some small importers dropping out," says William Thomas, president of Pathcom Inc., which sells radios under the Pace brand name. Tandy's Mr. Asher is more blunt: "The question is: Who's got the best banker?" He believes most CB companies are in deep financial trouble, and "it just depends on when the bankers pull the plugs."

"Industry Will Be Stronger?"

13. Most company officials believe that a shakeout, leaving about a half dozen major concerns in the CB business, would be good for the industry, which has grown more quickly than have its management skills. "When the dust settles, those that are left will be stronger and the industry will be stronger," says Johnson American's Mr. Insel.

14. Under FCC regulations, 23-channel models can't be sold in the U.S. after Dec. 31. Some companies petitioned for an extension of the deadline, but were overruled. Generally, the industry is hoping that prices of 40-channel radios thus will stabilize next year and perhaps edge up a bit. There is agreement that a sizable market for CB radios remains but that the boom days of 1975 and 1976 won't return. Accordingly, companies are searching for ways to reduce their dependency on CBs by expanding other divisions and by examining the possibilities of stock acquisitions or mergers that will allow diversification into related fields. Such maneuverings, though, may be coming too late. "Why should anybody merge with a CB company right now, and why would two CB companies merge? They'd just compound the agony," asserts one skeptic.

15. Another relief measure has been to produce "Cadillac" CB models, high-priced products for the well-heeled customers who don't mind paying more for something unique. The hotest items currently are microprocessor-based radios that provide such features as push-button controls and automatic fine tuning. These radios start at about $250 retail, around three times the price of many discounted 40-channel regular models, yet consumer acceptance had been strong.

A New Competitor?

16. Indeed, the market for these fancier radios looked so good that Texas Instruments Inc., a big concern currently without any CB products, earlier this year announced plans to enter the market in the fall with a $325 model. Three months later, however, it decided to delay the move until "early 1978," and officials have declined to elaborate. Despite the delay, Texas Instruments' reputation as an aggressive, price-cutting company frightens some CB concerns. "The last thing the competitors in this industry need is a Texas Instruments," worries SBE's Mr. Robi-

chaux. He believes Texas Instruments "could probably shake out all the major competitors in six months if they wanted to."

17. Others question whether Texas Instruments could become a dominant force in the CB business, which depends less on semi-conductors than do calculators and digital watches, the two consumer markets where it has achieved much success. Some doubt Texas Instruments is even interested in waging an aggressive fight. "The indication is that they might tread a little more carefully because they will enter the market at the high end," says an official from another company.

18. Those searching for any sign of hope for the industry see a positive sign in Texas Instruments' interest.

When such a company invests in a new business, it indicates the industry must be viable, they argue. And the company's technological skills could help develop a more sophisticated product, and so create a new replacement market of CB owners wanting to upgrade their equipment, they believe.

11

Price Setting by Firms: Noncompetitive Conditions

Aaron and Nick, roommates who took economics together, were studying for their next exam. They were sharing notes because when they learned their class was at 8:00 A.M., they agreed to take turns going to class and taking notes. Now they were trying to combine these notes into some useful information for the exam.

Aaron, after reading Nick's notes, scratched his head and asked, "Nick, are you sure that maximum competition exists when all firms sell at the same price?"

Nick went over his notes. "That's right. I remember the instructor said that when the number of firms is so large that no one firm has any market power, all firms must sell at the same price. What's wrong with that?"

"Well, today the instructor said that when there are only a few firms in the industry, they find it fairly easy to agree to sell at the same price. But he said this was illegal. Did the instructor say it was illegal when all those firms you were talking about sold at the same price?"

Nick thought for awhile, then answered, "I can't remember too well, that was the morning after we had that big party. What are we going to do, Aaron, if I don't do well on this exam, you'll have a new roommate next semester!"

"Don't worry, Nick, I just figured it out. We know its illegal when an extremely small number of firms charge the same price. So it is probably illegal when an extremely large number of firms charge the same price. See, the point is the government doesn't like extremists. This economics is just a little logic and some common sense!"

Although Aaron's answer is incorrect, their discussion has pointed out a curious situation in our economy. Firms in the most competitive situations sell at the same price; at the same time, firms in the least competitive situations frequently also sell at the same price. Moreover, we find that some of the latter sell at the same price because they have conspired to fix their prices,

96

whereas others are forced to sell at the same price because of the nature of the industry.

In this chapter, we will learn about some types of noncompetitive behavior and also examine some noncompetitive situations.

CHECKLIST

Definitions of New Terms

1. Cartel--a formal, open agreement to control prices, usually by controlling output.
2. Price-fixing scheme--a secret agreement to control prices.
3. Collusive price leadership--when one firm changes product price for the entire industry either because that firm is able to force all others to follow or because all firms--at least the major firms--have agreed that prices should be changed. All collusive leadership is illegal.
4. Barometric price leadership--when one firm leads a change because conditions in the industry warrant the new price. This is not considered illegal.
5. Shared monopoly--when, because of the industry's structure and conduct, several large firms act in unison. The government has been examining this type of situation to determine if it should be subject to antitrust charges.

Concepts

1. Interdependency leads to parallel behavior in an industry. When an industry is dominated by a few large firms who sell a fairly standardized product, each realizes that its price and output decisions will have a major impact on the economic activity of other firms. Moreover, they all realize that price differentials cannot be maintained for very long periods without creating havoc in the industry. Therefore, this type of industry structure usually leads to parallel (common) behavior among all firms in the industry. In general, this type of parallel behavior is not considered to be a violation of antitrust laws.
2. Interdependency might lead to noncompetitive behavior. Certain aspects of an industry's structure make noncompetitive behavior more likely. Noncompetitive behavior has a greater probability of occurring:
   A. the fewer the number of firms;
   B. the greater the similarity of each firm's size, costs, market share, and product;
   C. the more stable the demand for the industry's product;
   D. the greater the difficulty new firms have entering the industry (i.e., barriers to entry).
3. Common prices might result from several different types of situations, some legal, some illegal.
   A. Illegal situations include:
      i. cartels;
      ii. price-fixing conspiracies;

      iii. collusive price leadership;
   B. Situations with questionable legality include:
      i. shared monopoly.
   C. Situations generally considered to be legal include:
      i. barometric price leadership.
4. Firms which conspire to fix prices can achieve maximum
   economic profits for the group included in the conspiracy.
   Assume Firm A and Firm B in Figure 1 decide to fix prices in
   order to earn maximum monopoly profits. They meet and select
   a coordinator. The coordinator sums the marginal costs of A
   and B (ΣMC), then determines the output at which ΣMC =
   industry MR, which is Q_{10} in Figure 1(C). This output will
   be sold at price P_1 by both firms. Maximum monopoly profits
   will be earned in the industry.

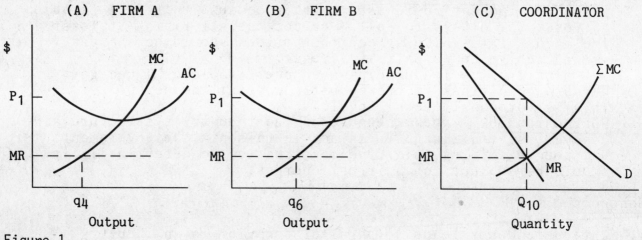

Figure 1

   The most difficult job for the coordinator is setting and
   maintaining output quotas. Quotas are set by equating
   industry MR (at the MC = MR level) with the MC of each firm.
   Thus the quota for Firm A is q_4 and for Firm B it is q_6.
   If either firm sells more than its quota, total industry
   output will exceed Q_{10} and price will fall.

                  GUIDE FOR ANALYZING ARTICLES

1. Identify the product and the producers.
   A. Is the product differentiated or uniform?
2. Determine the type of noncompetitive behavior found in the
   industry.
3. Determine if any aspects of the industry's structure make
   noncompetitive behavior likely.
   A. Is there a small number of large firms?
   B. Are each firm's size, market share, operating costs, and
      product relatively similar?
   C. Is market demand relatively stable?
   D. Is it difficult to enter the industry?
4. If some type of parallel behavior exists, determine if:
   A. there is a price leader, and if so, who is the leader, why

is the leader being allowed to lead, and how effective has
the leadership been?
B. there is a shared monopoly, and if so, how have the major
firms maintained control?
C. price has changed, and if so, was it an attempt to adjust
to changes in operating costs, to a change in demand, or an
attempt to improve the rate of return in the industry?
5. If a collusive agreement was used to coordinate activity,
    determine:
    A. the type of coordination and how it was achieved;
    B. how successfully the group coped with changing conditions;
    C. how members were disciplined;
    D. how outsiders were kept outside;
    E. if all members of the group profited equally;
    F. what caused the breakup of the agreement.
6. Determine the overall economic effect of noncompetitive
    behavior.
    A. How were consumers affected?
    B. How were firms affected?
    C. Is the reappearance of noncompetitive behavior likely?

Articles

AN ANALYZED ARTICLE: OVERVIEW

This article presents a fairly complete case study of one of the largest and longest price-fixing schemes in U.S. history. A court indictment on December 27, 1973, charged six firms in the gypsum industry with conspiring to fix prices for over 13 years.

Busting a Trust: Gypsum Trail Shows How Price-fix Plan Supposedly Operated

By DAVID MCCLINTICK
Staff Reporter of *The Wall Street Journal*

Hotel Meetings, 'Accident' At Plant Figured in Case Against Big Companies

Jail Sentences Suspended

1. It was a raw, bleak Monday, Feb. 15, 1965, in Portland, Ore. Two conservatively dressed businessmen arrived at the airport on separate flights, met and drove into the city to join a third man. Then, for four hours, the three conferred over dinner at Canlis, a plush restaurant atop the Portland Hilton.

2. The out-of-towners were Robert C. Gimlin, a vice president of U.S. Gypsum Corp., the nation's largest manufacturer of gypsum wall and ceiling board, and John W. Brown, a senior vice president of National Gypsum Corp., U.S. Gypsum's prime competitor. They dined with William H. Hunt, executive vice president of Portland-based Georgia-Pacific Corp., which was then on the verge of entering the gypsum business.

3. More than 10 years have passed, and Mr. Brown is dead. But the meeting in Portland still is haunting Mr. Gimlin, Mr. Hunt and a lot of other people. The Justice Department has alleged in court that the meeting was a small but important part of a nationwide conspiracy, lasting at least 13 years through 1973, to fix prices illegally in the gypsum industry. The conspiracy allegedly involved sabotage, intricate scheming among executives and managers and an array of cover-up ploys ranging from falsely documenting prices to lying under oath by executives.

Six Big Companies Convicted

4. All in all, authorities say, the conspiracy was one of the largest and longest-lived price-fixing schemes in U.S. history. And they say it cost consumers of gypsum board, a staple in countless homes, office buildings and other structures, many millions of dollars in inflated prices.

5. Over the past several months, the nation's six largest gypsum makers and 10 of their highest executives or former executives have pleaded no-contest to federal criminal charges or have pleaded innocent and been found guilty by a jury in Pittsburgh of taking part in the scheme. The companies are U.S. Gypsum; National Gypsum; Georgia-Pacific; Celotex Corp., a subsidiary of Jim Walter Corp.; Flintkote Co., and Kaiser Gypsum, a subsidiary of Kaiser Cement & Gypsum Corp., 37% owned by Kaiser Industries Corp. Two other big companies, Johns-Manville Corp. and Fibreboard Corp., and 146 individuals were named in an indictment as unindicted co-conspirators.

6. During the alleged conspiracy, the companies together sold more than $4 billion worth of gypsum, over 90% of the industry's total volume.

7. The companies and individuals convicted by the jury still protest their innocence, and they are appealing their convictions. Among other things, they point out that some gypsum prices actually were lower at the end of 1973, when the government brought its charges, than in earlier years. The government doesn't deny that, but argues that without price fixing, prices would have been even lower.

The Companies' Argument

8. In court, the defendants' lawyers also argued that, if the companies seemed to violate the Sherman Antitrust Act, it was only because they were trying to comply with another federal law. That law, the Robinson-Patman Act, generally permits a manufacturer to sell to one customer at a lower price than to other customers only

when the lower price is necessary to meet competition for the first customer's business. So when the companies conferred with each other about prices, the argument went, they were merely trying to verify the prices being charged such customers.

9. This rationale, the government alleged, was cooked up after charges were brought. If the companies' contracts with each other had been legitimate, prosecutors said, the companies would have kept careful records of their discussions instead of destroying many records. The jury apparently accepted the government's view.

10. Despite criminal prosecution and civil lawsuits, price fixing is considered widespread in some industries, partly because its rewards—higher prices and bigger profits—often may seem worth the seemingly small risk of getting caught and penalized for violating the antitrust laws. In the gypsum case, Judge Hubert I. Teitelbaum gave only suspended prison sentences and imposed fines ranging from $50,000 to as little as $1,000. Still, the companies have paid out about $70 million in damages to gypsum dealers who filed private civil suits to recover the money they lost in paying illegally high prices.

Back to 1951

11. How the conspiracy worked can be pieced together from court records—a 15,000-page trial transcript, 5,000 documents put in evidence, the grand-jury indictment, a 350-page government bill of particulars and other material.

12. Because of the statute of limitations, the prosecutors, led by Justice Department antitrust specialist John C. Fricano, had to prove that violations occurred within five years prior to the date of the indictment, Dec. 27, 1973. But they were allowed to present voluminous evidence that the alleged conspiracy began earlier. Price fixing on gypsum, the government says, began before 1951. In that year, a federal court in the District of Columbia, enjoined U.S. Gypsum, National, Celotex and other companies against it.

13. Later in the 1950s, the government said in court, U.S. Gypsum's current chairman, Graham J. Morgan, executive vice president Andrew J. Watt and, by implication, executives in most of the rest of the gypsum industry, knew that prices still were being rigged.

14. So were other sales terms that affected the gypsum companies' revenues and earnings, the government said. A former credit manager for Oakland-based Kaiser Gypsum, Richard L. Downing, testified at the Pittsburgh trial that in 1957 or 1958, he and credit managers for other gypsum companies with West Coast operations met at a hotel in Long Beach, Calif., and agreed to raise the interest rate charged to customers who bought on credit to 6% from 5%. It is illegal not only for companies to band together to charge the same prices but also to fix other sales terms that deprive customers of the benefits of competition.

15. There was testimony that the companies knew they were risking antitrust violations. The government alleged that U.S. Gypsum, based in Chicago, declined to send a representative to the Long Beach meeting because of the "danger" that the agreement would be detected. But U.S. Gypsum's credit manager later agreed to impose the credit terms set at the meeting, the prosecutors said.

16. Testimony also suggested that the companies fixed uniform methods of shipping wallboard to customers. Usually the companies would deliver only by rail, so that a construction company or retail-supply customer would have to locate on a rail spur or truck its gypsum-board shipments from a rail yard. Fixing the delivery method, the government said, stifled competition.

17. When a producer stepped out of line, the government tried to show in court, other producers got tough. In 1960, a Texas building contractor, Claude Huckleberry, built his own gypsum plant in El Paso. Because his competitors weren't trucking material to customers, Mr. Huckleberry figured—correctly, it turned out—that he could win a lot of their business by trucking gypsum board directly to customers at no extra charge.

Sabotage At A Plant Opening?

18. Though the El Paso market was relatively small, the big companies apparently considered Mr. Huckleberry's company, Texas Gypsum, a serious threat. In growing, Texas Gypsum might encourage other small companies to deliver by truck and ultimately cost the major producers a lot of business or force them to offer truck delivery themselves.

19. In December 1960, one month before Texas Gypsum's plant was to open, Martin Hardin showed up in El Paso to visit Mr. Huckleberry. Mr. Hardin was president of American Gypsum, a small Albuquerque producer, but the evidence showed that his visit was made on behalf of other gypsum companies, too.

20. Over coffee at a bowling alley, Mr. Huckleberry testified, Mr. Hardin delivered a message: "U.S. Gypsum, National, Celotex, Flintkote—he named them all—had agreed that if I didn't stop trucking they would move in and kill me"—meaning, drive him out of business.

21. Undeterred, Mr. Huckleberry went ahead. In January 1961, his gypsum plant was ready. He invited a New York banker, an El Paso newspaper reporter and several other guests to the plant for a demonstration. Suddenly the machinery in the plant began running in reverse, slopping "slurry," a plasterlike ingredient of gypsum board, onto the floor. "We were waist deep in slurry before I could get everything shut off," Mr. Huckleberry recalled.

The "Quality" Tests

22. Mr. Huckleberry fired Texas Gypsum's plant manager, William A. Kincaid. The government implied in court that it was more than coincidence that Mr. Kincaid previously had worked for U.S. Gypsum and returned to U.S. Gypsum after he lost his job at Texas Gypsum.

23. The Texas Gypsum plant started operating anyway, and the company won 72% of the gypsum-board market in the El Paso area in a few months. At the same time, the lackluster competition in the area grew fierce. U.S. Gypsum, National and Kaiser rented warehouse space in El Paso, filled it with 150 to 200 railcar loads of gypsum board, slashed prices well under Texas Gypsum's and hired trucks to deliver the board.

24. Nor was that all. According to a Texas Gypsum customer, salesmen from five major gypsum companies asked him for samples of Texas Gypsum's board to test for quality. "I began to get the drift of what was going on," said the customer, John D. Tinsley, a Dallas lumber dealer. He said he gave four of the five salesmen samples of their own companies' board. Some salesmen, he says, reported back that the "Texas Gypsum" board was inferior. "I doubt if anyone knew which board was which," Mr. Tinsley testified.

25. Texas Gypsum lost much of its new business. Because deals between companies to drive a competitor out of business are as illegal as price fixing, Mr. Huckleberry filed a private antitrust suit against his big competitors. Eventually he sold his company and got out of the gypsum business. The buyers settled the suit out of court.

Fixing Kickbacks

26. Demand for gypsum was rising in the late 1950s when Mr. Huckleberry was planning to enter the business, which he did in 1961. By 1965, however, construction activity in the U.S. had become less stable, and demand for gypsum board was diminishing. But the government says the gypsum companies stepped up their efforts to keep prices high. It was at this time that Mr. Brown of National Gypsum and Mr. Gimlin of U.S. Gypsum flew to Portland and met with Mr. Hunt of Georgia-Pacific.

27. Mr. Gimlin testified that his encounter with Mr. Brown was a coincidence, the dinner with Mr. Hunt was impromptu, and nothing illegal was discussed. In any case, on July 1, 1965, with demand for gypsum wallboard at one of its lowest points in some time, Georgia-Pacific announced a price increase of $4 a thousand-square-feet on fire-resistant board, effective Sept. 1.

28. In mid-July 1965, Mr. Watt, of U.S. Gypsum, traveled to the West Coast. On July 14, he had breakfast in Portland with Mr. Hunt of Georgia-Pacific. Mr. Watt then went to Oakland to confer with Claude E. Harper, a senior executive of Kaiser Gypsum. A few days later, U.S. Gypsum announced a price increase comparable with Georgia-Pacific's. By Aug. 27, four days before these increases were to take effect, all major producers had announced similar increases.

29. At the same time, according to the prosecution, even kickbacks were fixed. The big companies agreed to pay $2 a thousand-square-feet to wallboard installers in Oregon and Washington who purchased the companies' gypsum board through dealers. The kickbacks were paid by cashiers' checks that didn't show the original source of the funds.

Tightening Credit

30. A few months later, the government alleged, in September and October, the companies agreed to adjustments, to take effect in December, that would again boost prices more than 15% in some parts of the country.

31. From Oct. 12 to Oct. 15, the Gypsum Association, the industry trade organization, had a semiannual meeting at Ponte Vedra, a Florida resort. Mr. Watt of U.S. Gypsum was named chairman of a task force to, among other thing, plan the December price increase, the government said in court. A group of U.S. Gypsum executives refined the plan at several meetings between Oct. 25 and Nov. 5 in Mr. Morgan's office at U.S. Gypsum. Details of the increase were coordinated by telephone, the government alleged, between Mr. Morgan and National Gypsum's chairman, Colon Brown, in Buffalo.

32. To effect the increase, the government said, the companies decided to eliminate kickbacks and cancel industry-wide discounts from list prices, leaving list prices themselves unchanged. On Nov. 17, U.S. Gypsum announced its new terms. The other companies announced similar terms by Dec. 1. The companies also agreed to centralize pricing decisions in top management in order to police their agreements better, the government said.

33. Shortly after Dec. 15, when the changes took effect, the companies announced another change; on March 1, 1966, they would tighten and make more uniform the credit terms extended to customers.

34. This threatened a California wallboard dealer, Richard L. Downing, the former Kaiser Gypsum credit manager. Mr. Downing met with James D. Moran, chairman of Flintkote, and told him tighter credit terms would force his company out of business. Flintkote agreed to impose the new terms on Mr. Downing's company over a two-year period to give the company time to adjust. On Feb. 21, Mr. Downing persuaded Kaiser to consider giving his company the same treatment.

A Deal Called Off

35. But when Mr. Downing met with National Gypsum officials on Feb. 23, they rejected his request that National Gypsum extend similarly easy terms. Mr. Downing hinted to National officials that the other two companies had agreed. National, according to testimony, quickly accused Flintkote of violating the industry's agreement. The government said it was a typical display of the industry's clout in policing its deals when, the next day, officials of Flintkote and Kaiser phoned Mr. Downing to back out of their deal with him. Later, Mr. Downing sought easier terms from Fibreboard, which also refused him. The government said Mr. Downing's company, and others, were forced out of business by the new and stringent credit terms.

36. The 1965 and 1966 price and credit agreements, the Justice Department alleged, set a pattern for illegal arrangements that were "conspiratorily achieved and maintained" into the 1970s. The gypsum companies appeared to be aware that they were on dangerous ground. In November 1966, Georgia-Pacific's lawyer urged Mr. Hunt to insure that the company's contacts with competitors were legal. The lawyer also recommended that Georgia-Pacific change the title of its "pricing administrator" to "something less suggestive."

37. The government charged also that some of the companies later tried to conceal their price-fixing contracts from the court handling civil suits against them and from the federal grand jury investigating them. National Gypsum was fined $5,000 by the federal court in Washington, D.C., for criminal contempt of court. The company at first failed to produce subpoenaed desk calendars of its chairman, Colon Brown. The calendars, later produced, were used to help reconstruct Mr. Brown's movements and contacts with executives of competing firms.

Prison Terms Suspended

38. Mr. Brown was convicted of conspiring to violate the Sherman Act, fined $50,000 given a six-month suspended prison term and put on probation for three years. Jay P. Nicely, a vice president of National Gypsum, was fined $1,000, given a six-month suspended prison sentence and put on probation for one year. Mr. Watt, of U.S. Gypsum, was fined $10,000, given a six-month suspended prison sentence and put on probation for one

year. Convicted separately as corporate defendants were U.S. Gypsum, National Gypsum, Georgia-Pacific and Celotex. (Mr. Gimlin, of U.S. Gypsum, and the late John W. Brown, of National, who took part in the 1965 Portland dinner meeting, were named unindicted co-conspirators.)

39. Other defendants didn't contest the charges. They were fined, given suspended prison sentences of either 30 days or six months and put on probation. These defendants were Mr. Morgan, of U.S. Gypsum, fined $40,000; Mr. Hunt, not retired from Georgia-Pacific, $40,000; William D. Herbert, president of Celotex, $20,000; Mr. Harper, former president of Kaiser Gypsum, $40,000; Robert A Costa, former vice president of Kaiser Gypsum, $20,000; George J. Pecaro, retired chairman of Flintkote, $20,000; and Mr. Moran, chairman of Flintkote, $20,000.

40. The gypsum companies have paid $70 million in damages from private, civil antitrust suits. Ordinarily, such damages would be deductible from taxable income; but the criminal convictions, if upheld on appeal, would make two-thirds of the damages nondeductible. That could cost the companies about $22 million in extra taxes.

41. If the convictions are overturned, the big gypsum makers still face trouble. Sources say it's likely that the Justice Department soon will file a civil antitrust suit seeking to force them to divest themselves of certain manufacturing facilities and end certain joint operating agreements in order to create, one source says, a "more competitive environment" and a greater number of "aggressive single-plant producers."

Analysis

Gypsum board is a fairly standard building item used in homes, office buildings, and other structures. It is a fairly uniform product of the gypsum industry. There are six major producers; the remaining producers account for only 10 percent of total output.

All six major producers participated in a price-fixing scheme (a type of noncompetitive behavior) that fixed the price of gypsum for over 13 years.

We now want to determine if the industry's structure was conducive to this noncompetitive behavior. From the information we have, we know that only six firms produce 90 percent of this fairly standardized building material. We also learn that during the period when the conspiracy was formed, the demand for gypsum was rising, but it probably rose at a fairly stable rate (par. 26). Moreover, although no natural barriers appear to exist, the members of the conspiracy were able to keep out new entrants (par. 17 - 25). Therefore, while admitting that our information is limited, it seems there was some probability that noncompetitive behavior would be used in this industry.

Since a collusive agreement was used to coordinate activity, we will proceed to examine how this coordination was achieved. First, we find that the agreement fixed prices, credit terms, kickbacks, and delivery methods (par. 7,16,29,30, and 33). At least some of the coordination was handled by a task force established at a semiannual meeting of the Gypsum Association (par. 31). Further coordination was carried out at the offices of the U.S. Gypsum Corp., the largest producer in the industry (par. 31). According to the government, the members of the conspiracy "agreed to centralize pricing decisions in top management to police their agreements better" (par 32). In fact, Georgia-Pacific had a "pricing administrator" until its lawyer suggested the company should find a less suggestive title (par. 36).

From all indications, the conspiracy handled changing market conditions quite well. For example, in 1965, a time when demand was declining, all major producers increased their prices by $4 per thousand-square-feet (par. 28,29). As another example, when the wallboard installers needed special considerations, the group gave them a fixed kickback (par. 29).

To illustrate how the conspiracy handled firms that tried to upset their scheme, we will cite the experiences of Texas Gypsum. Before we begin, we should point out that one provision of the price-fixing agreement required all members to standardize their total costs by adding a transportation cost equal to the freight rate between shipping points (par. 16). When Texas Gypsum entered the industry, it decided that the best way to attract customers was to offer free delivery. Very soon, Texas Gypsum had 72 percent of the gypsum business in the El Paso area (par. 23).

Needless to say, the conspiracy was upset. They retaliated. First, a quirk accident occurred during a demonstration run of Texas Gypsum's new plant. Sabotage was suspected (par. 21,22). Texas Gypsum bounced back from the accident and continued to offer free delivery. At this point, three of the major gypsum producers, all members of the conspiracy, began shipping their gypsum into the El Paso area and selling it for less than Texas Gypsum's price, with free delivery included (par. 23). Then, to make matters even worse for Texas Gypsum, these companies circulated rumors about the quality of its product (par. 24). After losing a lot of its business, the company sold out (par. 25). The conspiracy won! (However, Texas Gypsum later received an out-of-court settlement in its antitrust suit against the members of the conspiracy (par. 25).)

Another example of how the conspiracy disciplined its members is found in its enforcement of a new credit policy in 1966. A wallboard buyer convinced one conspirator, Flintkote, that he should be given two years to adjust to the new credit policy (par. 34). Kaiser Gypsum also agreed to give the buyer time to adjust (par. 34). However, when another member, National Gypsum, heard about the deal the other firms were giving to one of their customers, it "quickly accused Flintkote of violating the industry's agreement" (par. 35). Flintkote and Kaiser dropped the deal with the customer the next day.

As to the question of whether all members of the conspiracy profited equally, the article provides no information. However, the group broke up only after the government was able to gather enough evidence to bring a charge of price-fixing against the conspiracy.

The conspiracy "cost consumers many millions of dollars in

inflated prices" (par. 4). On the other hand, the companies have paid $70 million in private, civil antitrust suits to date; they may also owe the government $22 million in extra taxes because these payments may be disallowed as business expenses (par. 40). Finally, the article says the Justice Department plans to ask for some changes in the industry which should create a more competitive environment (par. 41).

TWO ARTICLES WITH QUESTIONS

Steel-Price Rise Prompts Inquiry By Justice Unit

By A WALL STREET JOURNAL
News Roundup

1. WASHINGTON—Federal antitrust officials are examining the recent price boost by the nation's steel producers to determine if U.S. antitrust laws were violated. The inquiry by the Justice Department's Antitrust Division doesn't represent a formal investigation, officials said, but merely the initial step to see if a full-scale inquiry is warranted.

2. Hugh P. Morrison Jr., Deputy Assistant Attorney General for antitrust, said that a "preliminary review" of the Dec. 1 steel-price increase, which averaged 6% on sheet and strip products, is under way. "The Antiturst Division has been closely monitoring this steel-price increase since its inception," Mr. Morrison said. "Staff attorneys responsible for steel-industry matters are currently reviewing information pertaining to the price increase."

3. The preliminary inquiry includes a review of data submitted by the steel companies to the government's Council on Wage and Price Stability. The wage-price council requested the data after the price increases were announced.

4. Steel producers aren't being asked to furnish additional information or material to the Justice Department, an official said.

5. Disclosure of the Antitrust Division's inquiry was made in a letter to consumer advocate Ralph Nader and the Corporate Accountability Research Group, a Nader organization. Mr. Nader had urged the Antitrust Division to investigate the steel-price increase.

6. In his letter, Mr. Morrison said if the division's preliminary review discloses facts that suggest antitrust laws may have been violated, "We will not hesitate to institute a full investigation of this matter."

7. Justice Department attorneys are attempting to determine if steel producers conspired to fix prices in violation of federal antitrust laws. Antitrust officials emphasize their inquiry so far is preliminary.

8. Reports of the Justice Department's inquiry apparently took the steel industry by surprise. Edgar Speer, chairman of Pittsburgh-based U.S. Steel Corp., the nation's largest producer in terms of shipments, said he didn't know anything about the investigation except what he'd read in the press. "We haven't been served with any papers up to this point," he said during a press luncheon in New York yesterday afternoon.

9. Mr. Speer of U.S. Steel added: "I can tell you very definitely there isn't a problem here as far as U.S. Steel is concerned."

10. Other producers also said they hadn't known of the investigation and hadn't been contacted by the government about it. They were Bethlehem Steel Corp., Bethlehem, Pa., Wheeling—Pittsburgh Steel Corp., Pittsburgh, and the Youngstown Sheet & Tube Co. unit of New Orleans-based Lykes Corp.

11. Eight industry producers surveyed declined to comment on the inquiry. Most echoed Bethelem, the second-largest U.S. steelmaker in terms of shipments, which said simply, "We have no knowledge of any investigation, and we have no comment to make."

12. The industry's controversial Dec. 1 price rises for flat-rolled products, widely used in automobiles, appliances and other consumer-related industries, had been led by Pittsburgh-based National Steel Corp. the day before Thanksgiving. It promptly was followed by several smaller producers before the two industry leaders, U.S. Steel and Bethlehem, joined the move.

13. U.S. Steel, however, conceded it was "surprised" by the timing of National's move. Just a few weeks earlier, in November, Mr. Speer had said any price activity would come next year. In recent months, industry sources have complained of softened demand for some consumer-related steel products, as well as continued lagging demand by manufacturers of capital goods.

Inland Steel Co. Lifts Most Prices An Average 5.4%

A WALL STREET JOURNAL
News Roundup

Move Joins 5.5% Increase Of Bethlehem Steel; U.S. Steel, Others Are Silent

14. Inland Steel Co., the nation's fifth largest steelmaker, joined No. 2 Bethlehem Steel Corp. in announcing base price increases on a broad range of steel products.

15. Chicago-based Inland said its increases will average 5.4%. The new base quotes on sheet, bar and plate products will take effect Feb. 1, while the boosts on structural items will take effect March 1.

16. Inland said new base prices on specific products weren't available, but a spokesman said that the size of the increases paralleled those made public Monday by Bethlehem on most products.

17. Bethlehem had said its increases, which affected nearly all its steel products, averaged 5.5%. The move by the Bethlehem, Pa., steelmaker came on the heels of a Sunday announcement by financially troubled Wheeling-Pittsburgh Steel Corp. that it was boosting sheet steel prices by an average of 7%, effective Jan. 3.

18. U.S. Steel Corp., the nation's largest steelmaker in terms of shipments, and other producers, remained silent yesterday. If Pittsburgh-based U.S. Steel should follow the boosts posted by Bethlehem and Inland, past practice would indicate that the rest of the industry would fall in line with the lower but broader increases announced by those two producers.

19. In Washington, a spokesman for the government's Council on Wage and Price Stability had previously suggested that Bethlehem's announced 5.5% average increase "isn't out of line with the general inflation rate." but the spokesman indicated that Pittsburgh-based Wheeling-Pittsburgh, the nation's ninth largest steelmaker, probably would have to ease the amount and effective date of its announced price boosts if other steelmakers fall in line behind Bethlehem and Inland.

20. Wheeling-Pittsburgh is more heavily dependent on sheet steel sales than either Inland or Bethlehem. Sheet products will account for about 78% of the company's shipments this year.

21. Inland's 10-K report to the Securities and Exchange Commission for 1976 shows that 47% of its sales were derived from shipments of sheet, strip and so-called "black plate" products. About 13% of its sales came from shipments of bars and semifinished steel products, with plates and structurals accounting for 12%.

22. The later March 1 effective dates that both Inland and Bethlehem posted for structural products appeared to reflect market conditions. Import competition and sagging demand in the heavy construction market for these products has led to price discounting by some producers in recent months. For example, Armco Steel Corp., Middletown, Ohio, has indicated that its discounts of wide-flange structural will be $30 a ton in January and $21 a ton in February.

Questions

1. Both articles are about price increases in the steel industry. Can you find any reason why these two articles were used?
2. Is it obvious that noncompetitive behavior led to the two price increases? What type of noncompetitive behavior was used, if any?
3. Does the industry's structure make noncompetitive behavior likely?
4. Which firm lead each of the price increases?
5. Do you think the 1976 price increase was the result of collusive price leadership or barometric price leadership or something else? Why?
6. Do you think the 1977 price increase was the result of collusive price leadership or barometric price leadership, or something else? Why?

A new and unique type of noncompetitive behavior--a shared monopoly--is presented in this article. The FTC contends that the top four cereal producers were able to keep cereal prices higher than competitive levels without engaging in formal price-fixing. In effect, the FTC believes that cereal makers were able to achieve results similar to those shown in Figure 1 (see Concept 4) without using a coordinator.

Antitrust: Snap, Crackle and Pop

By ALLAN J. MAYER
with JAMES BISHOP JR.
in Washington

People of the same trade seldom meet together even for merriment and diversion but the conversation ends in a conspiracy against the public or in some contrivance to raise prices.
—Adam Smith, "The Wealth of Nations," 1776

1. In judging antitrust cases, U.S. courts have generally insisted that Adam Smith's suspicions be backed by hard evidence of conspiracy before they would hand down convictions for price-fixing or restraint of trade. But now, in a massive monopoly suit being tried against the four biggest cereal companies, the Federal Trade Commission is testing out a new legal theory of conspiracy. "Even if they weren't meeting in smoke-filled rooms," says a top FTC official, "their behavior is the same as if they were."

2. The novelty in this notion is the concept of "shared monopoly"—an economist's theory that in some industries, a handful of firms can control the lion's share of the market without any overt conspiracy. If upheld, it could set a staggering precedent, since the FTC believes such concentration exists in many key industries, from autos to steel. "Should the courts side with the FTC," says Charles Mueller, an ex-staffer who helped launch the cereal case in 1969, "they would be declaring about one-third of the U.S. economy to be illegal."

Doing Penance

3. Among them, the four cereal companies—Kellogg, General Mills, General Foods and Quaker Oats—control 90 percent of the $1.5 billion-a-year market for ready-to-eat breakfast foods. This shared monopoly, the FTC says, costs consumers $128 million a year in higher prices. To spur competition, the FTC wants to break up General Foods, General Mills and Kellogg into five new companies. In addition, they would be forced to license to other companies any new brands they develop within five years of their introduction, and Kellogg, which controls 45 percent of the market, would have to license its existing brands immediately—all royalty-free. Quaker Oats, because it has only 9 percent of the market, would be spared the divestiture and licensing requirements, but the company would be prohibited from making any acquisitions for twenty years.

Such drastic remedies rest on some bold arguments.

4. The FTC contends that the four cereal companies maintained a tacit "gentlemen's agreement" for 30 years to minimize competition. As evidence, the FTC cites an internal memo from a Kellogg executive acknowledging the company's "responsibility to maintain a profitable price structure for the entire industry and to continue consistently to resist price-cutting." How was this done? The companies, the FTC alleges, persuaded supermarkets to arrange the cereals on their shelves by company name, rather than by cereal type—thus making comparison shopping difficult. More important, says the FTC, the companies introduced an array of new cereals—more than 150 between 1950 and 1970—that were essentially the same, but were differentiated by a bewildering proliferation of trade names. To support this illusion of intense competition and to discourage potential rivals from entering the business, the FTC charges, the cereal companies advertised heavily—up to $10 million for a new brand.

5. The cereal makers vigorously deny these charges. "Advertising was a means that permitted us to expand and become a real part of the market," says Quaker Oats vice president and special counsel Luther C. McKinney. "We gained entry, furthered competition—and now we're being sued. What kind of sense does that make?" McKinney's argument is partly supported by an internal FTC document obtained by NEWSWEEK questioning "whether advertising raises or lowers entry barriers." As for the control of shelf space, Albert R. Connelly, a lawyer for Kellogg, says: "It's not our shelf space . . . it is up to the retailer to decide how much space to devote to cereals."

Creative Law

6. The firms are especially irritated by what they regard as the shaky foundation of the suit. "The FTC has created an entirely new offense that they call 'shared monopoly'," complains Edward F. Howrey, a lawyer for General Mills. "That is a phrase found in no statute . . . It was designed and created for this case." And one FTC official concedes as much: "We are taking the law and stretching it a bit."

7. In antitrust cases, however, new law is regularly created by the courts, largely because many of the governing statutes, dating back to the Sherman Antitrust Act of 1890, are vague. And the shared-monopoly theory is supported by many congressmen, economists and lawyers who see it as the only way to break up industrial concentration. But there's no question that the cereal companies were singled out to test the doctrine. "I didn't pick the auto or petroleum industries," says Mueller, "because they have too much political clout."

8. Though the odds are against the FTC, a victory would undoubtedly open the door to more suits—or perhaps even invite legislation to break up concentrated industries. FTC economists estimate that excessive concentration costs consumers up to $45 billion a year in higher prices—a much disputed but still tempting target for government trustbusters. If the FTC manages to win the cereal case, the shared-monopoly doctrine would become a key weapon in a major new offensive against industrial concentration.

12

Resource Demand

"Look at this skimpy check--this is all I get for working all week at my miserable job. My brother makes twice as much and he's got a soft job. It isn't fair."

Tom, who has been listenting to his friend Larry's tale of woe, tries to console him. "I can see why you don't think its fair, Larry. But I don't know a fairer way to determine everyone's earnings. Do you?"

"Sure," replies Larry, "It would be fairer if I earned just as much as my brother."

Tom thinks about that for a few seconds, then smiles and says, "If you earned as much as your brother, you would complain because Robert Redford earns more than you."

Do you know anyone like Larry? Could you explain how wages are determined in the U.S. economy? If not, the next two chapters will provide you with a basic understanding of resource pricing. In general, you will learn that resource prices reflect a resource's worth to the employer. Although this explanation certainly does not cover all differences in resource earnings, it provides a better explanation of earning differentials than does any other explanation.

When we say that resource prices reflect a resource's worth to the employer, we are simply acknowledging that a firm cannot pay out more than it earns. Consequently, the selling price of a firm's product is one important determinant of how much a firm can pay a resource. A second determinant is the resource's productivity. Together these two determinants indicate what a resource is worth to the firm. Another way of saying this is that product price and productivity establish the firm's demand for the resource.

Resource supply, on the other hand, depends upon what each resource owner expects to be paid for his resource. It is the interaction of resource demand and resource supply in a resource market that, barring any outside interference, establishes resource price. Resource prices are customarily expressed as a wage rate, a salary, interest, or rent.

In this chapter, we will emphasize the theory of resource demand. In the next chapter we will deal with resource supply and the resource market.

CHECKLIST

Definitions of New Terms

1. Total physical product (TPP)--the level of total output produced at each level of the variable input when all other inputs are held constant.
2. Average physical product (APP)--a level of total physical product divided by the number of variable inputs employed to produce that level.
3. Marginal physical product (MPP)--the increase in total physical product that results from the use of one more variable input.
4. Value of marginal product (VMP)--marginal physical product multiplied by the market price of the product.
5. Marginal revenue product (MRP)--marginal physical product multiplied by the marginal revenue of a firm. VMP = MRP when market sets product price, but not when the firm sets product price.
6. Resource demand--a schedule or curve showing the units of a resource that firms will employ at each price. These prices may be expressed in such terms as a wage rate, salary, interest, or rent.
7. Derived demand--resource demand is referred to as a derived demand because it is directly related to the demand for the firm's product.
8. Resource supply--a schedule or curve showing the units of a resource that resource owners will offer to sell each price.
9. Marginal factor cost--the cost to the firm of each additional unit of a input.

Concepts

1. The relationship of total physical product (TPP), average physical product (APP), and marginal physical product (MPP). The output produced by adding successive units of one input (variable input), while holding all other inputs constant, may be shown either as total product (Figure 1(A)), or as average and marginal product (Figure 1(B). In addition, the concept of diminishing marginal product can be incorporated into the product curves as has been done in both panels (A) and (B) of Figure 1. Diminishing returns begins when more than OD units of the variable input are employed, and this causes TPP to increase at a decreasing rate after OD. Correspondingly, diminishing returns causes MPP and APP to decline after OD. MPP decreases more rapidly than APP because MPP absorbs the full impact of each input's lower output. On the other hand, the averaging process used to calculate APP spreads out the

impact of diminishing returns over all inputs and thus APP decreases more gradually. When no additional output is produced by another input, MPP falls to zero, and TPP reaches a maxium. (See OJ in Figures 1(A) and 1(B).

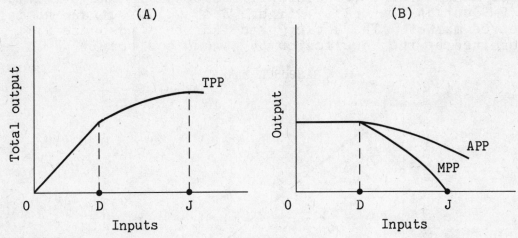

Figure 1

2. A firm's demand for a resource. If a firm wants to maximize profits, it should add additional units of each input so long as the cost of adding another unit (MFC) is less than the value of the output produced (VMP or MRP). Therefore, to maximize profits, the representative firm shown in Figure 2 should employ OB units of the variable input when the market price of that input is OE. Correspondingly, if the market price of the input rises to OF, the firm should reduce its use of the input to OA. Since quantity demanded at each price depends upon VMP (or MRP), we can conclude that VMP (or MRP) is the firm's demand for the resource.

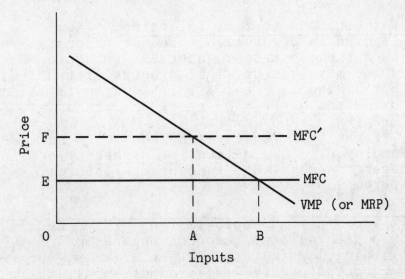

Figure 2

3. Market demand for a resource. We can predict that each and every profit maximizing firm that uses the same resource will calculate its employment level of that resource by following the MFC = VMP (or MPR) rule. It follows, therefore, that market demand for a resource will be equal to the summation of all VMP curves (or MPR)[1]. Figure 3 shows market demand in a resource market. The market price for this resource will be determined by the interaction of demand and supply.

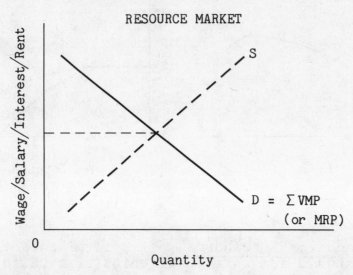

RESOURCE MARKET

Figure 3

4. Shifts in resource demand. Since VMP (and MRP) is determined by both product price and MPP, anything that affects either of these two variables will affect resource demand. Product price may change because of the reasons discussed in Chapter 2. Changes in MPP may be caused by either additions or improvements to complementary inputs or by improvements in the input itself. For example, adding more or better equipment will increase the MPP of labor. Labor's MPP may also be increased through training or by improving working conditions.

5. Input substitution and cost minimization. When more than one input is used in production, production costs are minimized when the least-cost input mix is employed. This occurs when the marginal physical productivity per dollar of each input is equal. That is, if two inputs, A and B are being used, the correct quantity of each exists when: $MPP_a/P_a = MPP_b/P_b$.
Therefore, if the price of A rises, less of A and more of B should be employed. In addition, at higher prices for A, it may be cheaper to substitute some other resource, say resource C, for resource A.

---

1. Summing provides only an approximation of the demand for a resource. To get the true resource demand, one must adjust for the following: when resource price falls, more resources are employed, output increases, product supply shifts left, product price falls, and VMP (or MRP) shifts left.

GUIDE FOR ANALYZING ARTICLES

1. Identify the product(s) being produced.
2. Determine the resource(s) being used as inputs.
3. Find information relating to the productivity of each input:
   A. Does this information relate to TPP, APP, or MPP?
   B. Is productivity changing?
   C. What is causing a change in productivity?
4. Find information about product price:
   A. VMP is relevant if a market sets product price; MRP if a firm sets product price.
   B. Is product price changing?
5. Combine the information on productivity and product price to learn about VMP (or MRP).
   A. Is the VMP (or MRP) curve shifting, or is a movement along the curve taking place?
   B. What is causing this change to take place?
6. Use the information about VMP (or MRP) to explain or predict:
   A. the price of a resource;
   B. changes in resource prices;
   C. relative differences in resource prices;
   D. changes in the quantity used of a resource;
   E. changes in the relative use of each resource.

Articles

AN ANALYZED ARTICLE: OVERVIEW

Productivity in the U.S. was increasing at a record pace when this article was written. The purpose of the article is to show how productivity gains were achieved by one U.S. firm, the Parker-Hannifin Corporation. The implication is that the productivity gains achieved by this firm are representative of those taking place throughout the economy. Our interest in the article is the opportunity it provides for applying a variety of resource demand concepts.

Grinding Out More: How the Current Gain In Productivity Looks From a Factory's Floor

By PHILIP REVZIN
Staff Reporter of *The Wall Street Journal*

At a Parker-Hannifin Plant, Rise in Skilled Workers, Better Maintenance Help

1. CLEVELAND—Standing at a screeching metal-cutting machine, Loretta Koss plucks a dumbbell-shaped aluminum part off the rotating turntable, blasts off stray bits of metal with an air gun, turns the part over, and replaces it just before the table moves and brings another part into sight. She repeats the process again and again.

2. Mrs. Koss has worked this and similar machines in the automotive division plant of Parker-Hannifin Corp. here for 24 years, turning out parts for compressor units of automobile air conditioners. On a typical eight-hour day in years past, Mrs. Koss, whose blonde hair literally sparkles with specks of aluminum, produced 1,800 of the parts.

3. Today she produces 2,250 parts.

4. Her foreman, Teofil Poremba, attributes this 25% increase in productivity—loosely defined as the amount of goods produced per worker per hour—to the simple expedient of running the parts turntable faster and thereby making Mrs. Koss work faster. At many companies, such a step might spur union complaints about a "production-line speedup."

5. But as everyone at Parker-Hannifin knows, business had been poor until very recently. So local union officials are actually heartened by the increased workload, and Mrs. Koss says she doesn't mind it. The work "isn't any harder, but it's still pretty monotonous," she says.

Important To Companies

6. While the productivity gains at Mrs. Koss's turntable may be unusually large, even smaller increases are important to Parker-Hannifin and to similar manufacturing companies. And the Labor Department says nationwide productivity figures began climbing in the second quarter of 1975 after more than two years of stagnation.

7. The statistics show that output per hour of work in the private economy in the second quarter rose at a 4.3% seasonally adjusted annual rate and in the third quarter surged at an 11% rate—the biggest increase since the second quarter of 1961.

*
*
*

8. Productivity increases in two major ways, experts say. One is long-term growth stemming from capital spending programs, on such things as more-efficient machinery and improved management controls. Most corporations constantly pursue such programs, but their exact contribution to productivity statistics at any particular time is impossible to calculate.

9. The second way that productivity changes is more calculable and shows up clearly in national statistics and in figures compiled by individual companies. This involves short-term increases or decreases in the goods that a factory worker, for example, can produce in a given time. It depends on such factors as the worker's alertness and attitude toward his job; how well the machinery is being maintained; the number of indirect workers, like janitors or

clerks, included in the statistical equation; and the tendency, in periods of high unemployment, for newer, less-skilled workers to be laid off and older, more-skilled workers to remain on the job and do more of the work.

A Look At One Firm

10. To appreciate the importance of such factors, consider the experience of Parker-Hannifin in the current business pickup. A detailed look at the company's operations illustrates the actual developments on a plant floor, particularly in terms of short-term changes in productivity, that lie behind national productivity statistics.

11. At Parker-Hannifin, as at many companies, the course of productivity is strongly affected by employe morale. "We feel there is a 10% to 15% area where the desire of our work force can make everything work right or not," Patrick S. Parker, president and chief executive, says. "That's our profit and then some. Increased productivity is really the key to whether we make it as a corporation or not."

12. Right now, Mr. Parker says, productivity is high. "For the next couple of quarters and possibly beyond that, we'll be at the maximum productivity we can get to in a normal business cycle."

13. Mr. Parker attributes the high productivity to several factors: "Our people are rested after a boom period about two years ago when they were working 10 hours a day, six or seven days a week. There is less of an 'interference factor,' that is, less-skilled people getting in the way of the more-skilled workers. In some cases workers are overskilled for jobs they are asked to do now, and they can perform them faster than the less-skilled people who used to do them. We can use our downtime to better maintain our machines, and we now are using new equipment which we ordered during the boom period and which hadn't been delivered until the depths of the recession hit."

14. Most of these factors can be seen at work at Parker-Hannifin's Cliff Impact division plant in the Cleveland suburb of Eastlake. Officials of the plant, which makes aluminum fire-extinguisher canisters and various tube-like parts for cars, trucks and industrial machines, are beginning to notice an increase in orders after a business slump that bottomed out last April.

15. According to company figures, the plant's productivity is directly related to business levels. From February through June of 1973, when the plant was swamped with orders, both the number of hours worked by employes and production were abnormally high; but the value of product produced per hour worked was as a low $35.15. In January through May this year, when business was severely depressed, both the hours worked and production were abnormally low; but productivity was high, at $52.29 an hour. As orders began strengthening in the June through September period, productivity increased further, to $57.20 of product per hour of labor. (The figures aren't adjusted for inflation, but officials say the effects of greater employee efficiency are far more important.)

Changes In Employment

16. Regis Minerd, operations manager at the Cliff Impact plant, says employment paralleled the level of orders on the way down the cycle. It fell from a peak of 200 hourly workers and 39 salaried support personnel in September 1973 to a low of 100 hourly and 26 salaried people last March. As orders, and production, picked up, however, the recall of laid-off workers lagged. The plant now employs 118 hourly and 33 salaried workers, and these 151 people "are producing about as much as the work force of 166 people we had last July," Mr. Minerd says.

17. Tracking a few products through the Cliff Impact plant underscores some factors involved in increasing productivity.

18. Near the middle of the big, warehouse-like plant, a row of large machines pound silver-dollar-sized aluminum disks into a variety of tubes and small canisters destined for parts of auto air conditioners. Not long ago a bin for feeding the disks into the impacting press was devised, so that parts wouldn't have to be fed in by hand. Now one operator handles two machines—keeping the feeding bin full—instead of one machine.

19. Nearby, Raymond Wesley operates a machine that can't be switched to automatic parts feeding. But he recently managed to speed up production a bit anyway. He now stacks aluminum disks on a ledge of the machine, so he can smoothly grab a disk, put it on the machine's die and take the finished cylinder off the machine shaft before the shaft crashes down again. Before he had begun stacking the disks, Mr. Wesley had to fish around for them in a big bin—a slower process.

Hard-Used Machines

20. Not far from Mr. Wesley, huge machines pound large aluminum disks into cylinders for fire-extinguisher canisters. When running full blast, the machines take a severe pounding, and they require a lot of maintenance. In the hands of a skilled operator, and when not being used 24 hours a day, the machines break down less frequently.

21. Mr. Minerd, the operations manager, says that two years ago, when the plant was running full throttle, a typical impacting machine would operate properly only 30% of the time. "Now it's going 48% of the time," he says. "That's still not terrific, since it is down more than half the time, but it's a hell of a lot better." Increased utilization of the machine, of course, boosts canister production without increasing the amount of labor, and productivity figures rise.

22. Moreover, the machines are being operated by more-skilled workers now, Mr. Minerd says. Two years ago Parker-Hannifin added a third work turn that inevitably was composed of mostly inexperienced people. "For a long time the first shift was coming in and spending most of its time repairing the damage to the machines done by the third shift," he says. When orders fell, the paring of less-skilled people helped productivity. During the boom "in many cases we were getting five days' work in six or

seven days," Mr. Parker, the president, says. "Now we're back to getting five days' work for five days' pay."

23.	Plant officials also say that as orders dropped they were able to consider a number of economies they had no time for when their chief concern was pushing finished products out the door. For example, recently much attention was paid to the placement of machines within the plant. The machine that finishes off fire-extinguisher canisters after they come off the impacting machines was moved closer to the impacters, and also closer to a machine that washes finished cans. The job of a materials handler who had carted bins of cans around was eliminated.

*
*
*

Analysis

We begin the analysis by noting that automobile air conditioners are produced at one of Parker-Hannifin's plants; aluminum fire extinguisher cannisters (plus other tube-like parts) at the other. Resources discussed include management (for example, as in par. 23), equipment (as in par. 13), and labor (par. 2 and 3).

If you recall the discussion of Concepts, you will remember that productivity can be expressed in total, average, or marginal terms. As we shall soon see, it is necessary to examine productivity data carefully before deciding which of the three terms is appropriate.

The first productivity data appears in paragraphs 2 and 3. Here we find that Mrs. Koss, a production worker at the automotive division plant, has increased her daily output from 1800 to 2250 parts. This productivity data, since it relates to what one worker has done to increase total output, is an example of marginal physical product. Figure 4 examines the implications of this data more fully. We will assume that Mrs. Koss is the Ath production worker and her earlier output of 1,800 units is shown by point A_1. Since Mrs. Koss's output would be located on the MPP curve for that period, we draw a dashed MPP curve through A_1. (A dashed line is used because we know only one point on the curve.) Next we show Mrs. Koss's current output of 2,250 units at point A_2; a second MPP curve is drawn through that point. Our analysis suggests that if Mrs. Koss is a typical

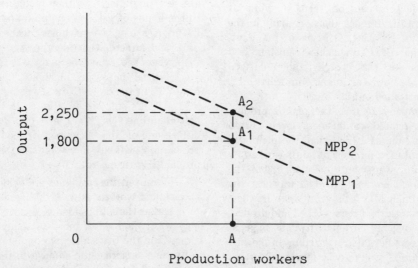

Figure 4

production worker, the MPP of production workers has increased (shifted upward) from the earlier period to the current period.

The second productivity figures are found in paragraph 7. Here we find that "output per hour of work" rose 4.3 percent and 11 percent in the second and third quarters respectively in 1975. Which of the three productivity terms--TPP, APP, or MPP--applies to these rates of increase? The key to the answer is the term, "per," in the statement. Since "per" suggests an average, the two rates of increase are most likely equivalent to APP.

If we know that APP rose during 1975, can we assume that MPP also rose? The answer to this question is that most factors which cause APP to rise will also cause MPP to rise. Therefore, MPP probably rose throughout the economy in the second and third quarters of 1975.

Our last task is outlined under Guide Step 3: we must explain why productivity has been rising. As we learned earlier, the productivity of any input, for instance, labor, will rise (1) when a complementary input (either management or equipment in this article) is either increased or improved, and/or (2) when labor itself becomes more productive. Examples of both are found in this article.

An example of (1) (above) is the increase in labor productivity that occurred when new equipment was installed (par. 13). Two examples of (2) are apparent. Mrs. Koss improved her productivity because she "doesn't mind" having the parts turntable run faster (par. 5 and 2). And Raymond Wesley improved his productivity by stacking aluminum disks on a ledge, making it possible to feed his machine much faster (par. 19).

In each of the three examples presented above, labor's MPP curve shifted upward, thus increasing the MPP of labor. A higher MPP for labor will also exist if labor is moved to a higher point on the same MPP curve. An example of the latter situation is found in paragraph 23. Here we find that management recently improved the "placement of machines within the plant," and thereby elimi-nated the job of materials handler. The article states that this is one of the "economies" achieved by plant officials. Question: did this change cause the MPP curve to shift upward or did labor simply move to a higher point on the same MPP curve?

The answer can be explained by using the MPP curve in Figure 5. Point B in Figure 5 is the MPP of labor before management elimi-nates material handlers. Does the "economy" referred to in paragraph 23 result in a move to Point C--a point on a higher MPP-or in a move to Point D--a higher point on the same MPP curve? The answer is Point D. By eliminating material handlers, the marginal productivity of the remaining workers will be higher because a higher point on the same MPP curve is now relevant.

Turning to the Guide Step 4, if the price of automobile air conditioners and fire extinguisher cannisters is determined by a product market, VMP is relevant. If not, MRP is relevant. Since it is probably safe to assume that these products are sold to only a few other producers, a market probably does not determine price. Thus, we accept MRP as the relevant concept, and we must next look for related data. However, the only data of this type is some-

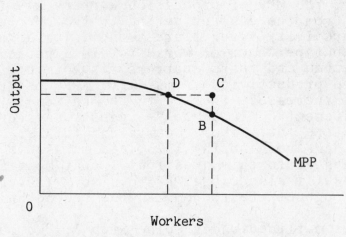

Figure 5

thing called "value of produce produced per hour worked" (par. 15). This term implies that the data combines revenue and output, which is what is done to determine MRP. However, before we can use this data, we have to determine if the data is related to marginal product or some other type of revenue product.

We handled a similar problem earlier when discussing productivity. At that time we said the term "per" meant an average. Accepting that interpretation again, we will assume the value of product data found in paragarph 15 relates to average revenue produce--a concept which has not yet been discussed--rather than MRP. Since MRP, not ARP, is the firm's demand for a resource, data on ARP is of use only if it provides information about MRP. Based on our earlier analysis of a similar problem, we can assume that, in most cases, MRP will change when ARP changes. Therefore, we will assume that MRP rose considerably from 1973 to early 1975 (value of product rose from $35.13 to $52.29) and then rose somewhat more during 1975 (value of product rose from $52.29 to $57.20).

As usual, we now want to determine the cause of that increase. According to our theory, an increase in MRP may be caused by an increase in product price, or productivity, or both. Since our analysis showed that productivity was increasing during the period, that would be one cause of the increase in MRP. Did product price also play a role? It would appear that the first increase in MRP (that is, from 1973 to 1975) was entirely due to increased productivity since "business was severely depressed" during this period and consequently product price was probably not increasing (par. 15). On the other hand, since "orders began strengthening" during the second period (during 1975), both produce price and productivity may have combined in pushing up MRP (par. 15).

We have reached the point when information about MRP will be useful in explaining and predicting changes in resource price, quantity of resources used, and resource mix. For example, can our economic theory be used to explain the statement that "151 people 'are producing about as much as the work force of 166 people'"? One way is to use total physical product curves. In

118

Figure 6, TPP_1 shows total physical product for 1973. At that time, OB workers were producing OC units of output. Then, as we determined in our analysis, productivity increased significantly. This increase in productivity shifts TPP to TPP_2. Now we see that a smaller number of workers, OA rather than OB, produce the same output.

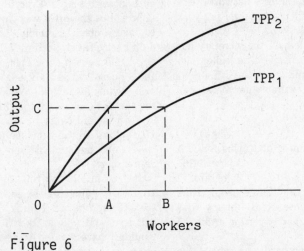

Figure 6

Explanations are relatively easier to make than predictions. Moreover, this article provides little information for making predictions. For example, although we know an increase in the MRP for labor will put some upward pressure on wages, we cannot predict an increase in wages unless we know much more about conditions in the resource market for labor. Nevertheless, our analysis uncovered some useful background information for anyone interested in making predictions.

AN ARTICLE WITH QUESTIONS

What Makes Barbara Walters Worth a Million?

By LES BROWN

The New York Times *(May 2, 1976). © 1976 by The New York Times Company. Reprinted by permission.*

1. Dinner was franks and beans, "the house specialty," a carryover perhaps from humbler times. But it came with candlelight and a good Bordaux, and Barbara Walters spoke of never having to confront again her old demon, insecurity. One might have expected manic conversation from a hard-working woman who had just struck it rich, but instead she was reflective in a muted tone that seemed out of character with her aggressive, and even at times shrill, television persona.

2. Flowers, some beginning to droop and sere, were banked against the wall like the hangover from a wedding. It was four days after the Big Decision and the front-page press reports that Barbara would be leaving NBC after almost two decades to become the co-anchor of the ABC evening newscast with Harry Reasoner for $1 million a year. The obvious questions were how was she taking it and what makes her worth such a royal paycheck?

* * *

3. "The night it all happened, the flowers began to arrive and the phone never stopped ringing. My friends were so pleased for me and so warm. And yet, through it all, I wondered why I was so unhappy," Barbara said.

4. She told of how her friends often joke about her inability to decide upon the smallest things, whether to buy the green dress or the blue. But this was one

119

the biggest decisions she had ever had to make—whether to switch to ABC for a million or remain at NBC, whose counter offer had also reached a million dollars. The difference between them was the immediate chance, at ABC, of becoming an anchorwoman.

5. Why the sadness? Part of it was leaving old friends at NBC for a lot of strangers at the new network. As if to illustrate, she recounted her secretary's faux pas with a call from a "Mr. Goldenson."

6. "What is it in reference to, please?" the secretary had asked, not recognizing the name. The caller was Leonard Goldenson, chairman of the American Broadcasting Companies, Inc., Miss Walters's new employer.

* * *

7. "But is was not just the sadness of leaving NBC. It was all the publicity about the million dollars, a kind of publicity I've never been used to," Barbara said. "I worried all night about public reaction. Some people were going to be resentful of me because of it. But my own feeling was, why should I quarrel about getting a raise? I didn't ask for it."

8. She feels somewhat less concerned now about the reaction, having sampled how the news was received by some of her public. "Most people, I found, were used to the idea of basketball players getting fantastic sums for a few ball games. My driver—we all have drivers and hairdressers on the show, there's nothing special about that—told me that none of his friends found it unseemly that ABC would pay me a million a year.

9. "Yet, I know there are many who believe news people should be more pure than show-business people. They seem to feel that if you get a million bucks, you're a superstar. And if you're a superstar, you're show biz. And if you're show biz, you can't be pure and can't do justice to the news."

10. Her agent, Lee Stevens of the William Morris Agency, had put it well, she thought. Why, he observed, should a good reporter get less on television than a good comedian when news executives at the networks don't get paid less than executives in other departments of the company?

11. "I don't worry about being able to do the job at ABC but only whether people will accept a woman on the news at night, and whether they feel a woman can have the proper authority," she remarked. "People tend to go to male doctors. We still have to learn whether they can accept the idea of going to a female."

* * *

12. She continued: "I know now that I'm totally professional and good at what I do. I may not be great at ABC, but I know I won't be terrible. This is the kind of confidence that men have always known but women are only just beginning to get. If I make it, there'll be other women in these anchor jobs all over the country. This was why I wanted Sally Quinn to succeed at CBS, but few people understood that."

13. Barbara reviewed the pros and cons of her heavy decision, as if making it all over again. "If I had stayed at NBC, I'd have been safe," she began. "No matter what I did—left the 'Today' show, conducted a new magazine, become eventually a co-anchor of the news—I could not be humiliated. This was home. Going to ABC is challenging, scary. Everyone is watching, looking for failure. But the offer was there, and I'm still young enough to take a chance. Finally, I knew I'd always regret it if I didn't seize the opportunity."

14. She paused for a cigarette. "I won't fall apart if this doesn't work. My entire life is not what I do for a living. Meanwhile, it's exciting to think about some of the things I'd like to do on the newscast."

15. What are some of those thing? Well, that's for later, closer to the time she joins ABC—sometime between now and when her NBC contract runs out in September.

16. "I can tell you this, though," she said. "For me, it's not going to be a matter of just reading the Teleprompter. I think Harry [Reasoner] and I will be balanced and will spark off good things in each other. I wouldn't have wanted this job if all it meant was reading the news.

17. "Look, this isn't to suggest that I want to do 'happy news' or that I would alter the integrity of the newscast, but we are beyond Watergate and Vietnam—those periods when the news was compelling and carried itself. What you find—what all the studies show—is that the three newscasts are about the same except for the appeal of the people before the cameras. As a team, Harry and I could be more interesting than the others.

* * *

18. Women viewers predominate before the sets in the periods before prime time when the newscasts are presented. Part of ABC's bet on Barbara is its belief that she will attract the viewers of her sex, and she appears confident of that.

19. "My biggest fans are women, and not men," she said. "I can tell from the mail and the people I meet that women do identify with me. I couldn't possibly have stayed on the air 12 years without being female. Other women tell me I ask the questions they wanted to ask. Quite frankly, although some people fault me for being aggressive, I can't stand not asking the questions that have to be asked."

20. All right, then what makes her—of all the journalist—worth a million a year? "If that's what two networks think I should get," she answered, "they'll get no argument from me. But the money was not what this was all about. It was about opportunity and challenge. I work hard and do good work, and I want to be judged by that and not by how much I earn."

* * *

21. The question was not for Barbara Walters herself to answer. Network television—a $2.5 billion industry in

which only three companies share—operates on a grander scale than most media. It responds, too, at every level, to the basic law of show business that governs the price of things: whatever the traffic will allow. To put it simply, the traffic has allowed Barbara Walters to be traded on the talent market for $1 million a year because she possibly will boost the news ratings a notch or two. At the high stakes the networks play for, the investment of a mere million toward lifting ABC's long-static news ratings is a minor gamble, indeed. A television personality overnight can add hundreds of thousands of households to a program simply through his or her presence. The gain of a single rating point puts the newscast in 710,000 additional homes, where it may be watched by approximately 1.2 million extra people. At the rates paid for commercials on the network newscasts in today's market, the gain of a single rating point should mean of gain of at least $1 million in revenues.

22. Thus, if by her presence Barbara Walters should improve the ratings for the ABC Evening News by a single point, she pays back her spectacular salary. If by two points, it's a bonanza.

Questions

1. What is the purpose of this article?
2. What product is being produced? (Hint: What does ABC get paid for?)
3. What inputs are used to produce the product?
4. What information in the article relates to the productivity of the inputs? Does it relate to average or marginal productivity? Are the curve(s) shifting?
5. Using the information you find about product price, can you determine whether VMP or MRP is relevant?
6. Is the MRP curve changing? (NOTE: Your answer here should conform to the way you answered Question #4.)
7. From your analysis of MRP, how do you explain Ms. Walter's $1 million salary?

AN ARTICLE FOR STUDENT ANALYSIS: OVERVIEW

After explaining why Barbara Walters is worth a million, you should be prepared to determine if O. J. is worth $2 million. In this article, you will find considerable data for determining the marginal revenue product of a football superstar.

Is O. J. Worth $2 Million? Well, That's Entertainment

By LARRY FELSER

Buffalo Evening News *(Sept. 18, 1976). Reprinted by permission.*

1. Is the Juice worth it?
   Is O.J. Simpson worth the estimated $2-$2.1 million
2. contract which Bills' owner Ralph Wilson gave him to return to a football career in Buffalo?
3. The answer depends upon which context is used to consider the question.
   If you ask whether O.J. or any athlete is worth more
4. than the combined salaries of the president of the United States and the secretary of state; far more than Jonas Salk or Albert Sabin; a hundredfold more than a cancer researcher or a person teaching deaf children, then the answer is, "No, of course not."

* * *

5. But in the context of Simpson's own element, the entertainment world, the answer must come in the form of other questions:
6. Is Elton John worth $400,000 for a concert which lasts less than 3 hours?

7. Is Steve McQueen worth $2 million for 3 week's work in front of a camera?

8. Are Crosby, Stills, Nash and Young worth $10.5 million for a 30-date concert tour conducted with 33 days?

9. Are Marlon Brando, Richard Burton, Elizabeth Taylor and Robert Redford worth more than $1 million each time they film a motion picture?

* * *

10. The answer seems to be that the public is willing to pay staggering amounts of money to be entertained; that promoters make staggering profits for staging the entertainment, and performers are demanding and receiving larger and larger shares of those profits.

11. In an even smaller context of the entertainment world, Simpson's own milieu of sports, O.J. is worth not only the money Wilson gave him, but is an excellent buy when compared to highly-paid basketball players such as Ernie DiGregorio and Bob McAdoo and the richest of the hockey stars, Bobby Orr.

12. For Wilson it is a matter of mathematics.

13. He has a sound knowledge of how much business Simpson brings to him. It has nothing to do with O.J.'s skill as a football player. The vital factor is his box-office value.

14. When the Bills' owner attempted to trade O.J. to the San Francisco 49'ers just before the deadline for transactions between Buffalo's American Conference and the 49'ers' National Conference, the San Francisco management expressed its doubt about an ability to pay Simpson.

15. Wilson tried to ease their fears.

16. "He means about 20,000 tickets a game to you," said Ralph.

* * *

17. In Rich Stadium, Wilson's home park, there are 10 games played each year. Multiply 10 games times 20,000 tickets and you have 200,000 tickets for a home season.

18. The Bills' average ticket price is somewhere between $8 and $9. Multiply 200,000 by $8.50 and Simpson has generated $1.7 million in revenues.

19. There are, of course, expenses to be subtracted, and the visiting team gets 40 percent of the gate receipts after expenses. But even taking that into consideration, O.J.'s financial value for the home schedule alone is impressive.

20. It doesn't end with the home schedule.

When Tampa Bay's expansion franchise mailed out its

21. first season-ticket sales flyer to prospective buyers, guess whose picture was on the cover? The Buccaneers front office feels that O.J.'s presence should mean an extra 20,000 filled seats a week from Sunday in Tampa.

22. Simpson could actually rescue the season for New England's owner, Billy Sullivan.

23. Sullivan took a $9 million loan from a Chicago bank in order to buy control of the franchise at the end of last season. A month ago, the Patriots admitted there was a danger of defaulting on the loan at one time in August.

24. The Pats' season ticket sale drooped drastically this season and the opening-game crowd of 43,415 was 11,000 under last year's opener and 18,000 under capacity.

25. If O.J. draws 20,000 more than what the Bills might attract without him, he not only will have eased Sullivan's worries but enriched Wilson by an extra $40,000 or $50,000 in the Bills' take-home check.

26. Then there is the matter of preseason games.

27. Since the teams arrange their own schedules, the franchises with the biggest stadiums bring in the best gate attractions.

28. Buffalo was booked into the Los Angeles Coliseum last month in the belief that Simpson would be in their starting lineup.

29. "O.J. would have meant an extra 20,000 sales for us," said a member of the Rams' front office. "No way we would have booked Buffalo without expecting O.J. to be with them."

30. The truth is that Buffalo is a colorless team without the Juice. Around the NFL the consensus opinion is that the Bills are on a par with the Detroit Lions, both artistically and the the area of glamour.

31. That glamour means instant recognition for the Bills, through mere association with O.J.

* * *

32. In a recent issue of the Ladies' Home Journal, a poll was taken of adolescents from the fifth grade through high school in all parts of the country to determine who are young America's heroes and heroines.

33. The poll excluded no one and the lists ranged from Ralph Nader to Oral Roberts, from Betty Ford to Patty Hearst.

34. The winners of the combined poll for boys and girls was O.J. Simpson.

35. The winner of the boys' poll was O.J. Simpson.

36. The winner of the girls' poll was O.J. Simpson.

37. Football tycoons are as astute as any other big businessmen. They recognize that today's hero worshiper is tomorrow's consumer.

38. That's why O.J. Simpson has his rich, new contract.

13

Resource Supply

Jim just met his old high school classmate, Pete. After high school, Jim went to college, Pete became an autoworker. Jim asked Pete about his union, then said, "After learning about all the benefits of market-determined prices, I feel less sympathetic toward your union, Pete. I think wages should be determined by the market and not by strikes."

"Wait a minute," replies Pete. "Let's look at this a little more closely. I'll agree that if we weren't unionized, all of us workers would provide a pretty good market supply. But since most of us work for only four firms, how can an effective market demand exist? So we match size with size--our big union bargains with the Big Four."

The last chapter deliberately avoided a variety of resource market complications so we could concentrate on the theory of resource demand. Jim and Pete have raised one type of resource market complication. Before becoming involved in their argument, we need to learn about resource supply and some common types of market supply situations. We will see that most resource pricing situations we read about involve some type of market intervention by firms, unions, or government policy.

CHECKLIST

Definitions of New Terms

1. Monopsonist--a term for a sole buyer in a resource market. Remember, a monopolist is a single seller in a product market.
2. Union--an organization of resource owners, usually owners of the resource of labor. Union officials represent the entire group of resource owners in all matters related to the employment of their resources.
3. Bilaterial monopoly--a situation in which a monopsonist and a monopolist face each other in the same market.

Concepts

1. <u>Resource supply may be shifted by resource owners, unions, or government policy.</u> We can use a specific resource, say race drivers, to explain each of these three situations. Let us first assume a rash of racing accidents causes some drivers to quit racing. What will happen to market supply? Simple; these resource owners shifted supply to the left. Second, suppose all race drivers decide to unionize and the union adopts a policy requiring that all drivers must either have three years experience or else serve a three-year apprenticeship before they can race. How does this affect market supply? Finally, what if the government passes a law requiring all race drivers to pass an examination and obtain a $500 license before being able to race? This too, will affect market supply. Although each of the three examples discussed above were different, in each case supply shifted to the left as shown in Figure 1(A).

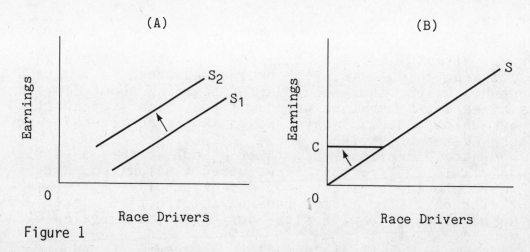

(A)   (B)

Figure 1

2. <u>A portion of the supply curve may be shifted to the left by government policy or union policy.</u> When government adopts a minimum wage or when workers unionize and demand a specific wage (a type of minimum wage), that portion of the supply curve below the minimum wage will, in effect, shift up to the level of the minimum wage. This effect is shown in Figure 1(B) where the original supply curve, OS, becomes the supply curve, CS, after a minimum wage of OC is established.

3. <u>For a monopsonist, marginal factor cost (MFC) is greater than the resource price shown by the supply curve.</u> When a market sets resource price, supply and demand determine the MFC for each firm, which may employ any number of resources at that price. However, since a monopsonist sets resource price, MFC will vary with the level of resource usage and will always be greater than the supply curve price. This situation is shown in Figure 2. Assume a monopsonist chooses to employ OB units--which is one more unit than OA--rather than OA units. The supply curve shows it would cost OD for each of the OA units; OD is the average cost-per-unit. However, if OB units are employed, each unit must be paid OE. But what is the MFC of

124

employing this last unit? That is, what is the total cost of employing one more unit? It is not only the OE cost, but also the additional cost of DE that must be paid for OA units. Adding OE + (OA times DE) yields OF, the MFC of OB units.

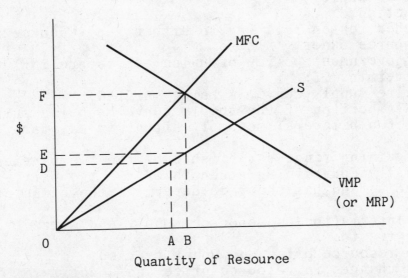

Figure 2

4. For a monopsonist, MFC determines an employment level, but S determines the payment rate. Firms which must pay market-determined resource prices and monopsonists determine employment levels by equating MFC with VMP (or MRP). However, a monopsonist pays only supply price, not VMP (or MRP). Consequently, the monopsonist in Figure 2 would employ OB units (that is, where MFC = VMP), but only pay OE per unit. As a result, although the resources produce a marginal product worth OF, they are paid only OE.

5. Economic theory is unable to predict resource price for a bilaterial monopoly situation. However, the range of price possibilities can be predicted. Everything else equal, the monopsonist in Figure 2 will pay resource owners OE. However, if a union represents resource owners, we would assume it would try to get its members a price equal to their marginal product, which is OF. Therefore, OE and OF become the lower and upper limits respectively of the bargaining range. The resource price finally established will depend upon the relative bargaining strength of each party. (NOTE: If VMP can be shifted to the right, the upper limit of the bargaining range is raised.)

GUIDE FOR ANALYZING ARTICLES

1. Identify the product(s).
2. Determine which resource(s) are being used as inputs.
3. Determine who demands and who supplies the resources.
4. Determine if resource price and/or quantity has changed, is changing, or will change.

5. Determine if the change above (Step 4) is being caused by a change in resource demand, resource supply, or both.
6. If resource supply has changed, determine if the change was caused by:
   A. government policy;
   B. union action;
   C. some other reason relating to either the resource itself or the resource owner.
7. If either government policy or union action are influencing supply, determine if:
   A. the entire supply curve is being shifted;
   B. the lower portion of the supply curve is being shifted;
8. Determine if a bilateral monopoly situation exists. If so, determine:
   A. the bargaining range established by the two parties;
   B. the relative bargaining strength of the two parties.
9. If resource demand has changed, determine the cause of the change.
10. Using the information on resource supply and demand you have developed, try to:
    A. explain resource price and quantity used;
    B. predict changes in resource price and quantity.

Articles

AN ANALYZED ARTICLE: OVERVIEW

The United Rubber Workers (URW), after striking for 16 weeks, reached an agreement on a new contract with one of the Big Four tire makers, and the other three firms are expected to sign comparable agreements soon. This article provides an opportunity to see the bilaterial monopoly model in action.

Rubber Workers Disclose Terms of Proposed Pact

By A WALL STREET JOURNAL
Staff Reporter

Big Tire Firms, Meanwhile, Raise Prices;
2 Makers Consider Further Boosts

1. CLEVELAND—The striking United Rubber Workers union disclosed the terms of a proposed settlement with the Big Four tire companies, and two of the companies indicated further tire-price increases may be coming.

2. Negotiators for the URW and Firestone Tire & Rubber Co. worked out the proposal early Thursday.

The URW made the terms public after its 20-member Firestone policy committee ratified the agreement Friday, setting the stage for industry-wide bargaining that is expected to settle the 16-week strike.

3. Meanwhile, all four major tire companies—Firestone, B.F. Goodrich Co., Goodyear Tire & Rubber Co. and Uniroyal Inc.—have raised tire prices substantially, in many cases, more than 10%, in the past few weeks. The companies announced the increases through trade channels, and none made the increases widely known at the time.

4. Despite those increases, spokesmen for Firestone and Goodrich said further increases may be necessary after negotiations on labor contracts are completed.

5. The terms of the proposed settlement call for a wage increase of 80 cents an hour in the first year of the three-year contract, 30 cents in the second year and 25 cents in the third. In addition, rubber workers would receive a cost-of-living adjustment for the first time.

Cost-of-Living Increases

6. In the first two years, wages would rise one cent an hour for each 0.4 point rise in the consumer price index. In the third year, wages would increase one cent an hour for each 0.3 point rise.

7. Additionally, pensions would rise 25% over three years. Goodyear employes, whose pension benefits are lower than those at the other companies, would receive immediate parity before the increases go into effect.

8. The URW didn't win a provision for worker retirement after 30 years service regardless of age, which many union members consider an important issue. Currently, rubber workers can't retire before age 55.

9. Industry sources said the package, if eventually approved by the union bargaining committees, could increase wage and fringe benefits about 36% over three years, assuming a 6% rate of inflation. Roughly half the increase would come in the first year of the contract, one fourth in the second year and one fourth in the third year, the sources said.

"Master" Agreements Sought

10. Separate negotiations are scheduled to resume today and tomorrow between the URW and each of the four tire makers. They will attempt to work out "master" agreements whose economic features will be essentially those worked out last week.

11. Such master agreements, however, also cover unresolved noneconomic issues. Among them are work rules, job security and health and safety issues. After master agreements are signed, the proposals will be submitted to the rank and file for ratification.

12. The package already worked out contains a proposal for a three-person study committee, composed of "distinguished experts in collective bargaining," which is designed to make future strikes less likely. The union, the rubber industry and the government each would

select one member.

Meanwhile, Firestone said it recently increased tire prices about 8% "almost across the board," effective today.

13.

14. Goodrich said it recently increased prices 7% to 20% within the past 30 days.

Recent Price Boosts

15. Goodyear said it already raised automobile-tire prices 12.5% to 16.5%. It also raised truck-tire prices 13% to 17% and raised prices on most farm-vehicle tires about 15.5%. Uniroyal said it raised automobile-tire prices last week 7.5% to 16.5%, some truck-tire prices about 13% and most large off-highway-tire prices about 17%.

16. Spokesmen for several companies attributed the boosts to increased prices for raw materials, distribution and other costs, and anticipated higher labor costs.

17. Despite the recent increases, a Firestone spokesman said: "Obviously, tire prices will have to go up further to cover anticipated costs of the settlement. But for a specific percentage (increase) hasn't been determined."

18. Patrick Ross, president of the Goodrich tire division, said, "Further price increases may be necessary when the current contract negotiations have been completed."

19. A Goodyear spokesman said he didn't know of plans to revise tire prices. A Uniroyal official wouldn't comment on the possibility of further increases.

Analysis

Tires for automobiles, trucks, farm vehicles, and other vehicles are produced by firms in the tire industry. Four major firms, referred to as the Big Four, produce most tire products in the U.S. Although these firms use a variety of inputs to produce tires, only one of these inputs, labor, is discussed in this article. Since the Big Four are the major producers, most rubber workers are employed by these firms. The URW (United Rubber Workers) represents these workers.

Resource price will soon change: rubber workers are to receive annual wage increases of 80¢, 30¢, and 25¢, respectively, for the next three years (par. 5). In addition, fringe benefits will be increased (par 9). Despite these increases, resource quantity is expected to remain unchanged.

The reason for this resource price increase is simple to explain--the union was successful. We can show how this union affected resource supply by constructing Figure 3. We begin with an underlying supply curve; this curve is shown as OS in Figure 3. Next we add the wage rubber workers received before the strike; we will assume this was OC. The effective supply curve

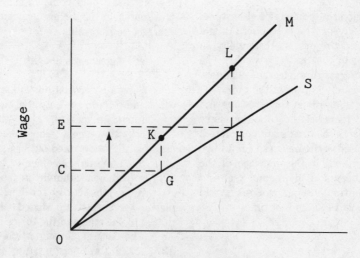

Figure 3

would therefore be CGS and the corresponding marginal factor cost curve would be CGKM.

Once the new contract is accepted, the minimum wage will increase to OE. As a result, the effective supply curve will become EHS and the corresponding MFC curve will be EHLM.

Thus far we have determined that resource price increased because the union was able to shift the lower portion of the supply curve upward. It is interesting to note that the union attempted to shift the entire supply curve to the left by bargaining for an early retirement clause in the current contract (par. 8), but the clause was rejected by the firms.

We have worked our way to Guide Step 5 which requires us to determine if a bilateral monopoly situation exists. On the one hand, the entire supply of rubber workers available to the Big Four firms is represented by a single voice, namely, the URW. On the other hand, the Big Four are the major employers of all rubber workers. Therefore, the URW is a monopolist selling the services of rubber workers to the Big Four, and the Big Four firms act as a monopsonist buying those services. Thus, the situation presented in this article is an excellent example of bilaterial monopoly. Unfortunately, since the strike was virtually settled at the time the article was written, no information about the initial wage positions or the relative strength of the two parties is contained in the article.

Up to this point, only the resource supply curve has been analyzed. Guide Step 9 indicates resource demand must also be considered. Can you find anything in the article which suggests a change in resource demand? Remember, this change will occur if there is a change in either worker productivity or product price.

Two observations about resource demand can be found in paragraph 3, which informs us that all Big Four companies raised product prices during the past few weeks. First, since the firms, not the market, determine tire prices, we know that MRP, not VMP, is the relevant resource demand curve. Second, since product price increased, resource demand shifted to the right, as shown in Figure 4.

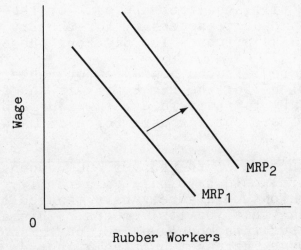

Figure 4

By combining the information developed separately in Figures 3 and 4, we'll create Figure 5. With this figure, we hope to provide an explanation of the change in resource price that just occurred and in addition attempt some predictions about future changes in resource price and quantity.

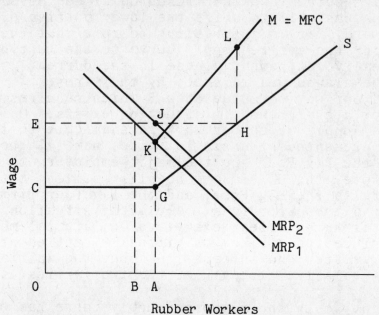

Figure 5

In Figure 3 we assumed a pre-strike wage of OC, making CGS the effective supply curve and CGKM the corresponding marginal factor cost curve. In Figure 4 we used MRP_1 as the resource demand curve for the period prior to the tire price increase. These curves from Figures 3 and 4 have been transferred to Figure 5. Using the intersection of MFC and MRP_1 to determine the number of rubber workers employed prior to the strike, we find an employment level of OA[1].

We can now use our model to explain two items reported in the article. First, the Big Four are about to agree to raise wages. Second, the Big Four recently raised tire prices--some by more than 10 percent. We will show that the size of the wage increase demanded by the union made it necessary for the Big Four either to lay off workers or raise prices. The Big Four chose the latter. The analysis follows.

Assuming OE in Figure 5 is the new wage for rubber workers, can you see the implications for the Big Four? If the tire companies pay this wage when MRP_1 is their relevant resource demand curve, they will be paying their current work force of OA workers more

---

1. Given the construction of the curves, OC happens to be the wage that the firm would have paid voluntarily. You might argue that the union would surely have managed to bargain for a higher wage than that for its members. This argument is probably valid, but this model was set up to show the consequences of the wage increase, not the situation before the current negotiation.

than their MRP. The companies have two alternatives: reduce employment to OB (MFC = MRP_1), or raise tire prices sufficiently to shift MRP out to point J (MFC = MRP_2). Which alternative would you recommend if you were an economic advisor to the Big Four? Before you answer, be sure to recognize that the short- and long-run implications are different.

The trick of raising product price to avoid laying off workers will only work if quantity demanded does not fall. Since quantity demanded probably will not fall in the short run, raising prices is a tempting alternative for firms that have not produced any tires for sixteen weeks.

However, if tire prices increase significantly, but not other prices, quantity demanded will probably fall in the long run. If this occurs, tire companies may either lay off workers or shut down for a period of time to allow inventories to be sold.

This analysis has provided one explanation for the almost simultaneous increase in tire prices and rubber worker wages. It has also predicted that unless other changes occur, the tire price increase could eventually result in less employment for rubber workers and lower tire sales for the Big Four.

AN ARTICLE WITH QUESTIONS

Quick Adjustment: Fast Food Chains Act to Offset the Effects of Minimum-Pay Rise

By PAUL INGRASSIA
Staff Reporter of *The Wall Street Journal*

Fewer Hours, Higher Prices, More Automation Due; But Layoffs Are Avoided

1. HANOVER PARK, Ill.—Cheryl Anders, an 18-year-old part-time hostess at a Kentucky Fried Chicken restaurant here, won't be losing her job after all.

2. Earlier this year, executives in the $16 billion-a-year fast-food industry tried to forestall the increase in the federal minimum wage to $2.65 an hour from $2.30 by warning that many people like Miss Anders would have to be laid off. The increase was enacted anyway, and yet few layoffs are likely.

3. Unions that lobbied for the increase, on the other hand, predicted that people like Miss Anders would get a well-deserved 15% pay increase. And that generally won't be happening, either.

4. Miss Ander's employer, the KFC subsidiary of Heublein Inc., for example, is tightening work schedules at the stores it owns to help offset the effects of the higher wages. In the case of Miss Anders, she will now be working 18 hours a week instead of 23, and earning about $48 a week after Jan. 1, down from the $53 a week she has been averaging.

5. "I don't mind getting fewer hours because I have more time for other things," she says. "But some people in the store don't like it."

Coping With Costs

6. KFC's tighter scheduling is but one example of the steps that fast-food chains are taking to deal with the higher labor costs. Also being considered or implemented are such things as more automotion—and, not surprisingly, higher prices.

7. The fast-food companies aren't the only employers with a lot of workers paid the minimum wage, by any means. The Labor Department estimates that 4.5 million workers will be eligible for the automatic increase to $2.65 an hour on Jan. 1, or about 4.5% of the U.S. labor force. Besides fast-food and other restaurants, the industries feeling the greatest impact will be department and grocery stores, hotels, service stations, cleaners and custodial

services. Low-wage manufacturers such as textile and apparel companies will also be hit, the Labor Department says.

8. The new law calls for further increases in the minimum wage, to $2.90 an hour in 1979, $3.10 in 1980, and $3.35 in 1981. Some States, moreover, have minimums above the federal level.

9. The fast-food industry, which has seen a tripling of sales since 1970, was clearly alarmed by the potential effects of the new pay increase, as most of its employes earn little more than the minimum wage. Last summer, when the legislation was taking shape, executives of the hamburger and chicken chains were forecasting that hundreds of thousands of teen-agers would be thrown out of work.

Shorter Hours Considered

10. But such giants as KFC, McDonald's and Hardee's now say they don't plan any layoffs. Instead, for the fast-food industry and its customers, the net result of the minimum-wage increase will generally be that the late-night hamburger probably will become a little harder to find and a few cents costlier to buy.

11. Not that the pay raise won't cost the U.S. economy any jobs. Even the Carter administration, which strongly backed the increase, estimated it could cost some 90,000 jobs through 1981. But the fast-food chains are planning to avoid layoffs with selective price increases, massive marketing efforts to increase sales volume and technological gains in the kitchen to boost productivity—all on the theory that customers will take more kindly to higher prices than to lousy service.

12. Mostly because of the higher minimum wage, the fast-food industry's total wage costs are expected to rise about 12% next year, industry analysts say. Wages represent about one-fourth of the restaurant's expenses, so a 12% wage increase means a 3% rise in total costs. And that's about how much prices will go up, analysts predict. Jerrico Inc. recently raised prices in its Long John Silver's restaurants by about 2.5%, indicating the prediction is on target.

13. Though price rises may average 3% overall, they won't be that amount on all items. McDonald's, for instance, is considering "where we can raise prices without dropping customer acceptance" according to Edward H. Schmitt, president.

Holding The Line

14. And KFC, beset by flat sales in the last three years, says it won't raise prices at all. The company won't give figures, but it says reducing off-peak work crews has saved more money than the minimum-wage boost will cost—making a price increase unnecessary.

15. Instead of just sending some workers home earlier, as KFC is doing, some companies may actually close shop earlier. "With the minimum wage going up, hours that once were marginally profitable might become unprofitable," says John Toby, a vice president of Jerrico, which is considering closing earlier.

16. Taking another tack, McDonald's has launched a companywide campaign to reduce crew turnover, which now averages three times a year at each restaurant. "Hiring and training costs us money," McDonald's Mr. Schmitt says. "If we can cut down on our turnover, we can reduce a major operating cost."

17. McDonald's and other companies hope the higher minimum wage will bring in more homemakers, who generally don't come and go as quickly as teen-agers and college students. But "housewives feel out of place working with kids," says Donald Trott, a restaurant analyst with Blyth, Eastman Dillon & Co. "Past minimum-wage increases didn't get them to leave their homes to cook hamburgers or chicken."

18. Another cost-cutting gambit is a 1974 minimum-wage law provision that allows a restaurant owner to hire up to six students to work up to 20 hours a week at 85% of the minimum wage, provided their work hours don't amount to more than 10% of a company's total.

19. Because of the six-student limitation, the provision is useless to big employers like the fast-food companies, but it can be attractive to their franchisees. "I hadn't taken advantage of this before, but I plan to now," says Stacy Smith, who owns six Dairy Queen restaurants in Decatur, Ill.

20. Fast-food chains also will try to offset higher costs by boosting sales. Hardee's recently started a series of discount and two-for-one sales, which it hadn't tried before. Many of the promotions will involve its recently introduced roast-beef sandwich. KFC is switching advertising agencies to try to perk up sales.

21. Some fast-food chains are turning to machinery to boost productivity. Indianapolis-based Steak n Shake Inc., for example, has installed new automatic cash registers that it expects to save the chain about $840,000 a year by eliminating mistakes—or almost as much as the extra $1 million Steak n Shake expects to pay in higher wages.

22. Hardee's is getting new cash registers that will be tied into a computer, to track the stores busiest hours and permit more-efficient scheduling.

23. Bishop Buffets Inc., a chain of 20 cafeterias in the Midwest, is testing overnight slow-cookers to reduce early morning work to prepare roast beef. The idea is to have some early-shift workers start at 7 a.m. instead of at 6 a.m., cutting their work weeks by five hours. Bishop employes now working 45 hours a week at the minimum wage would get only an extra $2.50 a week—$106 compared with $103.50—after the minimum wage goes up and their hours go down.

24. The quest for labor-saving machines will continue. "Higher labor costs intensify the search for productivity, and we'll be putting more money into research," says McDonald's Mr. Schmitt. "But I can't tell you that tomorrow we'll be installing machines that cook hamburgers without us having to turn them. It just doesn't work that way."

132

Questions

1. What is the purpose of this article?
2. What products are being produced?
3. What resources are being used as inputs?
4. What firms demand the resources and who supplies them?
5. Are resource price and/or resources usage changing?
6. Are the changes you found in question #5 the result of changes in supply, in demand, or in both supply and demand?
7. If supply has changed, what caused the change and what type of change occurred?
8. Does any type of bilateral monopoly situation exist?
9. Has resource demand changed? Why and in what way has it changed?
10. Can you use the information you have found to explain the changes which have taken place in resource price and quantity? Can you make any predictions about future changes in resource price and quantity?

AN ARTICLE FOR STUDENT ANALYSIS: OVERVIEW

Before you begin your analysis of this article, review Concept 5 on input substitution and cost minimization found in the Chapter 12. This article presents a situation where the higher wages appear to be causing growers to substitute machines for farm laborers.

Coast Farm Workers Begin Fight on Machine Harvesting

By ROBERT LINDSEY
Special to *The New York Times*

The New York Times *(Nov. 18, 1977). © 1976 by The New York Times Company. Reprinted by permission.*

1. LOS ANGELES, Sept. 17— A curious battle of man against the machine is shaping up in the rich agricultural valleys of California. Having won wars against growers and the teamsters' union, Cesar Chavez's United Farm Workers has opened fire on mechanical harvesting machines, which are fomenting the same kind of revolution in agriculture here that the assembly line prompted in Detroit 60 years ago.

2. To a large extent, the improved, wages won only recently by farm workers after almost a decade of strife, have created a backlash, accelerating the development of machines that will put more and more farm workers out of jobs.

3. University of California agricultural researchers, who have a world reputation for innovation in farming, now find themselves under attack for helping develop machines that can reduce manpower needs in the fields and automatically pick, sort and otherwise harvest a wide range of crops in California, the nation's richest agricultural state.

4. A special investigation of the university, focusing on the role of agribusiness interests in supporting some agricultural research, is being conducted by the state's Auditor General, partly in response to pressure from organized farm workers and sympathetic state legislators.

'Human Needs' Given Precedence

5. Lieut. Gov. Mervyn Dymally, noting that electronic sorting machines introduced this year in the harvesting of tomatoes would displace more than 11,000 farm workers in 1977, has demanded that the university end its research in agricultural automation. "Human needs" of farm workers must be given precedence," he said.

6. At a recent convention of the United Farm Workers in Fresno, what the organization called a "rapid and reckless" trend toward mechanization was denounced as perhaps the most significant single threat to farm workers.

133

7. If unchecked, the union founded by Mr. Chavez contends, mechanical harvesting equipment would lead to elimination of 100,000 of the 250,000 farm labor jobs in California over the next decade.

8. In a resolution at the close of the convention, delegates said that mechanical harvesters were being developed "solely for the purpose of increasing the p... "its of corporate growers at the expense of the farm workers" and demanded a moratorium on future research in agricultural mechanization until it was assured that the interests of farm workers would be protected.

9. Although it is too soon to determine if the growing pressure will have any effect, remarks by some University of California agricultural researchers indicate they have become more timid in undertaking some new mechanization projects. At the same time, they say that if they drop out, private business researchers will take over the role.

10. Organized agricultural interests assert that without increased mechanization the United States would lose parts of the agriculture industry to low-wage areas of the world, particularly Mexico, Central and South America and the Orient. And, they contend that increasing field workers' productivity results in more jobs in food canneries and allied food industries.

11. "Mechanization in agriculture hasn't reduced the number of workers in the labor force," Frank Heringer, president of the California Farm Bureau Federation, said. Since the universities developed a mechanical harvester in the 1960's, he said, the amount of acreage in tomatoes in California has doubled. The same number of people are employed, he added, "and they have less strenuous jobs."

12. The new tomato sorting system, which employs electronic sensors to determine the color, ripeness and condition of newly picked tomatoes, has reduced from 20 to four or five the number of people needed on each tomato harvesting machine.

13. The confrontation of man and machine is expected to heat up still more soon. The University of California and the United States Department of Agriculture recently developed the first promising lettuce harvesting machines, which use an electronic eye to inspect a head of lettuce as it grows in the field, determines its ripeness, and—if the time is right—orders it cut off and taken by conveyor belt to a hopper.

14. In its trials so far, the system has worked so fast that existing packing systems cannot deal with it efficiently, but this problem is being researched.

15. The machine, which costs more than $60,000, has yet to have a major impact on lettuce production, but its existence looms over future negotiations between lettuce growers and the United Farm Workers.

16. Mechanization is far from a new phenomenon in farming. Harvesting machines, combines and other machines have long cut manpower needs in production of wheat and other grains. But, only fairly recently has technology produced machines that can harvest soft, easy-to-bruise crops such as tomatoes, lettuce, peaches and prunes.

17. Research by scientists at the University of California's Davis campus, near Sacramento, is generally regarded as one reason why California, which has only 2 percent of the nation's farms, produces about 9 percent of its total farm income, although another reason is the prevalence here of large corporate-owned farms.

18. In recent years, economic motives have increasingly supplanted the fear of labor shortages as the main thrust behind the drive to automate. As Mr. Chavez and the teamsters' union (which this year bowed out of their long, bitter competition to organize farm workers) sign more and more farm workers to labor contracts, the wages of farm laborers began to climb to more than $3 an hour.

134

14

International Trade

Alex watches as his friend, Gary, drives up in a new car. As Gary
climbs out, Alex greets him, "I see you bought yourself a new car!
An Audi Fox! Who makes these?"
  "They are made in Germany," replies Gary.
  "Germany!" exclaims Alex. "You are just making work for the
Germans when you buy one of these. Why don't you buy an American
car and make work for Americans?"
  "I did make work for Americans--myself," answers Gary. "The
company I work for sells a lot of its products to Germany. If
Americans don't buy from Germany, Germans won't buy from America,
and then I'll be out of a job."
  Alex's argument against international trade reveals one of a
number of popular misconceptions that exist in this area of
economics. Although a few situations warrant restricting
international trade, in most cases trade benefits both parties.
When nations trade, each is able to specialize in what it does
best. In this chapter, we will show that, in theory, trade will
provide more goods and services for everyone. In addition, we
will examine some of the various issues and situations that
complicate the flow of trade.

CHECKLIST

Definitions of New Terms

1. Absolute advantage--a nation has an absolute advantage when
    its real costs of production (i.e., its costs in terms of
    units of resources used) are less than those of another
    country.
2. Comparative advantage--a nation has a comparative advantage in
    producing a product when the opportunity cost of producing the
    product in that nation is less than another nation's opportu-

135

nity cost of producing that product. Therefore, comparative advantage is based upon a nation's relative internal efficiency.

3. Infant Industry--a domestic industry that has just begun production and, consequently, may have higher operating costs than a well-established foreign industry.

4. Quota--a specific limit on either the number of units or the total value of products that may be imported.

5. Revenue tariff--an excise tax or duty placed upon imported products for the purpose of raising revenue.

6. Protective tariff--an excise tax or duty placed upon imported products to shield domestic producers from foreign competition.

7. Trigger prices--a unique method of implementing protective tariffs that was devised by the U.S. in 1978 to deal with steel imports. If imported steel is sold below the trigger price, special tariffs may be imposed and investigations may be launched.

Concepts

1. Economic arguments for trade
    International trade is advantageous because it is simply an application of the principle of specialization and exchange. When any individual unit--be it a person, state, or nation--concentrates its efforts on what it does best and then exchanges the goods or services it produces for those of other specialists, everyone can have more goods and services. A simple illustration will be used to explain this principle. Assume two neighbors each have a small 10 square foot garden plot for growing tomatoes and peppers. Figure 1(A) presents the productivity per square foot for these two garden plots. Ms. Greenthumb can grow 15 tomatoes and 9 peppers per square foot; Mr. Brownleaf can grow 10 tomatoes and 8 peppers per square foot.

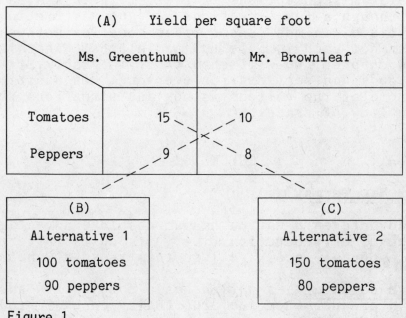

Figure 1

A. The principle of absolute advantage: Ms. Greenthumb has an absolute advantage in growing both tomatoes and peppers; she can grow more of either than Mr. Brownleaf can.

B. The principle of comparative advantage: Although Mr. Brownleaf's garden is less productive than that of Ms. Greenthumb, Mr. Brownleaf has a comparative advantage over his neighbor in growing peppers. Correspondingly, Ms. Greenthumb has a comparative advantage in growing tomatoes. One way to explain this comparative advantage is by comparing the opportunity cost of growing peppers. If Greenleaf grows peppers instead of tomatoes, her unit yield per square foot drops by 40 percent. On the other hand, Brownleaf's yield drops only 20 percent when he switches to peppers. Another way to explain this is to compare the results of Alternatives 1 and 2 in Figures 1(B) and 1(C). Alternative 1(A) has Greenthumb specializing in peppers; Brownleaf in tomatoes. Together they produce a total of 190 units of produce. If they switch their specializations, as shown in Alternative 2, they can produce a total of 230 units. Therefore, Ms. Greenthumb should grow only tomatoes; then when she picks her tomatoes, she should trade some for some of Mr. Brownleaf's peppers. It is easy to show that after trading each will have more of each vegetable than they would have if they each grew all of their own vegetables.[1]

2. Economic arguments against trade

The gardening example can be used to explore some of the following more popular arguments used to oppose international trade:

A. Infant industry argument: Mr. Brownleaf just started gardening last year and wants to grow both tomatoes and peppers so that he can develop gardening skills and prepare his soil for growing both vegetables. He is not ready to compete with the advanced gardening skills and superior growing soil of Ms. Greenthumb. A similar argument has been used by some U.S. firms to gain protection from foreign competition. The first problem with this argument is that we do not want to protect firms unless they are producing a product for which the U.S. has a comparative advantage. After this issue has been settled and protection is advised, the U.S. should select the most economically efficient method and length of protection.

B. Protect domestic jobs: Mr. Brownleaf's son grows the tomatoes; his daughter grows the peppers. Consequently, if Brownleaf "imports" all his tomatoes, his son will be out

---

1. There are some trading ratios (or terms of trade) that would make both neighbors better off. One such ratio is 1 pepper for 1.3 tomatoes. On the other hand, there are also trading ratios that would provide greater benefits to one neighbor at the expense of the other. For example, if the trading ratio were 1:1, Brownleaf would be better off, Greenthumb worse off, than if each grew their own.

of a job! Following this same logic, if the U.S. imports
footwear, some domestic shoemakers will be forced out of
their jobs. The fact of the matter is that imports offer
some benefits but result in some costs. We can point to
at least three benefits: consumers can buy lower-priced
footwear, the domestic industry is forced to be more
competitive, and exporters are able to export products for
which the U.S. has a comparative advantage. These benefits
must be compared with the economic, social, and political
costs of domestic jobs and sales that will be lost.
C. Maintain military self-sufficiency: If Mr. Brownleaf
   gets into an argument with his neighbor, ending their
   relationship, he will not get any tomatoes. Consequently,
   since Brownleaf's recipes require tomatoes, he may decide
   to grow some of his own tomatoes, just in case! So too,
   the U.S. may decide to protect some domestic producers from
   foreign competition because their products are vital to the
   military. If certain products are vital, the problem is
   to decide on the most efficient method and level of
   protection.
D. Protect high domestic wages: Some argue that if products
   produced by low-paid foreign labor are imported, U.S. wages
   will be driven down. It is easier to argue that a country
   with low wages simply has a comparative advantage in
   producing products that are labor intensive.
3. Economic measures used to discourage trade:
   A. Protective tariff: The economic effect of a protective
      tariff is shown in Figure 2. In the absence of imports,
      domestic supply and demand would set price OC, but we will
      begin by assuming that foreign competition has forced the
      pre-tariff domestic price down equal to the world price,
      OA. At this price, domestic producers sell OE units,
      foreign producers sell EH units. If a tariff of AB is
      added to imports, domestic price rises to OB. Domestic
      producers now sell OF units and foreign producers sell FG
      units. Tariff revenue collected by the government will be
      AB times FG units.

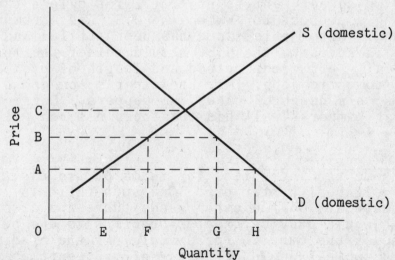

Figure 2

138

B. Import quotas: Quotas and tariffs both reduce imports, but a quota does not bring in any government revenue. The economic effect of a quota expressed in units is shown in Figure 3. We begin with Figure 3(A), which shows the supply of imports when an import quota of 100 units exists. Assuming price is OA, the supply of imports will be horizontal out to 100 units, then it will become verticle. Figure 2(B) begins with the domestic supply curve. At price OA, domestic producers will supply 200 units. Since foreign producers will add 100 units, total supply at price OA will be 300 units--this is shown by constructing a total supply curve, S'. S' is 100 units to the right of S at all prices. Consequently, if price rises to OB, domestic producers will sell 250 units of the 350 units that will be sold in the U.S.

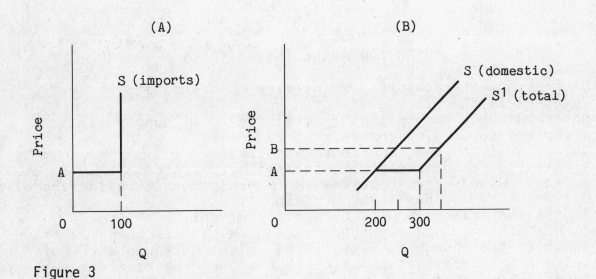

Figure 3

4. Economic measures used to encourage trade
   A. Subsidies to domestic firms to help them meet foreign competition: Government can grant subsidies to domestic firms, thereby making it easier for them to compete with imports or improving their export opportunities. Figure 4 shows the economic effect of a subsidy to firms selling in the domestic market. In effect the subsidy lowers costs, resulting in a shift to the right of domestic supply from S to S'. If the world price is OA, domestic producers will increase their sales from OE to OF and imports will be reduced from EG to FG.
   B. Subsidies to domestic producers and employees displaced by imports: One way to take advantage of another country's comparative advantage without requiring one industry and its employees to bear the full effect of the resulting costs is to provide government subsidies for retraining, relocation, etc. The U.S. provides this type of subsidy if the industry can prove it has been displaced by imports.

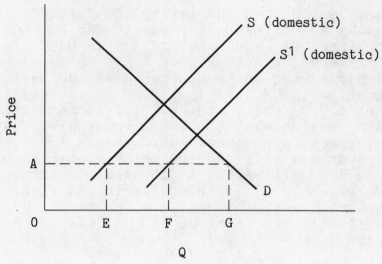

Figure 4

GUIDE FOR ANALYZING ARTICLES

1. Determine what countries, industries, and products are
    involved in the discussion.
2. Determine what proportion of total demand or supply is
    accounted for by international trade.
3. Determine if anyone is encouraging trade.
    A. Are the reasons economic, social, or political?
    B. What methods are suggested as a means of encouraging trade?
4. Determine if anyone is discouraging trade.
    A. Are the reasons economic, social, or political?
    B. What methods are suggested as a means of discouraging trade?
5. Consider the economic, social, and political aspects of this
    trade and determine the policy that offers the greatest net
    benefit for the U.S.

Articles

AN ANALYZED ARTICLE: OVERVIEW

Footwear imports have attracted the attention of a wide variety of
U.S. citizens, companies, and organizations. Some favor importing
footwear, others are opposed. The controversy discussed in this
article began a year earlier when President Ford decided against
restricting footwear imports. At the time of the article,
President Carter had to decide whether to continue that policy.

Controversy Over Trade: Carter Must Decide Soon on Strengthening Import Curbs on Shoes, Sugar, and TV Sets

By RICHARD J. LEVINE
Staff Reporter of *The Wall Street Journal*

1. WASHINGTON—Along with advice on abstruse subjects like arms control and Mid-east peace formulas, Jimmy Carter is getting an earful about shoes.

2. From the governors of 26 states and three territories comes a petition demanding that he "take action now to provide effective import relief to the footwear industry before more jobs are lost, more plants are closed and more communities are afflicted by the current tidal wave of footwear imports."

3. From AFL-CIO President George Meany comes a warning that unless the White House imposes tough restrictions on imports, the U.S. shoe industry faces "slow but certain death."

4. From the study commissioned by U.S. shoe retailers comes the opposing message that restrictions could cost American consumers an added $500 million a year, making it more difficult for consumers to "stretch their limited resources."

5. This verbal cross fire arises from well-organized rival campaigns to influence Mr. Carter on an issue with delicate economic, political and diplomatic implications: whether to protect the U.S. economy from imports—not only of shoes but also of sugar, steel and television sets.

6. For months, a series of cases involving demands by U.S. producers for protection from foreign goods has been moving toward the President's desk through the complicated machinery of the U.S. International Trade Commission and the courts; he must begin making decisions within a few weeks. Senior administration officials are concerned that these cases, if mishandled, could lead to a wave of retaliatory protectionism abroad or nasty battles with Congress and organized labor.

7. "Government agencies tend to look at these as narrow, technical decisions," a White House official says. "But the U.S. has a special role in the world, and one has to understand what forces would be unleashed."

8. Major U.S. allies are also worried about the protectionist pressures building here and abroad. "I feel deep anxiety about the social and political consequences for the world if we slide once again into protectionism or a breakup of the world economy into rival trade blocs," Japanese Prime Minister Takeo Fukuda said at the National Press Club yesterday. "Surely we have learned by now that such a course can only exacerbate world economic conditions."

The Shoe Case

9. The withering cross-pressures being exerted on foreign-trade issues stand out vividly in the shoe case—a problem that President Carter inherited from his predecessor. Last April, Mr. Ford, looking for a way to put his free-trade hat back on after deciding to impose quotas on specialty-steel imports, came out against restricting imports of footwear. Such restraints, he said, would be "contrary to the U.S. policy of promoting the development of an open, nondiscriminatory and fair world economic system."

10. The Ford rejection of import restrictions on shoes angered some members of Congress. And the Senate Finance Committee last year directed the trade commission to undertake a new investigation of whether the domestic producers were entitled to "import relief" under the 1974 trade act.

11. In January, the commission called for a combined quota and tariff arrangement that would allow 265.6 million pairs of shoes a year from about 20 countries to enter the U.S. at current duties, which average about

10%; imports above the quota would be subject to a duty of 40% for three years, the rate dropping to 30% in the fourth year, to 20% in the fifth year and lapsing thereafter.

12. That put the case in Mr. Carter's lap, and he has been getting conflicting advice from all sides ever since.

13. Both organized labor and domestic shoe producers want the President to adopt stronger restrictions than the commission recommended. In a letter to Mr. Carter, AFL-CIO President Meany contended that a direct quota system "would be the most effective and least expensive remedy for workers, employers, consumers and taxpayers."

14. However, American shoe retailers maintain that quotas would be self-defeating in the end. Import curbs, says the Volume Footwear retailers of America, "would trigger inflationary price increases, would impair our international regulations and could cause a net loss in American jobs."

Estimating The Bill

15. The trade-commission staff has estimated that American consumers could pay an extra $190 million a year if the tariff-rate quota system is put into effect. But shoe retailers and consumer groups content that the bill for import restrictions could end up much higher.

16. Andrew Brimmer, the former Federal Reserve Board governor who now is a Washington-based financial consultant, recently produced a study for retailers showing that the additional bill could come to $500 million rather than $190 million a year.

17. The solution, as the retailers see it, is federal "adjustment assistance" to shoe workers and companies hurt by imports; this includes retraining and relocation aid to workers and technical assistance and loans to companies switching to new lines.

18. But the unions, the shoe producers and their supporters in Congress argue that such help is inadequate. "Trade-adjustment assistance is a dole," says Sen. William Hathaway, a Maine Democrat. "It doesn't create jobs for the 26,000 shoe workers now unemployed," he says, and confirms it is a costly and time-consuming process that leads to loans at usurious interest rates."

19. Caught in the middle of this debate, the administration is trying to find a solution by working quietly with all the partiess. Early this month, the administration's economic-policy group, headed by Treasury Secretary Michael Blumenthal, met with representatives of industry and labor and with interested Senators.

20. At that meeting, participants say, the administration officials didn't provide any strong clues to their thinking. However, economic adviser Schultze did say at one point, "I'm not going to use the dirty word adjustment assistance," indicating that the Carter economic team is well aware of the political hazards of such an approach.

21. If President Carter should reject or significantly soften the trade commission's shoe-import recommendation, he might face a fight with Congress. But a congressional move to override the President would be even more likely if he veered away from the proposed tariffs on TV sets. "That's where the real crunch could occur," suggests a top AFL-CIO official, who notes that unions in the electronics industry are much larger and more politically powerful than in the shoe industry.

Analysis

U.S. shoe retailers do not want to restrict footwear imports. They argue that if the proposed tariff-quota plan is enacted, U.S. consumers will pay $500 million a year more for footwear. U.S. allies also oppose restrictions on imports. They share the concern expressed by the Prime Minister of Japan, who warned that the U.S. must resist those who seek to erect trade walls because "such a course can only exacerbate world economic conditions" (par. 8).

Those who support trade suggest having the government provide federal adjustment assistance to compensate those shoe workers and companies hurt by imports (par. 17). In this way, shoe workers and shoe companies could relocated into activities in which the U.S. continues to have a comparative advantage.

On the other side of the issue, we find a varied group of vocal and politically powerful opponents of footwear imports. The first opposition--outside of the opposition from the industry itself-- came from some members of Congress who were angered because President Ford accepted restrictions on specialty-steel imports, but rejected restrictions on footwear imports. Congress called for a trade commission study. This resulted in a proposed quota and tariff plan. During the first four years, the plan would produce the import supply curve shown in Figure 5. A maximum 265.6 million pairs of shoes could be imported at the current 10 percent tariff. The price to American consumers would be the foreign price, P_F, plus 10 percent. All additional imports would be assessed at a 40 percent tariff (par. 11). After four years, the 40 percent tariff would be reduced. The trade commission staff estimated the cost of this plan at $190 million in added footwear cost (par. 15).

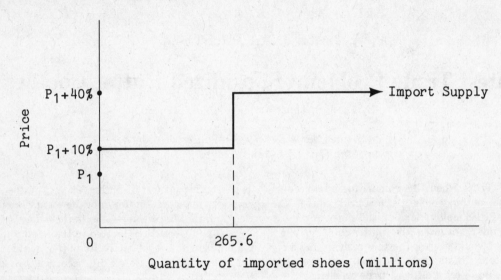

Figure 5

The governors of 26 states and 3 territories also oppose footwear imports (par. 2). They have petitioned Carter to act to save American jobs and companies. Labor is also opposed: AFL-CIO President George Meany warns that foreign footwear competition will result in "slow but certain death" for the U.S. footwear industry (par. 3).

As for the trade adjustment assistance plan suggested by the supporters of free trade, opponents argue that this plan is wholly inadequate because "it doesn't create jobs for the 26,000 shoe workers now unemployed" (par. 18).

In short, footwear imports have created unemployment, and, if unchecked, may cause the demise of the U.S. shoe industry. On the other hand, using the proposed plan to support the shoe industry will cost U.S. consumers between $190 and $500 million annually in added shoe costs. In addition, we may jeopardize other trading possibilities.

Before we can truely decide on the net benefits in this situation, we need to know the full economic and social costs of relocating workers and companies. Economic costs include such things as retraining, retooling, moving, etc. But, in addition to these costs, we must also include the social costs that result from uprooting families from relatives and friends, from forcing older workers to learn new skills, etc. And, finally, President Carter will most likely add the political cost of losing the support of the shoe industry and its friends.

When putting all this together, President Carter should adjust for a political bias that probably favors the footwear industry over consumers as a group. This bias exists because each individual associated with the footwear industry has more to lose than any single consumer has to gain. Think of it--would you be more likely to write your Congressman if you were a footwear employee about to lose your job because of imports, or if you were a consumer who might be forced to pay a higher price for shoes?

AN ARTICLE WITH QUESTIONS

Latest Trade Problem: Subsidized Butter Cookies

By The L.A. Times-Washington Post Service

Buffalo Evening News *(Dec. 19, 1977), Reprinted by permission of the Times-Post News Service.*

1. WASHINGTON—When it comes to international trade, the butter cookie is a David among the Goliaths of steel, color television and shoes.

2. And no one, not even the butter-cookie makers themselves, would suggest the tiny industry has a big enough stone in its sling to knock off the steel industry as the world's most difficult trade problem.

3. Nevertheless, the rich little Danish-type butter cookie that comes in the shiny blue tin or foil-wrapped in the blue box, is a big problem right up there with steel.

4. By Dec. 28, the U.S. Treasury must decide whether to slap special, contervailing duties on the butter cookies this nation imports from Denmark.

5. The decision threatens to have a wide-ranging impact, not only on the narrow concerns of the butter cookie industry, but on the complicated series of subsidies Europe uses to make its "Common Agricultural Policy" work as well as on the four-year-old multi-lateral trade talks that finally seem to be getting untracked in Geneva.

* * *

6. It's not that the butter cookie industry is a big one. While the United States imports hundreds of millions of dollars of color television sets a year, it buys little more than $6 million of Danish butter cookies. The American Deer Park Baking Co. makes the remaining $2 million.

7. Hundreds of thousands of Americans alone owe their livelihoods to the steel industry. At best several thousand workers across the world account for every Danish butter cookie sold here and about 150 work at Deer Park.

8. There are lots of "Danish" assortments around, but they are usually less expensive and—to hear cookie buffs tell it—are made with inferior ingredients such as shortening instead of butter. The key to the high quality cookie is the word "butter" not the word "Danish" and the rich morsels sell for about $4 a tin these days.

9. When Deer Park—located in Hammonton, N.J.—begin to market aggressively its butter cookie about eight years ago, sales took off, according to vice president William Crothers.

* * *

10. But, recently, as the price of U.S. butter has soared, sales that had doubled every year leveled off. "We cannot compete with the Danes on price because the European Community's common agricultural policy subsidizes the butter the Danish cookie makers use," Mr. Crothers said.

11. The Treasury Department also found that the European Community gave export rebates on the eggs, flour and sugar the Danish cookie makers used.

12. "Eight years ago, we paid 40 cents a pound for butter, Now it is $1.06. They're (the Danes) probably not paying more than 30 cents," Mr. Crothers said.

13. The Treasury Department already has decided that the rebates Danish manufacturers get as well as access to low-priced butter are indeed a "bounty or grant" that the nation's countervailing duty laws prohibit.

* * *

14. If the department does impose such duties (in 1975, it saw fit not to in a similar case, that of table quality Emmenthaler cheese from Switzerland), Europeans are fearful that it could trigger similar complaints against a host of processed foods Europeans ship here every year.

15. When a European trade team was here last month, it took some time out to talk about the little cookie decision. An attack on internal European policies

could make it difficult to negotiate an international code on agricultural policies and subsidies, already the most harrowing part of the Geneva negotiations.

16. But these matters of international diplomacy don't sway Mr. Crothers.

"All I want is a fair shake," Mr. Crothers said. "Any

17. product that is subsidized by a foreign government should have the amount of that subsidy added to its price by a countervailing duty.

"If I sell my cookie in Denmark, I've got to face a 35

18. percent tariff. Here they come in at 3 percent. That's not fair."

Questions

1. What countries, industries, and products are involved in the trade discussed in this article?
2. How significant are the imports relative to U.S. supply?
3. Who feels this trade should be encouraged? Why?
4. Why should this trade be restricted?
5. Summarize the economic, social, and political issues involved.
6. Should the countervailing tariff be imposed?

AN ARTICLE FOR STUDENT ANALYSIS: OVERVIEW

This article discusses the implications of a new type of tariff plan--trigger prices--for steel producers and consumers (see Definitions of New Terms). After analyzing this article, you might compare the economic effect of trigger-prices with that of the other trade restriction plans discussed in the first two articles.

Steel Importers Fear Trigger-Price Plan by U.S. May Mean a "Practical Embargo"

By DAVID IGNATIUS
Staff Reporter of *The Wall Street Journal*

1. A leading spokesman for steel importers warned that the trigger prices announced earlier this week by the Treasury Department could mean a "practical embargo" on foreign steel and a "windfall" for domestic producers.

2. Kurt Orban, president of the American Institute for Imported Steel and head of a major importing concern, said in an interview yesterday that at the $330 a ton average trigger price level set by the Carter administration, steel imports are likely to drop sharply in 1978. He said that such imports could plunge to between five million tons and 10 million tons, or about half the estimated 1977 total of 18 million to 19 million tons.

3. While the Carter administration's plan clearly has upset importers and free-trade advocates in Washington, major domestic steelmakers continued to withhold formal endorsement of the plan. Most steel companies, including industry leader U.S. Steel Corp. and No. 2-ranked Bethlehem Steel Corp., continued to study the trigger-price data yesterday.

4. A tentative expression of support for the plan came from Armco Steel Corp., the nation's seventh-largest producer in 1976. In Middletown Ohio, Armco's chairman, William Verity, said the partial list of trigger prices released last Tuesday reflected "a serious effort by the administration to achieve its stated objective of reducing imports to a level of 12% to 14% of the domestic market."

5. Other steelmakers, including Republic Steel Corp. and Inland Steel Co., said they couldn't evaluate the trigger-price plan until the government announces the minimum charges it will post for "extras" on steel imports for special treatment or handling.

6. Strong criticism of the trigger-price approach is expected soon in a study by the staff of the Federal Trade Commission in Washington. FTC sources said

145

yesterday that the authors of the steel study believed that trigger prices "weren't a desirable import-control device."

7. By raising the cost of steel sold here, the system could cost domestic consumers "on the order of $1 billion annually," these sources said.

8. FTC sources added that the study—in preparation for two years and expected to be released soon—also rebuts the domestic industry's case that high-import levels have resulted from systematic dumping by subsidized foreign producers. Instead, the sources said, the study argues that import levels generally appear to reflect cost advantages abroad.

9. Mr. Orban, chairman and president of Kurt Orban Co., a steel-importing concern based in Wayne, N.J., said the trigger-price system could "wipe out" some independent importers and brokers. He said that the system wouldn't allow importers much spread between their steel-buying costs and selling prices.

10. He predicted that even after the average 5.5% price increases for domestic steel, which will take effect beginning next month, foreign mills will still have difficulty wooing customers. The trigger-price system will mean that foreign steel will sell at an average discount of only 5% below the new domestic list prices, he added.

11. "With a 5% differential, it would seem to me that very little imported steel will be bought or sold" unless a domestic shortage develops, Mr. Orban said. He said that a saving of 10% below domestic prices has generally been required to lure buyers to foreign mills.

12. Mr. Orban said that "until the dust has settled"—after at least six to eight weeks—we don't see anyone wanting to buy" foreign steel at the trigger-price levels.

13. The importer said that there wouldn't be any "sudden drop" in imports during the first quarter, because of orders already placed for first quarter delivery. First quarter imports, he predicted, would total three million to four million tons, compared with 3.3 million tons a year ago.

Exchange Rates and the Value of the Dollar

Like many Americans, Mrs. Sibley enjoys watching the national news each evening before dinner. Recently she started noticing that each evening the broadcaster would report what was happening to the value of the dollar. She really didn't pay much attention to what was being said until one evening she heard that the value of the dollar was at an all-time low. Being a senior citizen, she found this news disconcerting since most of her wealth was in her savings account. She wondered whether she was going to be in financial trouble. The next day she made an appointment with her local banker.

"What should I do?!" she frantically asked her banker. "Will I have to move into a cheaper apartment?"

"Calm down, Mrs. Sibley," her banker replied. "Things aren't as bad as they look. You see, the dollar has essentially two values. The first value depends on the amount of domestic goods it can buy. Your rent, food, and most of your clothes are domestically produced, so that if their prices don't rise faster than your pension checks, you should be okay. The second value of the dollar depends on the amount of foreign currency it can buy. Since you need foreign currency to buy foreign goods, if your dollars buy less foreign currency, they'll buy less foreign goods. When they talk about the dollar losing its value, they are generally referring to its value with respect to purchasing foreign currency and foreign goods. Since you don't buy many foreign goods, the drop in the value of the dollar shouldn't be too harmful to you."

"I think I understand," Mrs. Sibley responded and then perceptively asked, "But won't the price of my oil go up?"

"Yes, it is quite possible," her banker replied, "but remember you won't be hurt as much as people who like to buy foreign cars or take vacations in Europe."

Feeling more assured, Mrs. Sibley left her bank to return home. On her way, she remembered that she had neglected to ask her banker what caused the value of the dollar to rise and fall in the first place. Rather than making a return visit and taking more of her banker's time, she decided to find the answer by herself. She bought a large calendar and each day kept track of the value of the dollar and the reasons given for any changes taking place. After about three weeks she noticed some patterns, and by the end of a month she could predict fairly accurately how certain events would affect the value of the dollar. Although she didn't realize it at the time, Mrs. Sibley was also learning quite a bit about supply and demand while watching the rise and fall of the value of the dollar. This was because the present international monetary system allows the value of different currencies to change according to supply and demand conditions. Since you already know a lot about supply and demand, you should be able to analyze articles on exchange rates and the value of the dollar without having to buy yourself a large calendar. Nevertheless, before doing so there will be some new terms and concepts to learn. These will be the main focus of this chapter, along with a list of the different shifts in supply and demand you will most often encounter.

CHECKLIST

Definitions of New Terms

1. Exports--the sale of goods to foreign purchasers.
2. Imports--the purchase of goods from foreign sellers.
3. Appreciation--the rise in the value of a currency.
4. Depreciation--the fall in the value of a currency.
5. Balance of Payments--a statement describing a country's international transactions.
6. Balance of Trade--a term describing a country's international trade position.
7. Fixed Exchange Rates--an international monetary mechanism which guarantees that exchange rates will remain unchanged.
8. Flexible Exchange Rates--an international monetary mechanism which allows exchange rates to vary as demand and supply conditions change.
9. Devaluation--the intentional lowering of the exchange value of a currency when fixed exchange rates are operating.
10. Foreign Exchange--foreign currency.
11. International Reserves--foreign currency held by central banks.
12. Reflation--inflating one's economy in order to cure balance of payments surpluses.
13. Trade Surplus--a surplus in the balance of trade occurs when exports are greater than imports.
14. Trade Deficit--a deficit in the balance of trade occurs when imports are greater than exports.
15. Key Currency--a currency which most countries accept as payment in international transactions.
16. Float--letting exchange rates fluctuate according to demand and supply conditions.
17. Dirty Float--when a country interferes with the value of a currency by becoming a demander or supplier of that currency.

This will often occur when a country does not want its currency to appreciate in fear of losing some of its exports.

Concepts

1. Suppose a United States company wants to buy something from a French company. Since the U.S. company has dollars and the French company wants francs, a mechanism for exchanging dollars for francs must be available in order for this transaction to take place. One of the important parts of this mechanism is a means of determining how many francs one dollar will buy. The number of dollars one franc will buy or the number of francs one dollar will buy is called the exchange rate between dollars and francs. If the exchange rate is one dollar = 5 francs, then the price of one franc to an American is twenty cents, and one can buy five francs for one dollar. Likewise, the price of one dollar to the French is five francs.

2. The effects of exchange rate changed on trade: The exchange rate between two currencies is very important because it has a large effect on the amount of imports and exports a country will have. If, for example, the exchange rate is 1 dollar = 5 francs, a French shirt valued at 20 francs will cost an American $4 to buy. If the exchange rate were 1 dollar = 4 francs, the same 20 franc shirt would not cost an American $5. Likewise, if 1 dollar = 10 francs, the shirt would cost an American $2. Thus a change in the exchange rate can make the purchase of the shirt more or less attractive to an American. Since the American demand for the French shirt is downward sloping, it's reasonable to expect that as the dollar becomes more valuable (one dollar buys more francs), our imports will rise, and as the dollar becomes less valuable (one dollar buys less francs), our imports will fall. The same analysis holds true for French people who want to buy American shirts. As the franc becomes more valuable in relation to U.S. currency, French people will import more American shirts, and as the franc becomes less valuable, French people will import fewer American shirts. In summary,

If	Then	Causing
The U.S. dollar appreciates	Foreign currency depreciates	Exports to go down and imports to go up
The U.S. dollar depreciates	Foreign currency appreciates	Exports to go up and imports to go down

3. Since exchange rates are merely the price of one currency in terms of another currency, exchange rates will be determined by the demand and supply of the two currencies. The demand and supply of the two currencies (say dollars and francs) are related in the following manner.
    A. If people want dollars they must be willing to give up francs. Therefore, the demand for dollars is the same as the supply of francs.
    B. If people want to get rid of dollars in order to purchase

francs, it means that the supply of dollars is the same as the demand for francs.

4. How the value of the dollar changes: Unlike in the past when exchange rates were fixed, the present international monetary system allows exchange rates to fluctuate or float according to market conditions. Therefore the value of the dollar will change in the following ways.

   A. If United States exports are rising, and/or foreign investment in the United States is increasing, the demand for the dollar is increasing, and the value of the dollar is rising.

   B. If United States exports are falling, and/or foreign investment in the United States is falling, the demand for the dollar is decreasing, and the value of the dollar is falling.

   C. If United States imports are rising, and/or United States investment in foreign countries is increasing, the supply of the dollar is increasing, and the value of the dollar is falling.

   D. If United States imports are falling, and/or United States investment in foreign countries is decreasing, the supply of the dollar is decreasing, and the value of the dollar is rising.

   E. If it is expected that the value of the dollar will rise, the demand for the dollar will rise, the supply of the dollar will decrease, and the value of the dollar will increase.

   F. If it is expected that the value of the dollar will fall, the demand for the dollar will fall, the supply of the dollar will increase, and the value of the dollar will decrease.

5. A. United States exports will rise if United States prices are rising more slowly than foreign prices and/or if foreign economies are growing faster than the United States economy.

   B. United States imports will rise if United States prices are rising faster than foreign prices and/or the United States economy is growing faster than foreign countries.

   C. United States investment in foreign countries will increase as our interest rates increase less than or are below foreign interest rates.

   D. Foreign investment in the United States will increase as foreign interest rates increase less than or are below United States interest rates.

   E. Expectations of changes in the value of the dollar will depend upon what currency dealers feel will happen with respect to (A) - (D) above and are also based on current changes in the value of the dollar.

6. Because the supply and demand for a currency can be influenced by many factors, the exchange rates between two countries are rarely constant under a system of flexible exchange rates. Generally they do not fluctuate a lot, but in 1977 and 1978, the value of the dollar dropped continuously because of the large deficit in the United States' balance of trade. A continuously dropping dollar can cause some problems. First, any foreign country holding dollars as reserves will find them

losing value. This could cause them to try to get out of dollars and consequently the value of the dollar will be pushed still lower. As a result, the dollar could lose its appeal as a key currency, and if the dollar fell far enough, the international monetary system might undergo a drastic change. Second, although our exports will be increasing, our trading partners will find theirs decreasing. Some countries will not want this to happen and may artificially keep the value of their currency from rising or they may even place tariffs on their imports. Third, since the dollars foreign countries receive when we import goods are losing value, they may raise their prices. And fourth, Americans who want to buy foreign goods and Americans who live abroad, but are paid in dollars, will find they will be able to purchase fewer goods and services with their dollars. Thus, although a decline in the value of the dollar may be good for restoring a balance of payments deficit, it does so with a cost.

GUIDE TO ANALYZING ARTICLES

1. Make a list of those variables changing in the article and/or variables which policy makers are proposing to change.
2. Determine how each of these variables affects the demand and supply of currency (Concepts 4 and 5 should be especially helpful here).
3. Shift the demand and supply curves appropriately and note their effect on the value of the currency.
4. If the change in the exchange rate is given, determine whether it is consistent with the above analysis.
5. If the change in the exchange rate is not given, try to predict what will happen to the exchange rate from the above analysis.
6. If the article makes policy recommendations, use your supply and demand analysis to predict what would happen if the recommended policy were enacted.

Articles

AN ANALYZED ARTICLE: OVERVIEW

This is an interesting article for two reasons. First, it shows that the value of the dollar can be rising and falling at the same time, depending upon which exchange rates are examined. Second, it shows that there is at least one country, Canada, which seems to be having more problems with its currency than the United States is having. In analyzing this article, let's examine what is happening with respect to the Canadian dollar and the Japanese yen separately, and then try to determine whether the changes in the value of the dollar with respect to these currencies is consistent with a supply and demand analysis of the situation.

Canada Dollar Lowest Since Depression

By UNITED PRESS INTERNATIONAL

Buffalo Evening News (Mar. 28, 1978). Reprinted by permission, courtesy of United Press International.

1. TORONTO—Pressured by continuing erosion of confidence in the Canadian economy, the Canadian dollar Monday plunged to a post-Depression low on North American money markets. European markets were closed for the Easter holiday.

2. After a day of light trading, the dollar changed hands at 88.36 U.S. cents—its lowest since 1933.

3. Earlier, it opened at 88.68 cents—its closing price on Thursday and the year's previous low—before beginning a 32-point slide.

   The Canadian dollar also fell again today in Buffalo.

4. Marine Midland's international department announced that it was buying Canadian drafts at 87.75 cents and currency at 86.75 cents, down from 88.25 and 87.25, respectively, on Monday.

5. Local traders were baffled by the sharp downturn, apparently sparked by massive divestitures of Canadian dollars on Chicago markets, in favor of U.S. currency.

* * *

6. Chicago Monetary experts said holders of Canadian funds dumped the currency as a hedge against expected action by the U.S. Federal Reserve Board to strengthen the U.S. dollar, which also fell sharply Monday against the Japanese yen.

7. In addition, traders were disappointed with Canada's failure to make significant headway in the fight against unemployment and inflation, aggravated by continuing uncertainty about Quebec separatism, one Chicago trader said.

8. His words were echoed by New York financial experts, who attributed the dollar's decline to the long-term flight of capital out of Canada.

9. Meanwhile, speculators today dumped more than 1 billion unwanted U.S. dollars on the Tokyo foreign exchange, sending the American currency to a new postwar low despite massive buying by the Bank of Japan.

10. Banking sources said transactions totaled $1.063 billion. There were almost no customers for dollars except the Japanese central bank.

11. The dollar ended the day at a price of 225.02 yen, but almost all transactions were at a price of 225 yen, which also was the opening price today.

12. The turnover was the second highest in history, topped only by the $1.18 billion traded during the dollar's decline in August 1971.

13. The previous low for the greenback in Tokyo came Monday when it touched 225.25 yen before closing at 225.30, a 6.8-percent drop in the dollar's value since the first of the year when it was traded at 241.10 yen.

Analysis

In paragraphs 1,7, and 8 we are told that there are some negative signs in the Canadian economy. We find high levels of unemployment and inflation, and uncertainty about whether Quebec will separate from Canada. This had made investors very unconfident about the future of the Canadian economy, and they are apparently decreasing their investments in it. This will lower the demand for the Canadian dollar. There also seems to be some feeling that the Fed will intervene to strengthen the value of the United States dollar (par. 6). Consequently many holders of Canadian dollars will probably switch to the United States dollars in hope that the value of the United States dollar will rise. This will increase the supply of the Canadian dollar. We can put these effects on a supply and demand graph, where the price of the Canadian dollar started at 88.68 United States cents. This is shown in Figure 1.

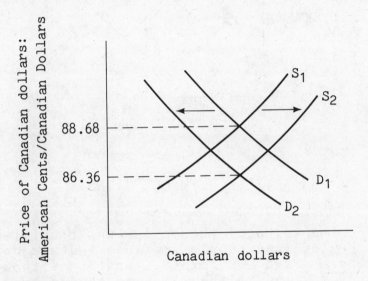

Figure 1

From our graph we can see that the increase in supply and the decrease in demand will in fact lower the value of the Canadian dollar from $1 Canadian = 88.68¢ United States to $1 Canadian = 86.36¢ United States. This also tells us that the value of the United States dollar with respect to the Canadian dollar has risen. Therefore, it appears that the reported change in the value of the Canadian dollar is consistent with the reasons given for that change.

Japan
Paragraph 9 indicates that speculators have dumped more than $1 billion United States' dollars on the Tokyo foreign exchange market. This is probably because they expect the value of the dollar to fall even further. (It is interesting to note that Canadians expect the value of the dollar to rise at the same time the Japanese expect it to fall. Does this seem logical to you? Why?) This dumping of dollars will increase the supply of dollars. At the same time there has also been a "massive" purchase of American dollars by the Japanese central bank. This will cause the demand for the dollar to rise. We can assume, however, that the central bank is buying fewer dollars than the speculators want

to sell. This can be seen in Figure 2 which shows that the only way the value of the dollar can fall from $1 = 225.3 yen to $1 = 225.02 yen when the supply of the dollar is increasing is if the demand increase is less than the supply increase.

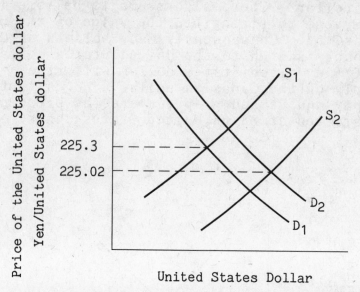

Figure 2

AN ARTICLE WITH QUESTIONS

During early 1978, the value of the dollar was consistently falling. This troubled many people and in a feature article U.S. News and World Report asked four experts what they thought were the reasons for the decline in the value of the dollar and what could be done to alleviate this problem. This article contains the responses of two of these experts.

4 Experts Tell How To Rescue the Falling Dollar:

"Massive" Buying of Dollars

By ROBERT V. ROOSA
Partner in Brown Brothers, Harriman & Company,
former under secretary of Treasury for monetary affairs

U.S. News & World Report *(Mar. 13, 1978). Copyright ©*
U.S. News & World Report, Inc. Reprinted by permission.

1. I support the idea that the United States should try to stabilize the dollar by intervening heavily in foreign-exchange markets. We should be prepared to cooperate with foreign governments in selling massive amounts of foreign currencies in exchange for U.S. dollars. This would push up the value of the dollar.

2. However, I do not believe that the U.S. should try to peg a rate for its currency. The reason we had to switch to a fluctuating-rate system is that relationships among national economies change so swiftly that it is impossible to establish and hold fixed rates between currencies.

What is necessary though is intervention to prevent

3. the kind of cumulative development where fear builds on fear and you have a run against or into a particular currency.

The dollar is especially vulnerable to this kind of
4. development because there are so many dollars in so many hands, abroad as well as here at home. The only way to prevent currency swings from exceeding all bounds of reason is for people to know that there is somewhere out there a boundary zone where they are going to have some protection from official sources that can overwhelm whatever the private sector can pour into the market on any given day.

The drop in the value of the dollar relative to the
5. mark and yen is a reflection of foreign concern—I think rightly expressed—that our own domestic economic program is so far quite unsatisfactory. So besides taking a more active role in the foreign-exchange markets, the U.S. must also come up with an energy program that eventually would contain inducements for additional investments designed to conserve energy and find alternatives to oil.

By our failure to enact an energy bill, we present a

6. rather sorry spectacle to the world. We go on paying 45 billion dollars a year for imported oil. The net effect of that is that we are running a 19-billion-dollar balance-of-payments deficit. That spills out as liquidity on a world that already has more dollars than it needs for international transactions. So it becomes a source of inflationary pressure all across the world.

Although it will be difficult, I hope we can begin to
7. make some progress in reducing oil imports this year.

There is still a tremendous amount of room for conservation. To encourage that, it will be necessary eventually to deregulate the price of oil and natural gas so that American consumers pay the full cost.

The Carter administration is wrong to blame the
8. Germans and Japanese for not stimulating their economies. They make the mistake of believing that just because a particular set of policies would work here, they are valid for other countries. But given the present structure of the German and Japanese economies, the only way they can increase economic growth is to increase exports. And that's the last thing we want them to do now. We have to encourage them to increase imports.

"Enact an Energy Bill"

By ROBERT SOLOMON
Senior fellow at the Brookings Institution
formerly an adviser to the Federal Reserve Board

U.S. News & World Report, (Mar. 13, 1978). Copyright ©
U.S. News & World Report, Inc. Reprinted by permission.

For the immediate future, there isn't much we can do
1. about the dollar except to enact an energy bill that will help improve market expectations about our future balance of payments.

If German Chancellor Helmut Schmidt had instead of
2. rebuffing our Treasury Secretary the way he did last month, made it clear that he was going to see to it that Germany would have a healthy expansion in the year ahead, that too, might have affected expectations.

Germany and Europe should be expanding faster, not
3. in order to help the U.S. or the dollar, but because they're wasting their income in unemployment and idle factories. And we in turn need an energy program not for balance-of-payments reasons primarily but for other reasons.

I don't believe the U.S. should intervene more heavily
4. in the foreign-exchange market by buying dollars and selling marks and other currencies. I don't think that really does the trick. We certainly learned from the experience of the 1960s and the early 1970s that countries just can't hold an exchange rate when the market expects the rate to move the other way.

The major influence on the dollar is that the rate of
5. growth of the German and Japanese economies has been very, very slack while the American economy has enjoyed a healthy expansion. I know many people believe it odd or paradoxical that a nation with a strong economy should have a weak currency and vice versa. But this is pure and simple economics. It happens again and again.

An economy which is expanding faster than others is
6. going to have imports expanding faster than the imports of others. But its exports will rise more slowly. So it will tend to develop a deficit in its trade account.

Now that would not necessarily push down our
7. exchange rate if there were enough investment capital flowing back into the U.S. to offset the trade deficit. But that is not happening even though U.S. interest rates are 3 or 4 percentage points higher than in Germany.

The only way you can explain that is to say that
8. exchange rates are being driven by expectations that exchange rates will move.

It's a self-fulfilling kind of prophecy. The expectation
9. of a movement in the deutsche mark and the yen and other currencies has outweighed the normal pull of higher interest rates in the United States. Once those expectations turn around, I would expect to see quite a sharp reversal in capital movements.

Questions - Roosa Excerpt

1. What does Roosa feel are main causes of the depreciation of the dollar? (Par. 5,6.)
2. Are these causes consistent with a supply and demand analysis of the problem?
3. What does he specifically say is not the problem? (Par. 8.)
4. What solutions does Roosa propose? (Par. 1,4,7.)
5. Does supply and demand analysis indicate whether these policies would be successful?

Questions - Solomon Excerpt

1. What does Solomon feel are the major causes of the depreciation of the dollar? (Par. 1,3,5,7,8.)
2. Are these causes consistent with a supply and demand analysis of the problem?
3. What solutions does Solomon propose? (Par. 1,9.)
4. Does supply and demand analysis indicate whether these policies would be successful?
5. What does Solomon say we should not do? (Par. 4.)

Questions - General

1. On what points do Roosa and Solomon disagree? Who do you think is correct? Why?

AN ARTICLE FOR STUDENT ANALYSIS: OVERVIEW

In early 1978, the value of the dollar kept falling to record lows. Since the dollar has been the key currency in international trade, and since the United States has a large amount of political influence, many countries were persuaded to try to help push up the value of the dollar. Switzerland was one of these countries, and this article describes some of the policies of the Swiss government. You should try to determine why these policies helped increase the value of the dollar in European markets. (In doing so, remember that any time the value of the Swiss Franc decreases with respect to the dollar, the value of the dollar will increase.) You may also want to consider why the dollar did not do as well in the New York market although there isn't enough information presented to do a complete analysis.

Dollar Gains in Europe on Swiss Action, But Later Is Mixed in New York Dealings

A WALL STREET JOURNAL
News Roundup

Reprinted by permission from The Wall Street Journal,
(Feb. 28, 1978), © *Dow Jones & Company Inc. 1978.*
All rights reserved.

1. The U.S. dollar jumped sharply in Europe on the announcement of further Swiss government moves to slow foreign demand for its currency. But the surge was short-lived, and by late in the day in New York the dollar was mixed against other major currencies.

2. In addition to the imposition of the second set of new controls in four days, Switzerland also called for a new international conference to discuss monetary problems and criticized the U.S. for failing to agree.

3. Finance Minister Georges-Andres Chevallez said on Swiss radio that his government, backed by West Germany and France in particular, is "urgently" calling for the monetary conference. But, he said, the plan "unfortunately is opposed on the other side of the Atlantic for reasons that are either deliberate or due to lack of understanding."

4. Dealers in Europe predicted the dollar's easing off, saying that the Swiss moves and the dollar's subsequent gains were only superficial. "Nothing has been proved. People aren't buying back into the dollar as violently as they sold out," commented one London banker. "The dollar has received a small plus but the basics are unchanged and will be until the U.S. acts to correct its balance of payments deficit and enact an energy bill."

Steps To Protect Swiss Franc

5. The new Swiss measures, which are effective immediately, included a ban on the purchase of Swiss securities by nonresident foreigners. They also reintroduce a limit on the amount of foreign currency that may be brought into the country by nonresidents and authorize the central bank to engage in forward transactions of up to 24 months on money markets.

6. The steps followed the imposition last Friday of a negative interest commission of 40% annually on large Swiss franc deposits held in Switzerland by nonresident aliens.

7. "This is all Switzerland can do at this time to safeguard the Swiss franc and the national economy," a central bank spokesman declared. "Now there is an urgent need for greater international cooperation to stabilize exchange rates."

8. The central bank spokesman said the new law forbidding the purchase by nonresident foreigners of all Swiss securities means that an American in New York, for example, can't legally even buy one share in a Swiss company.

9. "The ban was decided because of the fear that, faced with a 4% negative interest annually on any Swiss franc deposit, the nonresident foreigner would simply switch the money into Swiss securities," the spokesman explained. There isn't any exact figure available on the value of Swiss securities held by non-resident foreigners, the spokesman said, "But the figure is definitely very high." Swiss banking secrecy regulations prevent the government from determining an exact amount.

10. The government set a new limit of the equivalent of 20,000 Swiss francs on the amount of foreign currency that may be brought into Switzerland by nonresident foreigners, per person per quarter. This amount at current exchange rates equals $10,589.

Similar Limit Imposed in '76

11. A similar limit was imposed in 1976 and lifted last fall after one year. Authorities generally conceded that it never worked properly because of the difficulties of inspecting the baggage of every nonresident foreigner entering Switzerland. "We have to rely on the customs authorities to make the limit effective," the central bank spokesman stated.

12. The third new measure authorized the central bank to engage in forward transactions on money markets of up to 24 months. The law, which enhances the central bank's influence on market rates, previously restricted the bank to forward transactions of three months or less.

13. At a news conference, Finance Minister Chevallaz said the ban on purchasing Swiss securities applies to all persons and institutions outside Switzerland with the exception of Swiss nationals. Mr. Chevallaz said any contravention of the ban or assistance in contravening it, will be punishable by a fine of up to 100,000 Swiss francs ($53,000) or imprisonment of one month.

14. In Zurich, where the Swiss moves had the most impact, the dollar surged to 1.8888 Swiss francs. It later fell back in New York to 1.8693 francs, but remained, nonetheless, ahead of Friday's New York quote of 1.8489 francs.

15. The dollar also ended with a gain against the British pound, as sterling dropped in London to $1.9323.

The pound recovered in New York to $1.9405, but that still was below Friday's rate of $1.9415 in New York.

16. In Frankfurt, the U.S. currency climbed to 2.0510 West German marks from 2.0462 marks in New York Friday. In New York yesterday, however, it lost that gain, dropping 2.0423 marks.

17. The dollar weakened steadily against the French franc both overseas and in New York. The American unit dropped in Paris to 4.7950 French francs from 4.8263 francs in New York Friday. In New York yesterday, it tumbled further to 4.7585 francs. Dealers said there wasn't any specific reason for the French franc's firmness, although one trader in New York suggested that the market may have completed its adjustments in advance of the French elections next month and that there "isn't much more downward pressure."

18. In Tokyo Monday, the dollar dropped to 238.33 Japanese yen from 239.69 yen Friday. It later recovered in New York to 238.83 yen.

19. In Toronto, the Canadian dollar eased to 89.65 U.S. cents from 89.69 cents in quiet trading.

20. Gold's price bounded about but ended the day ahead only five cents an ounce. The five major London bullion dealers boosted their common quote $1.35 at their morning meeting, but cut $1.30 in the afternoon, to $180.80 an ounce.

Answers

CHAPTER 1

Answers to Questions on "Paragraphs from the Authors--Part II."

1. The Nobel Prize winners may not know anything about the effects of
   marijuana, but we cannot determine this since their names are not given.
   Nor do we know what other experts are saying about marijuana.
2. Just because good times for the economy are associated with wars does not
   mean that the wars caused the economy to behave well. After all, if the
   money spent on the wars had been spent on highways, the same effect on the
   economy might have been achieved.
3. Not everybody who looks like Harry behaves the same way. Many people with
   long hair and beards do not smoke marijuana.
4. The speaker is generalizing from his one-time experience. He would be
   better off examining national statistics concerning the unemployment rate.
5. The speaker has a preconceived bias as to what is the public good. He
   might be asked how many people want the shows he is advocating. If no
   one wants these kinds of shows, then are they in the public good?
6. An analogy is being made between reading and math problems. Such an
   analogy is not proper since math is not just like reading. Some of the
   best writers were failures at math.
7. Even though tuition is high enough to afford a hockey team, one must
   consider the opportunity cost of doing so (that is, less money to spend on
   faculty, the library, etc.).

CHAPTER 2

Answers to Questions on Article, "Largest U.S. Harvest in History Threatens to
Drive Prices Down, Cut Farmer's Incomes."

1. The good harvests are causing decreases in the prices farmers receive for
   their products. This could lead to decreases in their incomes.
2. Corn, sorghum, wheat, and soybeans.
3. Our analysis should tell us why prices are falling.
4. A. The 1971 crop of corn, wheat, and sorghum is significantly larger than
       normal, while the soybean crop is somewhat larger than normal.

159

B. The world demand for soybeans has increased.
C. Corn, wheat, and sorghum acreage has sharply increased.
D. Growing conditions were nearly perfect across the country.
E. Many farmers want to store their crops in expectation of higher prices. (This may be impossible because of inadequate storage facilities in some areas.)
F. The shipping strike is making the exportation of wheat impossible.
G. Foreign buyers of U.S. wheat are beginning to buy their wheat from non-U.S. competitors.

5. It will increase (A,C,D) especially if farmers cannot find storage facilities.
6. It will increase (A,C,D) especially if farmers cannot find storage facilities.
7. It will increase (A,C,D) especially if farmers cannot find storage facilities.
8. It will increase (A,C,D) especially if farmers cannot find storage facilities.
9. It will decrease (F,G).
10. It will decrease (B).
11. Because there is nothing in our article which indicates that buyers want more of these goods at each and every price.
12.

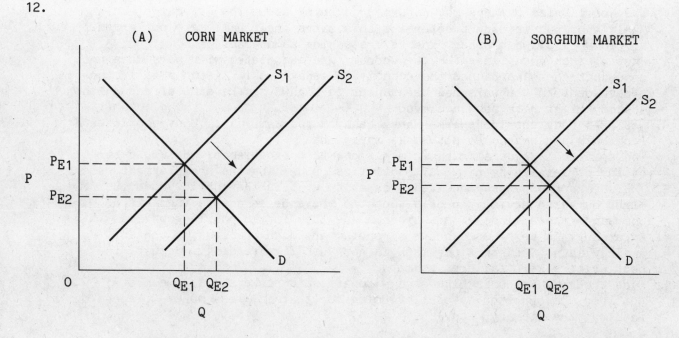

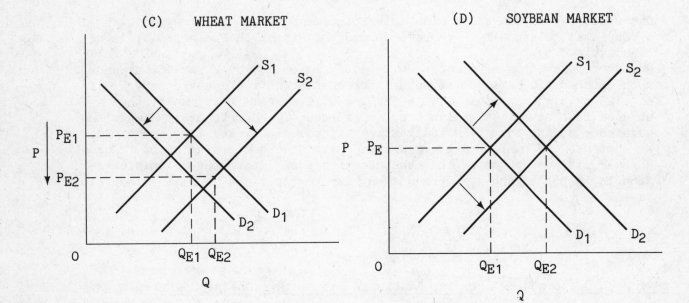

(C) WHEAT MARKET   (D) SOYBEAN MARKET

13. A. We would expect the price of sorghum to fall by less than the price of
       corn because the supply of sorghum increased by less (par. 1).
    B. The article states that the wheat harvest is up by 18%, so we can
       assume the equilibrium quantity has risen (par. 11).
    C. According to paragarph 7, the price of soybeans rose from $2.95 to
       $3.15, so that it appears that the increase in demand was greater than
       the increase in supply. (You might want to redraw the graphs to
       reflect this information.)
14. Prices are falling for all the products except soybeans. Consequently,
    the corn, sorghum, and wheat farmers appear to be in trouble unless the
    percentage increase in sales is greater than the percentage decrease in
    price. (The significance of this last statement will be discussed in the
    next chapter.) We would also expect that the sorghum farmers are hurt
    less than the corn farmers, and that the soybean farmers are going to find
    themselves in very good shape.

CHAPTER 3

Answers to Questions on Article, "30-cent Gasoline Tax Hike Studied."

1. The Carter administration is trying to decrease the country's gasoline
   consumption.
2. The proposed solution is a 10¢ increase in the gasoline tax.
3. The goals are to cut down consumption by 2 percent each year between 1981
   and 1985, and to net the government $10 billion in taxes.
4. Price (due to the tax increase), quantity, and tax revenue.
5. The price elasticity of demand.
6. The average price of gasoline is 61.8¢. A 10¢ rise in this price will
   change the price by approximately 16 percent. The desired change in
   quantity is 2 percent. The needed elasticity is:

$$E = \frac{\%\ \Delta\ \text{in Q}}{\%\ \Delta\ \text{in P}} = \frac{2\%}{16\%} = .125$$

7. One would expect the price elasticity of demand to be very low and .125 is a very small elasticity. Therefore we might expect this elasticity to be reasonable.
8. Whether consumption of gasoline will actually be cut by 2 percent depends upon whether you believe the actual price elasticity of demand for gasoline is .125 or higher. If it is, the policy will work. If it isn't, the changes in consumption will not be large enough. Unfortunately, we do not have enough data to determine exactly what the elasticity is. Therefore, we must use our own judgment or examine past data concerning price changes. However, it must be noted that the more successful the Carter administration is in curtailing gas consumption, the less revenue it will raise in taxes.

CHAPTER 4

Answers to Questions on Article, "National Interest is Energy Priority."

1. Probably because the word "priority" indicates that the article might be about resource allocation. In addition, it appears the article is about energy (but it is really about cars and only indirectly about energy) and this is a product.
2. As we said above, priority would suggest resource allocation. Then, as soon as we read paragraph 3 we find the article is about allocation problems concerning small versus large cars.
3. GM wants to make as many big cars as the public wants; the U.S. government wants the public to drive smaller, more fuel-efficient cars. In other words, is it proper for a government in a market economy to reallocate resources from big to small cars?
4. Neither the U.S. nor any other economic system has a pure market economy; the government always plays a role in resource allocation in the U.S. economy. Critics frequently charge the government with unwarranted interference into market activity. But you must make your own decision in this case.

CHAPTER 5

Answers to Questions on Article, "Carey Tilts to Economy at Expense of Environment."

1. The residents of New York are consuming a product that we could call water purity. In this case, water purity depends upon the absence of PCB, an industrial chemical. The lower the level of PCB in the water of the Hudson River, the purer the water.
2. Although no traditional price and quantity data is given, we can substitute the degree of water purity for quantity. Statistics show that degree of water purity has increased. G.E. dumped 30 lbs. of PCB daily until recently; now it dumps only 2 to 3 lbs. daily (par. 11).
3. Governor Carey apparently believes the average citizen of his State would get very little marginal utility from further improvements in water purity. That inference is made from reading that he finds "the difference between zero and 3.5 ounces . . . largely symbolic" (par. 11).
4. We can employ the Law in a very general way. The marginal value of water

purity is found by dividing the marginal utility of water purity by its cost, which is in this case primarily lost jobs. As long as the marginal value of water purity is greater than one, further improvements are warranted because marginal utility is greater than marginal cost. However, Governor Carey apparently believes this value is now approximately one. That is one explanation for his interest in ending any activity that seeks to improve water purity any futher (par. 11).

5. Unless even a minute trace of PCB is hazardous, there is probably diminishing marginal utility for water purity. If so, Governor Carey may be correct in assuming there is no demand for further increases in water purity, given the cost.

CHAPTER 6

Answers to Questions on Article, "Another Energy Sleeper."

1. The major production concept discussed in this article is marginal cost pricing for electric utilities (par. 3). This is simply a plan for basing electric prices on the marginal cost of providing the service to each user. Peak load outputs are also discussed; this term relates to the short-run (par. 3 and 4). Finally, there is a brief point about expanding capacity (par. 2).

2. The marginal pricing proposal is included in the energy legislation being considered by the House. This article (which is a Wall Street Journal editorial) argues against marginal pricing, primarily because of the "truly gigantic problems that arise in implementation" (par. 6).

3. Both, but the only discussion of the long-run occurs in paragraph 2 where there is a reference to the "expansion of electrical generating capacity." The remainder of the discussion is about the short-run, specifically about short-run marginal costs.

4. No, the article merely implies there is a need to expand generating capacity. It does not indicate if this should be done by expanding existing plants or by building new plants, nor does it give any hints about potential economies of scale.

5. Economic capacity is the most economical level of output. Since producing peak loads requires using "excess generating capacity," it most likely requires operating above economic capacity (par. 3). In fact, producing for peak loads probably requires a utility to operate very close to physical capacity. (See Figure 2 under Concepts.) Although we can make some general observations about these capacity concepts, we do not have any specific data that relates to them.

6. Only short-run marginal costs are discussed in the article. Although there is no specific data on these costs, we can infer from paragraphs 3 and 8 that marginal costs probably rise rapidly near the peak load level of output. However, "nobody yet knows for sure how you calculate marginal costs" since four different methods have been presented in one rate case (par. 8).
(Question: do you think Figure 2 in the Concepts material is an appropriate representation of the short-run costs presented in this article? Where would the level of usage by residential users appear in the diagram?)

7. First, we must realize that the conclusions we reach from reading this article are based upon information presented in an editorial. Nevertheless, we can say that marginal costs probably vary considerably

over the range of output electric utilities are required to produce. We can also conclude that the Wall Street Journal believes it is impractical to compute and base prices on the marginal cost of providing electricity for each user.

NOTE: In addition to the information on production found in this article, you may also be interested in analyzing the information relating to distribution which is found in paragraphs 5, 8, and 9.

CHAPTER 7

Answers to Questions on Article, "Ranchers Face Bleak Future As Costs Soar While Prices for Calves Decline Sharply."

1. The principle product discussed in this article is feedlot calves. Ranchers raise these calves until they are large enough to sell to feedlot operators. The industry consists of about 500,000 ranchers who operate in more than 40 states.
2. Calves are a fairly homogeneous product which is produced by a relatively large number of producers.
3. The price of calves dropped to $25 from the previous year's record of over $70 (par. 9). There is a slight chance that a further decline in price might occur in the next two years.
4. The price of calves dropped because demand shifted to the left and supply shifted to the right. Demand shifted to the left when feedlot operators curtailed their buying (par. 5). Feedlots will operate at only 75 percent of their last year's capacity. The reason for this decrease in buying is not given in the article. In addition to this change in demand, supply has been increasing by more than 5 percent a year.

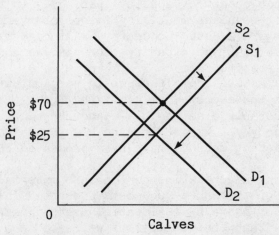

Figure 5

164

5. Ranchers are reducing the size of their herds because product price is falling while operating costs are rising. Operating costs which have increased include the cost of hay, feed supplement, grain, fuel, fertilizer, and labor. The cost of keeping a cow and calf until it is feedlot weight has doubled in the past year up to a cost of $190. Figure 6 was drawn with the assumption that ranchers were making some economic profit before price fell and costs increased. (NOTE: there is nothing in the article that supports that assumption, so you can begin with any level of demand you wish.) The diagram provides support for the statement in paragraph 10 that ranchers are selling off their animals in an attempt to "beat the squeeze."

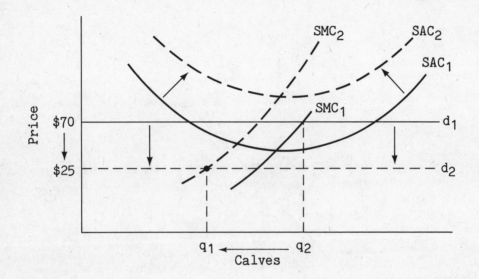

Figure 6

6. Rancher's profitability has fallen and is expected to fall still further. In fact, Mr. Monfort, a large feedlot operator, predicts that ranchers could lose billions (par. 13). If substantial losses occur, the smaller firms will probably be forced out of the industry. In any case, it is clear from the article that the industry's output will decline substantially.

CHAPTER 8

Answers to Questions on Article, "Striking Farmers Demand Law for Minimum Prices."

1. Apparently the policy being proposed would apply to all agricultural products and all producers of these products.
2. The American Agricultural Movement wants to establish a national board of agricultural producers within the Department of Agriculture. This board would establish annual production targets designed to provide farmers with

100% parity. Each farmer would receive a "selling right" which would
enable him or her to sell a certain proportion of the total targeted output.
3. Product price would rise as output falls to the amount set in the production target. Resources would be taken out of production as farmers cut
back production to the amount specified in their "selling rights." No
government money would be spent, but consumers would pay more for fewer
products. Farm income would rise to the point where each unit produced
would provide farmers with the same purchasing power it had in 1910 to
1914. Since agricultural prices have generally fallen relative to other
prices since that period, 100 percent parity would undoubtly increase their
incomes.
A. (See Figure 5.)

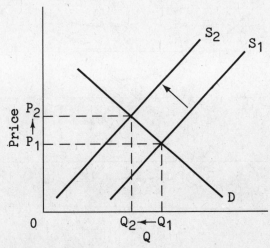

Figure 5

4. New producers cannot enter the industry without a selling right. So,
unless agricultural demand increases and additional permits are issued to
those now outside the industry, no new entry can occur. Of course, it
might be possible for someone to sell their selling right. One of the
major economic disadvantages of this plan is that it requires resources to
be unemployed. The public might well object to this waste. Another
economically inefficient provision is the attempt to freeze the relative
level of agricultural prices which is what 100 percent of partiy requires.

CHAPTER 9

Answers to Questions on Article, "TWA Attacks . . . ."

1. The product is passenger air service for the New York to California
market. Producers are TWA, American, and United, and in addition, a number
of charter operators. You might argue that there are really two markets

for this route, regular passengers and charter passengers. American's proposal is an attempt to gain some of the charter passengers (par. 6).
2. The Civil Aeronautics Board (CAB) is the regulatory agency.
3. American wants to offer discounts of up to 45 percent for New York to California flights. These discounts, called Super-Saver fares, would be limited to 35 percent of total seats. TWA is opposed because it believes these discounts will be money-losing propositions for the airlines.
4. American argues that its lower fares will "generate so much new traffic that any revenue losses would be more than offset" (par. 3). If their argument is correct, demand must be price elastic. Figure 2 shows what they are saying in a theoretical framework. As you can see in Figure 2, when price is lowered from OB to OA, the number of passengers will increase from OE to OF. If we use the elastic portion of this demand curve, the decrease in revenue from former passengers (AB times OE, or the area labeled "loss") is more than offset by the additional revenue from new passengers (OA times EF, of the area labeled "gain"). All we know from this exercise is that total revenue will increase if their assumption about demand is correct. To determine if discounts are profitable, one must compare this potential increase in revenue with potential increases in cost.

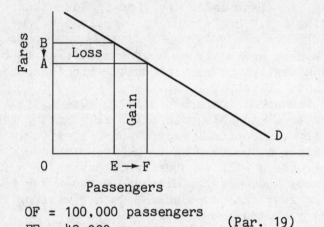

OF = 100,000 passengers
EF = 43,000 passengers   (Par. 19)

Figure 2

5. First, TWA believes these discounts could lead to a price war that could ruin all airlines. Second, TWA argues it is bad timing to introduce the discounts at the onset of the industry's peak passenger season. Third, TWA points out that since the CAB computes an airline's revenue on the basis of full-value of fares, any additional passengers gained by the discounts will "inflate" airline profits. As a result, the airlines will have more difficulty arguing for fare increases in the future. Finally, TWA believes that these discounts will cause passengers from cities other than New York, Los Angeles, or San Francisco to fly first to one of these cities before flying to the other. In other words, the discounts in one market will siphon off passengers from other markets. In summary, TWA believes it will lose $8 million in revenue and $2.3 million in profits if the CAB allows the discounts.
6. Although American has filed its proposal with the CAB, the latter had not yet acted at the time this article was written. However, it should be pointed out that the CAB approved reduced fares for charter flights—those which are booked 30 days in advance. In fact, American's proposal grew out

of its fear that these charter flights would attract many of its potential passengers.

7. This is all yours! The economic consequences part should give you a good workout.

CHAPTER 10

Answers to Questions on Article, "Razor Fighting."

1. The disposable razor market. The various disposal razors are apparently quite similar, differing mainly in certain trivial design features.
2. Conventional safety-razors provide a very close substitute.
3. The producers mentioned in the article are Bic, Gillette, and Schick. Gillette and Schick also make traditional razors; the disposalbe razor is the first shaving item by Bic.
4. Apparently the consumers view these disposable razors as essentially interchangeable.
5. One can assume that price competition occurred earlier; otherwise Gillette would not be selling its disposable razor for 5¢ less than its Trac II blades. After reading about Bic's marketing philosophy, we might expect further competition.
6. Future competition may be primarily product competition that is designed to draw the customer's attention to each product. Bic is spending $9 million to promote its product; Gillette, $6 million.
7. A number of alternative scenarios are possible. One is that consumers may begin to switch over to disposable razors for all shaving needs until finally the demand for conventional razors and blades will not support their production. Since it costs more to make a disposable razor than a disposalbe blade, consumers will eventually be paying more for shaving supplies than they would have if the disposable had never been introduced. Moreover, by throwing away the disposables, we are wasting resources, especially our vital petroleum resources.

CHAPTER 11

Answers to Questions on Articles, "Steel-Price Rise Prompts Inquiry . . ." and "Inland Steel Lifts Most Prices . . ."

1. Two price increases occurred in the steel industry, each roughly one year apart. The 1976 price increase led to a government investigation whereas the 1977 price increase probably will not be investigated. We want to compare these two situations.
2. Noncompetitive behavior is not obvious, but the government appears to be looking into the possibility of collusive price leadership in the 1976 price increase.
3. Steel is a fairly uniform product produced by relatively large firms. Do you know of any other facts about the steel industry that might make noncompetitive behavior likely?
4. National Steel, one of the smaller firms in the industry, led the 1976 price increase. Wheeler-Pittsburg, again one of the smaller firms, led the 1977 price increase, although its lead is not being exactly followed by the other firms.

5. The fact that demand was lagging in 1976 makes this price increase somewhat suspicious, although one can find other examples of prices being increased during periods of declining demand. It does not appear that U. S. Steel was a party to the conspiracy since if it had been, it probably would not have stated that no price activity would take place until next year. This seems to be a situation where the smaller firms may have felt that they needed a price increase and were not willing to wait for the larger firm. National may simply have been a barometric price leader.

6. In this case, Wheeling, since it was financially troubled, may have been in a good position to "test the air" for a significant price increase. Once the industry found out that the 7 percent increase announced by Wheeling was unacceptable to the government, Bethlehem tried a 5.5 percent increase. Since this increase is acceptable to the government, the other firms are falling in line. This seems to be clearly a case of barometric price leadership.

CHAPTER 12

Answers to Questions on Article, "What Makes Barbara Walters Worth a Million?"

1. To explain why ABC is paying Barbara Walters $1 million to do the ABC Evening News with Harry Reasoner.
2. The product could be expressed as audience viewership since the network gets paid from advertisers for the number of viewers it attracts.
3. News items are one input; television equipment is another. But the article is about a third input, a newscaster, Barbara Walters.
4. Barbara Walters's productivity is found in paragraph 21: "she possibly will boost the news ratings a notch or two." A notch is another term for a rating point, which is equal to approximately 1.2 million viewers. Since Ms. Walters is joining Harry Reasoner, not replacing him, this increase in rating points is the marginal productivity of adding one more input to the ABC Evening News. Given this interpretation of Ms. Walters's position, adding her to the Evening News would be viewed as an outward movement along the program's MPP curve. (NOTE: In this situation, we are taking liberties with the rule that inputs are of uniform quality.)
5. Paragraph 21 also provides a product price: "a single rating point should mean a gain of at least $1 million in revenues." Despite the statement that this rate is based on "today's market," in this type of business the rate is probably determined by the firm rather than by the market. Therefore, MRP is probably the most appropriate concept. Nothing in the article suggests that this rate is changing.
6. Since we decided to view Ms. Walters as an addition to ABC Evening News in Answer 4, the answer to this question corresponds to that of Answer 4--MRP is not changing; rather, there is a movement to another point on the existing MRP curve.
7. Our analysis shows that ABC is fairly certain that Ms. Walters will earn at least $1 million in revenues. Therefore, she is being paid the expected value of her marginal product.

CHAPTER 13

Answers to Questions on Article, "Fast-Food Chains Act to Offset the Effects
of minimum-Pay Rise."

1. This article shows how a variety of firms employing low-paid workers are
   reacting to the minimum wage increase. One point of the article is to
   disprove the contention that the minimum wage increase will seriously
   reduce employment.
2. The firms included in the article produce a wide variety of goods and
   services ranging from fast-food products to custodial services.
3. The major resource discussed is labor, specifically, labors who do menial
   jobs, and in many cases, work on a part-time basis.
4. Two different types of firms demand the resources discussed in this article.
   There are firms which traditionally employ a lot of young part-time workers.
   These firms include fast-food establishments, restaurants, department and
   grocery stores, and service stations. A second group of firms employ
   low-paid, full-time workers. Included in this group are cleaners, firms
   providing custodial services, textile, and apparel companies.
5. Resource price is changing for all workers covered by minimum wage
   legislation who earn less than $2.65 per hour. The Carter Administration
   predicted this wage increase "could cost some 90,000 jobs through 1981"
   (par. 11). However, at the present time at least, the fast food industry
   is not planning any layoffs.
6. Resource supply has shifted and resource demand--at least in the fast food
   industry--is expected to shift to the right.
7. Government minimum wage legislation caused the horizontal portion of the
   resource supply curve for certain types of low-paid workers to shift upward.
8. Although there may be monopsonists operating in some of the labor markets,
   most of resource supply consists of a large number of unorganized
   workers. Therefore, we would not expect bilaterial monopoly in any of
   these resource markets.
9. Resource demand in the fast-food industry is expected to shift to the
   right as a result of increases in product price and improved productivity
   (par. 11).
10. The resource price increase needs no further explanation. However, it is
   interesting to examine the fast-food industry's efforts to avoid layoffs.
   Figure 5 of Article 1's Analysis is relevant to the situation in this
   article. In Figure 5 you can see that when the government raises price
   from OC to OE, employers must either reduce employment from OA to OB or
   increase resource demand out to point J. The fast-food industry expects
   to accomplish the latter by some minor price increases and by a variety of
   improvements in productivity. Productivity will be increased by such
   things as "technological gains in the kitchen" and installing "new automatic cash registers" (par. 11 and 12). Although there are similarities
   between Articles 1 and 2, the potential long-run negative consequences we
   predicted for the rubber industry should not be a potential problem for
   the fast-food industry. The difference in predicted outcomes is based
   upon the way each industry adjusted to the wage increases each was forced
   to accept. Whereas the tire industry increased resource demand solely by
   increasing tire prices, the fast-food industry is concentrating on
   increases in productivity. The advantage of the latter method is that
   product demand is unaffected.

CHAPTER 14

Answers to Questions on Article, "Latest Trade Problem: Subsidized Butter Cookies."

1. Although butter cookies are apparently imported from several countries, Denmark is the only importing country mentioned (par. 7). The product, butter cookies, are a special type of cookie made by the cookie industry. Only one U.S. cookie producer, the American Deer Park Baking Co., makes Danish-type butter cookies.
2. The American producer sells $2 million dollars of butter cookies. Another $6 million dollars of imports are sold in the U.S.
3. U.S. consumers of butter cookies would be interested in encouraging trade so they could continue buying their butter cookies at current prices. On another level, Europeans would prefer if no restrictions were put on butter cookies because other exports would most likely be subject to the same restrictions.
4. The American producer is arguing that their Danish competitors use subsidized inputs. The Danish pay no more than 30¢ a pound for butter; the American producer pays $1.06 (par. 12). In addition, the Danish producer receives export rebates for eggs, flour, and sugar (par. 11). Although the American producer does not say this specifically, the implication seems to be that if countervailing duties are not imposed, it and 150 of its cookies makers will be forced to quit producing butter cookies.
5. In weighing the costs and benefits of imposing the countervailing duties, we must first point out that it is difficult to evaluate any subsidy argument. The problem is that most governments subsidize industries in various ways. For example, the U.S. has used a variety of methods to subsidize certain sectors of agriculture. Consequently, it is always difficult to determine whether a "true" comparative advantage exists. Nevertheless, it seems that the Danish government has provided substantial subsidies to the butter cookie industry, and these subsidies are providing their cookie producers with an unfair advantage in the American market. As a result, the U.S. producer may lose its $2 million in butter cookie sales and 150 of its employees may be forced out of their jobs. However, these workers may be able to find employment in other parts of the cookie industry since only one small segment of the cookie industry is affected by these imports. Another potential economic cost to consider is a Danish monopoly in the U.S. butter cookie market if the American producer is forced out.
6. It seems that one significant cost of not imposing duties is the loss of $2 million in sales and one significant benefit is the goodwill achieved in the Geneva trade negotiations. You are on your own in finding other benefits and costs and then reaching a decision.

CHAPTER 15

Answers to Questions on Roosa Excerpt.

1. A. Foreign countries are concerned with our future, causing them to be cautious about investing in the United States.
   B. Our $45 billion importation of oil has caused a balance of payment deficit of $19 billion.

2. The decrease in foreign investment causes the demand for dollars to fall while the balance of payment deficit causes an increase in the supply of dollars. (Actually both the supply and demand for dollars are increasing but since there is a deficit, the supply increase is greater than the demand increase. Consequently we will just shift the supply curve on the graph below so that it will be easier to read.) Both these effects will cause a decrease in the value of the dollar as can be seen on Figure 3.

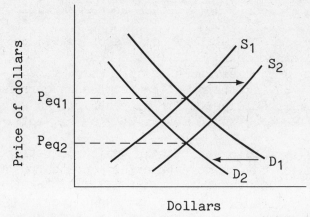

Figure 3

3. The lack of stimulation of the Japanese and German economy.
4. A. Intervene in the foreign currency market and buy dollars.
   B. Import less energy.
   C. Hope that both of the above policies will lead to expectations that the value of the dollar will soon rise.
5. If we buy more dollars, the demand for dollars will rise; if we import less energy, the supply of dollars will fall; and if we create expectations that the value of the dollar will soon rise, the demand for the dollar will rise and the supply of the dollar will fall. The net effect of these policies should be a rise in the demand for the dollar and a decrease in the supply of the dollar. The effect of these policies should be a rise in the value of the dollar as can be seen in Figure 4.

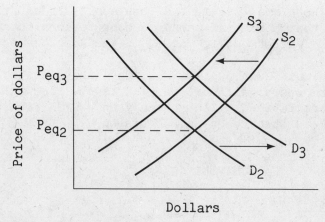

Figure 4

Answers to Questions on Solomon Excerpt.

1. A. Large amounts of imported oil.
   B. The lack of expansion in the German and Japanese economies.

172

C. A slowdown of foreign investment in the United States.

D. Expectations that the value of the dollar will fall further.

2. The importation of oil causes the supply of dollars to increase; the slowdown of the Japanese and German economies causes our imports from them to be greater than their imports from us, again increasing the supply of dollars; a slowdown of foreign investment in the United States causes the demand for dollars to decrease; and the expectation of further decreases in the value of the dollar causes the demand for the dollar to decrease and the supply of the dollar to increase. The net effect of these actions is a decrease in the demand for the dollar and an increase in the supply of the dollar. This will lower the value of the dollar as can be seen in Figure 5.

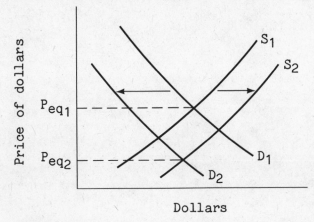

Figure 5

3. A. We should decrease our importation of oil.

B. We should try to get currency dealers to expect the value of the dollar will rise. (He doesn't tell us how this should be done.)

4. The decrease in our oil imports will lower the supply of dollars while if expectations change, the demand for dollars will increase and the supply of dollars will decrease. The net effect of his policy recommendations are an increase in the demand for dollars and a decrease in the supply of dollars. This should raise the value of the dollar as can be seen in Figure 6.

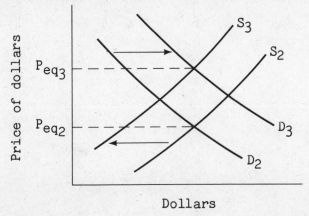

Figure 6

Answers to General Questions on Roosa and Solomon Excepts.

1. Roosa thinks we should buy more dollars in the currency market, while Solomon thinks that such a policy would not work. Solomon places part of

173

the blame on the German and Japanese leaders for not stimulating their economies while Roosa feels that they are not at fault. Our analysis indicates that Roose is correct in suggesting we buy dollars in the currency market. This action should increase the demand for dollars and raise the value of the dollar. It may also be helpful in turning around the expectations of the future of the dollar. Solomon also seems to be correct for placing part of the blame on the slow expansion of the Japanese and German economies. These slow expansions cause our imports from them to rise relative to their imports from us, the net effect of which is to cause the supply of dollars to increase more than the demand for dollars, putting downward pressure on the value of the dollar.

79   80   81   82   10   9   8   7   6   5   4   3   2